STEALTH

KAMALA HARRIS'S COMMUNIST ROOTS

D1607600

TREVOR LOUDON

Stealth – Kamala Harris's Communist Roots by Trevor Loudon

Cover Design: W. Rainier
Typesetting: W. Rainier

ISBN: 9798340336217
Independently published

While the author has made every effort to provide accurate internet addresses at the time of publication, neither the publisher nor the author assumes any responsibility for errors or for changes that occur after publication. Further, the publisher does not have any control over and does not assume any responsibility for author or third-party websites or their content.

www.TrevorLoudon.com
www.keywiki.org

To Renee Nal, who helped so much with the research and writing of this book.

Also, a huge thank you to the US military and its supporters who saved my home country of New Zealand from invasion during WWII.

Thank you also for bravely defending freedom across the globe for more than a century.

While the US military has been betrayed and misused many times by cowardly Republicans and communist Democrats for decades, we all owe those who served the deepest gratitude.

It is fashionable these days, on both right and left, to criticize the "US military industrial complex". We must all ask ourselves why the "Evil Empire" agents in this country, including many in the highest reaches of our government, are doing so much to misuse and undermine those who protect us.

I thank God every day for the men and women of the US military - past, present and future.

—Trevor Loudon
Free Florida
September 23, 2024

CONTENTS

FOREWORD

Is KAMALA HARRIS a "communist"?

I will prove to you that indeed Kamala Harris is a stealth communist.

I use the word "communist" deliberately because it is accurate. Kamala Harris is not just a "liberal", or a "progressive" or even a "socialist" – though she is all those things.

Kamala Harris is a communist. As is her running mate, Minnesota Governor Tim Walz.

Kamala Harris has probably never held an official Communist Party card, but she is ideologically in sync with communist goals and objectives. She was raised in a family that admired Third World communists and revolutionaries. She has worked with "actual" communists her entire life and has been supported by communists at every stage of her political career.

Kamala Harris does not say "I am a communist". Regardless, Kamala Harris *is* a communist.

A very few American communists are open about their ideology, as most operate in stealth.

Every year, millions of young Americans are indoctrinated by stealth Marxist teachers and professors. Read anything by the great James Lindsay if you are dubious about this claim.

Every Sunday millions of American Christians attend stealth Marxist (woke) churches – see our 2021 documentary "Enemies Within the Church" for confirmation of this painful fact.

For years now, far-left elements in the US Government have waged a stealthy (and sometimes open) war on Christianity. See Julie Behling's excellent documentary "Beneath Sheep's Clothing" if you want to understand how this works.

Every election cycle, tens of millions of US voters unknowingly cast their ballots for hundreds of stealth socialist and communist candidates running on the Democratic Party ballot line.

For detailed insights into this the leftist infiltration of the Senate and the House, I recommend reading my recent books, "Security

Risk Senators" Parts 1 and 2, along with the ongoing series "House UnAmericans," which currently spans Parts 1 through 4, with Parts 5 and 6 forthcoming. These works delve into the backgrounds and affiliations of currently serving Senators and members of Congress, highlighting security risks within the legislative body.

Kamala Harris and Tim Walz, along with many of their colleagues in the "commanding heights" of the Democratic Party, are "stealth communists".

The purpose of this book is two-fold.

Firstly, I want provide Americans with a greater understanding of what "communism" means in the modern context.

Secondly, I want to expose some of the extensive infiltration of institutions, initiated by the former Soviet Union and nearing "critical mass" under the guidance of the Chinese Communist Party and its army of domestic collaborators.

Kamala Harris is not a "stand alone" candidate. She is not where she is today based on her personal talents and abilities. She is the product of a "movement". Kamala Harris is a "manufactured" candidate, whose only qualifications for public office are her gender, her racial background and her revolutionary sympathies.

A BRIEF EVOLUTION OF STEALTH COMMUNISM IN AMERICA

The movement that "made" Kamala Harris can be traced back, at every turn, to US "Maoists" and supporters of the Chinese Communist Party - and before that to supporters of the former Soviet Union.

While the Communist Party of the Soviet Union ruled the Communist Party USA with an iron first from 1921 until 1991, American communism certainly did not die when the "Soviet Bloc" went into retreat in the early 1990s.

The Socialist Party USA, which was even older than the CPUSA, maintained an alternative revolutionary current, which manifests today in groups like Democratic Socialists of America.

In the very late 1950s, some American communists, inspired by Chinese leader Mao Tse Tung, began to split from the tired, stale and discredited CPUSA, to form new, pro-China revolutionary groups.

By the mid-1960s, influenced by the Chinese "Cultural Revolution" and the anti-Vietnam War movement, thousands of young college activists, mainly in the Students for a Democratic Society, turned to "Maoism".

Pro-Soviet communism was seen as boring and even too "conservative". Young '60s revolutionaries were far more excited by Cuba's Fidel Castro, North Vietnam's Ho Che Minh and China's Mao Tse Tung than they were by the Soviet Union's Nikita Kruschev or Leonid Brezhnev.

Who could be inspired by stone-faced, bushy eyebrowed, dark-suited, fur hat wearing, nuclear missile loving Soviet leaders who mostly weighed less than their wives?

While many white college kids were ingesting Mao's "Little Red Book", there was a parallel revolution going on in the working class "communities of color".

Young black revolutionaries began to form Maoist-oriented groups like the League of Revolutionary Black Workers and the Republic of New Africa in Detroit, or the Black Panther Party in the San Francisco Bay Area and Chicago.

At the same young Hispanic radicals were setting up the Raza Unida Party in the Southwest and converting the Young Lords gang in Chicago to a simplified version of Maoism.

Young Chinese and Japanese Americans, mainly in California, Boston and New York, established several Maoist groups, including the Red Guards, Yellow Seed, Seize the Time Collective and I Wor Kuen (Righteous and Harmonious Fists).

By the 1970s, with the collapse of Students for a Democratic Society, American Maoists began to coalesce into a series of pro-China, cult-like parties including the October League/Communist Party USA (Marxist-Leninist), Communist Workers Party, League of Revolutionary Struggle, Proletarian Unity League, Revolutionary Workers Headquarters, Line of March, etc.

All the main groups were competing among themselves to earn the coveted Chinese "franchise" – to become the "official" American representative of the Communist Party of China.

The Maoist groups – collectively known as the "New Communist

Movement", differed from their Communist Party USA counterparts in their greater propensity for violence and their stronger emphasis on racial and minority agitation.

However, by the 1980s, traditional Maoism was on the wane. In China, Deng Xiaoping's "market socialism" represented the next stage of communist development – and was mistaken for a turn to "capitalism" by naïve Western businessman and politicians.

US Maoists also struggled with the changes.

Up until the early 1980s, most US Maoists were active in factories, campus politics and social movements, working with race-based radicals, building secret cells in preparation for a violent American communist revolution.

By the mid-1980s, the switch had been flipped. As the Chinese Communist Party changed tactics, so did American Maoists.

Most US Maoists, almost certainly at the direction of their masters in Beijing, began to abandon the streets and factories to get jobs in the non-profit sector, the professions, the business community, academia and the Democratic Party – all while maintaining their hard-left views and pro-China loyalties.

The new Maoist goal was nothing less than the taking control of America through its institutions.

A young Maoist lawyer named "Ben Connors" (probably a pseudonym) laid out his party's new priorities in the pages of the February 1985 issue of "The Expert Red", a theoretical journal of the Communist Workers Party.

"Connors" explained what it was like to be Maoist revolutionary in the '70s and early '80s:

> To comrades who left home…who left family to live secret lives
> in unknown places, calling home from pay phones, comrades who
> gathered each and every week, to study Marx, Lenin, Mao, and
> to train one another in theory and practice, going to work every
> morning and studying on the job as well; comrades who tried to orga-
> nize workers into unions during bathroom breaks, and who lived
> collectively and helped raise each other's kids, comrades who lied,
> picketed, and fought against police and strike breakers, comrades

who left prosperous careers to fight the Klan in Greensboro, North Carolina, some of whom lost their lives...[1]

He also laid out the Chinese Communist Party's new road to a socialist America:

Just over a year ago, right before I joined the Communist Workers Party, a now very dear comrade exclaimed to me, 'To be a Communist in the eighties, wow!' Neither of us realized even then that a little more than a year later our thoughts would be turning to something called 'center stage.' Organizing other leftists like ourselves seemed sufficiently important at the time. We came to learn, however, that it was indeed important, but hardly sufficient. It was time to assume leadership over the whole society.

We are now 'cleaning up our act' in a sense. Rather than storming City Hall, we are donning tuxedoes and preparing to enter by special invitation. We are learning to use our skills and power in ways that are proving far more dangerous to the ruling class and far more beneficial to the masses.

For me, a young lawyer, new to the Party, this process is all very natural. Just point me in the right direction. You want me to be a Congressman? Fine, it's what my mother always wanted for me anyway. It's all very legitimate. For other new comrades, as well, the road is wide open—we can follow any career path we choose, so long as it helps the Party lead and serve the American people...[2]

At a convention in mid-1985, the Communist Workers Party formally dissolved itself, reorganizing itself into the "New Democratic Movement", which devoted itself to establishing "local power bases" and to infiltrating the Democratic Party.

At a New York City gathering, Jerry Tung, General Secretary of the former Communist Workers Party, explained the idea to the assembled faithful:

"[O]nce you get people elected or appointed to office, you can award contracts to friends.... When you can raise money for political purposes, when you do it in the right place in the right atmosphere, and look right, and the [mainstream] party bosses are there, then that money makes them take you seriously."[3]

Communism and corruption always go hand in hand.

Those few comrades and their miniscule sects who continued to work at street level, merged again in 1985 to form the Freedom Road Socialist Organization. This group absorbed displaced comrades from other dying organizations to become the most influential US "Maoist" group of the 1990s. Today it is known as Liberation Road and features heavily in this volume.

By the early 2000s, the Communist Party USA was reoriented towards China and starting to recover from its long term, almost terminal decline. Most of the pro-China groups worked increasingly in unison.

When the rest of the world was celebrating the "collapse of communism", America's Chinese Communist Party loyalists were burrowing ever deeper into our institutions and rebuilding powerbases and recruitment centers on university campuses.

By the dawn of the 21st century, "Maoists" and their allies held influential positions in the law, philanthropy, academia, business, labor, non-profits and the Democratic Party – even in some churches.

After China was admitted into the World Trade Organization in 2001 (with the help of the late Senator Dianne Feinstein of California), American Maoists in the Democratic Party, some labor unions and other institutions used every ounce of influence they could muster to integrate the US and Chinese economies. Many shortsighted businessmen, academics and Republican Party operatives happily jumped on the "gravy train" – as Chairman Mao and Premier Deng Xiaoping predicted they would.

By the mid-1990s, Maoist operatives and Democratic Socialists of America and Communist Party USA comrades had taken firm control of most US labor unions. By controlling organized labor, the communists were increasingly able to manipulate Democratic Party policy formation and ensure that more far-left candidates would be elected.

This long-term infiltration program is why the Democratic Party has moved increasingly to the left on issues like illegal immigration, education policy, defense policy and energy policy since the late 1990s.

Throughout this period, Maoist-aligned legislators also introduced

affirmative action bills and "hate speech" legislation across the country
to limit free speech and further undermine the Constitution.

Increasingly, there has become less and less daylight between
to policies of America's pro-China communists and those of the
Democratic Party.

KAMALA HARRIS AND TIM WALZ

This is the movement that raised, nurtured, promoted and is now
working to elect Kamala Harris and Tim Walz.

Of course, neither Kamala Harris or Tim Walz would dare to
publicly declare their communist sympathies – though the evidence
is copious and not hard to find.

However, Harris and Walz must continue to "dog whistle" and
drop enough hints to keep their socialist supporters enthusiastic.
Much like how American communists decoded the true implications
of Barack Obama's pledge to "fundamentally transform" America, or
when he chose the avowed communist Pete Seeger to perform the
pro-communist Woody Guthrie's "This Land is Your Land" at his
inauguration, signaling his ideological leanings without explicit dec-
laration. Read all the verses of this iconic song someday – you will be
surprised.

Many of Kamala Harris's campaign slogans and rallying cries come
directly from the communist movement.

"When We Fight, We Win" has been used by Harris and other
protagonists in this book such as Jesse Jackson and Van Jones,
reportedly comes from the Boston-based "social justice group" City
Life/Vida Urbana,[4] which is closely tied to the neo-Maoist FRSO/
Liberation Road organization.

According to writer/philosopher James Lindsay, the Harris/Walz
campaign's constant reference to "joy" refers to the concept "radical
joy," which is "a kind of religious ecstasy associated with believing they
are going to accomplish Communism, or at least their revolution."[5]

And Mao's words "bring joy" according to the Chinese Communist
Party.[6]

Even Kamala Harris's favorite slogan, "We're not going back" which
she used in the wind-up to the Trump-Harris presidential debate, is

identical to the name of the Communist Party USA's annual celebration of African American History Month held in New York City.[7]

Kamala Harris is indeed a communist. She has never been anything else. The mainstream media will never tell you this. Most Republicans either don't know the truth or are unwilling to state it. President Trump is the only major public figure to consistently call Kamala Harris a "communist".

Here is a question: If a candidate was raised by Nazis, was supported and promoted and endorsed by Nazis, associates with Nazis and spouts Nazi policies but did not explicitly say "I am a Nazi", would you think that person was a Nazi?

I wrote this book to give millions of American patriots the information they need to expose stealth communist candidate Kamala Harris for what she has always been, but few are willing to admit.

CHAPTER 1

GROWING UP RED

RED DIAPER BABY

KAMALA HARRIS WAS a red-diaper baby – the child of a Marxist father and a radical left mother. Her parents, Shyamala Gopalan, a biology student from India, and Don Harris, a Jamaican economics major, met at the University of California, Berkeley during the early 1960s.

"I came to study at UC Berkeley," Gopalan remembers. "I never came to stay. It's the old story: I fell in love with a guy, we got married, pretty soon kids came."[1]

Shyamala, Kamala and Don Harris

Those kids – Kamala (born October 20, 1964) and her sister Maya (born January 30, 1967) were "marching" in rallies and demonstrations before they could even walk.

Shyamala and Don Harris were very active during the civil rights and anti-Vietnam War protests of the era, often taking baby Kamala to protests in a stroller.[2]

AFRO-AMERICAN ASSOCIATION

At the start of the 1960s, black students began meeting at the Harmon Street, Berkeley house of Mary Lewis, an undergraduate from Detroit. Shyamala and Don Harris soon joined the group. Mary Lewis would become a close friend to Shyamala, and godmother to Kamala, known to her as "Aunt Mary". Her husband Sherman L. Williams would be known as "Uncle Sherman". Mary Lewis "laid the groundwork for what is now known as the African American Association [Afro-American Association]" at UC Berkeley:[3]

'I was awed by them,' says early group member Aubrey Labrie of the Harrises, 'They were intimidatingly smart. They had a determined kind of posture about them.'

Mary Lewis

'Fidel Castro and Che Guevara were the heroes of some of us,' Labrie recalls. 'We would talk about Black Muslims, the liberation movements going on in Africa, everything.' Labrie also referenced Mao Zedong as an 'admired' figure during their weekly meetings, which would 'later provide some inspiration to the founders of the Black Panther Party'.

Labrie was so close to the family that Kamala would call him 'Uncle Aubrey'.[4]

According to Donna Jean Murch, Rutgers University History Professor and author of "Assata Taught Me",[5] a glowing tribute to former Black Liberation Army terrorist Assata Shakur, convicted murderer and current fugitive in communist Cuba, the study group gradually developed "its own antiassimilationist ideology": "a reinvigorated , anticolonial Black nationalism," more Malcolm X than Martin Luther King, Jr."[6]

By 1963, the organization, now called the Afro-American Association, had grown to about fifty members. Guest speakers included civil rights militant Fannie Lou Hamer, radical poet Maya Angelou and LeRoi Jones – who later became a leader of the Maoist-oriented League of Revolutionary Struggle under his new name - Amiri Baraka.[7]

According to "Uncle Aubrey", Shyamala Gopalan was the original study group's only non-black member — the exception that proved the rule. "Her inclusion had a lot to do with the fact that we were really supportive of the Third World liberation movement, so we didn't really get into that whole debate who was 'black' or not," Labrie says. "But I will admit that a white person wouldn't have been welcome into that kind of setting. It wasn't because there was hostility towards them. We just felt more confident and comfortable getting our own thoughts and information together as black people."[8]

The Marxist character of this group is confirmed by the fact that Mary Lewis, Sherman L. Williams, the group's leader Donald Warden and Shyamala Gopalan were acknowledged as being pivotal in bringing Cedric J. Robinson's exhaustive history of the US black revolutionary movement: "Black Marxism: The Making of the Black Radical Tradition" to fruition.[9]

The Afro-American Association's leader Donald Warden took a particular interest in two young comrades - Huey Newton and Bobby Seale - who would go on to establish the Black Panther Party in 1966.[10]

The Black Panthers followed a Maoist philosophy. They also sent several delegations to communist China, North Korea and North Vietnam.

Inspired by Mao Zedong's advice to revolutionaries in *The Little Red Book*, Huey Newton called on the Panthers to "serve the people" and to make "survival programs" a priority within its branches. The most famous of their programs was the Free Breakfast for Children Program, initially run out of an Oakland church.[11]

The Black Panthers patrolled black areas of Oakland with visible, loaded firearms—which at the time was legal in California. The Panthers came to national prominence in May 1967, when they arrived armed at the California State legislature in Sacramento to protest a bill banning loaded guns in public places.

After multiple shootouts with police and constant exposure of their revolutionary and criminal activities, the Panthers were pretty much over by the late 1970s.[12] However, the Black Panthers still serve as a model for many in today's Black Lives Matter movement-right down to the Maoist guiding philosophy.

OBAMA CONNECTION

Years after the Harrises stepped into Mary Lewis's living room for the first time, Afro-American Association leader Donald Warden moved to Texas and adopted a new religion and a new name to go with it: Khalid al-Mansour.

In 2008, former NY1 reporter Dominic Carter interviewed former Manhattan borough president Percy Sutton on the show "Inside City Hall."[13] Sutton, who came from a San Antonio Texas Communist Party family, revealed his connections to then-presidential candidate Barack Obama.[14]

According to Investor's Business Daily:

> Sutton: 'I was introduced to (Obama) by a friend who was raising money for him.' He asked Sutton to write a letter in support of Obama's application to Harvard Law School.
>
> The friend's name is Dr. Khalid al-Mansour' Sutton said. 'He is the principal adviser to one of the world's richest men. He told me about Obama.'
>
> Sutton recalled that al-Mansour said that 'there is a young man that has applied to Harvard. I know that you have a few friends up there because you used to go up there to speak. Would you please write a letter in support of him?' Sutton did.[15]

According to Newsmax columnist Kenneth Timmerman, "At the time, Percy Sutton, a former lawyer for Malcolm X and a former business partner of al-Mansour, says he (al-Mansour) was raising money for Obama's graduate school education, al-Mansour was representing top members of the Saudi Royal family seeking to do business and exert influence in the United States."

Timmerman goes on to discuss a November 1979 column by TV commentator and respected Chicago Tribune columnist Vernon Jarrett entitled "Will Arabs Back Ties To Blacks With Cash?"

> *The late Vernon Jarrett was the father-in-law of Valerie Jarrett, who would go on to become…'the consigliere of the Obama White House'. Mr. Jarrett was a colleague and one of the best friends of Frank Marshall Davis, the former Chicago journalist and lifelong communist who moved to Hawaii in the late 1940s and years later befriended Stanley and Madelyn Dunham and their daughter Stanley Ann, mother of Barack Obama.*
>
> *Davis is known to have taken an active role in the rearing of young Obama from the age of 10 until he turned 18 and left Hawaii for his first year at Occidental College in Los Angeles in 1979. That was the same year al-Mansour was seeking Arab financial support for students such as Obama.*
>
> *Vernon Jarrett's column details how al-Mansour told him about a proposal he made to OPEC Secretary-General Rene Ortiz regarding a program to spend '$20 million per year for 10 years to aid 10,000 minority students each year, including blacks, Arabs, Hispanics, Asians and native Americans.'*
>
> *These minority students would then migrate through the political system promoting Palestinian and radical Islamist causes. Al-Mansour told Jarrett that the program had been endorsed by Ortiz and other OPEC administrators.*[16]

Timmerman didn't mention that Vernon Jarrett was also a Communist Party member in the 1940s and an activist colleague of Frank Marshall Davis.

Davis and Jarrett worked together on several Communist Party projects, including the Citizen's Committee to Aid Packing House Workers.

CITIZENS' COMMITTEE TO AID PACKING-HOUSE WORKERS

Organized to support the United Packing-House Workers of America C. I. O. now on strike

4859 So. Wabash Avenue   phones: Livingston 7365-7375

Chicago, Illinois

SIDNEY A. JONES JR.,
  Chairman
MRS. HATTIE K. BRYAN   April 12, 1948.
  Co-Chairman
THOMAS M. CLARKE   Dear Friend:
  Secretary
OSCAR C. BROWN
  Treasurer   The next meeting of the Citizens' Committee to Aid
MRS. LOUISE T. PATTERSON   Packing-House Workers will be held at Madam Walker's College,
  Asst. Treasurer   4703 South Parkway, Second Floor, Thursday, April 15, 1948, at
COMMITTEE MEMBERS   8:00 P. M. Please be present.
Sven Anderson
Joseph D. Bibb

Vernon Jarrett
Joseph Jefferson   PUBLICITY COMMITTEE: Vernon Jarrett, Chairman; Joseph D.
Horace Johnson   Bibb, Theodore Coleman, Charles A. Davis, Frank Marshall Davis,
Mrs. Marjorie Joyner   Mrs. Rebecca Styles Taylor.
B. F. Jones
Sidney A. Jones Jr.
Ulysses S. Keyes   The duty of this Committee is to give publicity to the
Rev. William Latham   facts with reference to the strike, the plight of the workers
Theophilus Mann   and the work of the Citizens Committee.
Mrs. Jackie Ormes
Mrs. Bertha Keith Payne

Vernon Jarrett remained at least a Communist Party USA (CPUSA) sympathizer for decades into the future.[17]

Dee Myles, Chicago-based chair of the education commission of the CPUSA, wrote an interesting obituary of Vernon Jarrett for the Communist Party USA's publication People's World dated June 4, 2004:

> Jarrett was fanatical about African Americans registering and voting in mass for socially conscious candidates... and this March, from his hospital bed, wrote an article appealing to Black Chicago to turn out to vote for Barack Obama in the Illinois primaries.
>
> Obama astounded everyone with an incredible landslide victory as the progressive, Black candidate for the Democratic Party nomination for the US Senate seat from Illinois. From his sickbed, Vernon Jarrett issued a clarion call, and the people responded.[18]

At every step of Barack Obama's career there was a communist there to help.

Kamala Harris's life follows a very similar pattern.

KAMALA HARRIS AND THE RAINBOW SIGN

The Outside of the Rainbow Sign, as Captured by a Local News Report, 1972

Shyamala and Don Harris divorced when Kamala was seven. The Harris girls would visit their father at his house in Palo Alto at the weekends, but their main social focus remained in Berkeley.

In the early 1970s, Shyamala Harris and her daughters were regular visitors at a local art gallery/ restaurant/ black cultural center, called the Rainbow Sign.[19]

Says Kamala Harris:

> My favorite night of the week was Thursday. On Thursdays you could always find us in an unassuming beige building on the corner of what was then Grove Street and Derby. Once a mortuary... My mother, Maya, and I went to the Rainbow Sign often. Everyone in the neighborhood knew us as Shyamala and the girls. We were a unit, a team, and when we'd show up at the Rainbow Sign, we were always greeted with big smiles and warm hugs.[20]

Though the venue only lasted from 1971 to 1977, it played a key role in the development of the Bay Area Black Left.

According to MSNBC's Trymaine Lee:

> And today, we're going into the little-known history of the Rainbow Sign and how it shaped a generation of Black creatives, activists,

*and politicians, including Vice President-elect Kamala Harris. So,
let's start in Berkeley, California, in the late 1960s.*

*The Rainbow Sign was the vision of Mary Ann Pollar, a leg-
endary Bay Area concert promoter who founded the place with a
group of other Black women.*

*They wanted to create a space where Black people and allies in
the fight for freedom could see a true reflection of themselves, unen-
cumbered by the white gaze…*

*For six years in the early 1970s, that beige building in the
Brooklyn, California, was the center of the universe, or at least the
section of it occupied by a constellation of Black luminaries like
Maya Angelou and James Baldwin, and a little, Black and Indian
girl would one day become a star of American politics.*

*Back then, that little building was home to the Rainbow Sign,
a cultural center that sat at the intersection of the Black Arts and
Black Power Movements. It was a social club, a concert space, the
kind of joint where you could find the first Black mayor of Berkeley
rubbing shoulders with Black Panthers over a plate of fried chicken
and collard greens while listening to Nina Simone pour her heart
out. It was that kind of Black.*[21]

It was that kind of Red, too.

Maya Angelou of course is notorious for her support for Cuba's
Fidel Castro. She was a veteran of the communist-controlled
California Labor School and the equally radical Harlem Writers
Guild.[22]

James Baldwin, a militant socialist was close at various times to the
Young People's Socialist League, the pro-Stalin Communist Party
USA and the pro-Mao Black Panthers.[23]

The Rainbow Sign featured a piece by communist sympathizing
sculptress Elizabeth Catlett.[24] Paintings by leftist artists Romare
Kofi Bailey and Cleveland Bellow adorned the walls.

Leftist folksinger Odetta performed there - she was a friend of the
owner's family.[25]

Early in its history, the Rainbow Sign became the main gathering
place of group of black women eager to shake up local politics.

Dezie Woods-Jones moved to the Bay Area with her family when she
was just six months old. After stints in the South organizing with the

communist-influenced Student Nonviolent Coordinating Committee (SNCC) she returned to help elect a black socialist to Congress.

Black Women Organized for Political Action (BWOPA) was founded in 1968, as an outgrowth of a group calling itself Bay Area Women for Dellums. The small group grew to over 200 black women from throughout the Bay Area - all diligently working to elect local activist Ron Dellums to Congress.

In 1970, they succeeded.

Dellums was openly pro-Cuba and unashamedly Marxist. He was a public member of the Democratic Socialists of America – even while serving on the House Armed Services Committee.[26]

Ron Dellums with Chicago DSA, 1983

Kamala Harris had some ties to Dellums.

In Mid-2008, Lenore Anderson, who served as Ron Dellums's policy aide on crime and public safety, jumped over to San Francisco District Attorney Kamala Harris's office.

Wrote the East Bay Express's Chris Thompson:

> *The Trib's story is chock-full of accolades for Anderson, which we can only echo, at least on a personal basis. We've been friends with Lenore Anderson for 13 years, going back to our youthful days as crazy Berkeley lefties, and she's every bit as smart and energetic as her fans say she is.[27]*

Lenore Anderson later became a founder of the Ford Foundation-funded, Soros-funded[28,29] and Facebook founder Mark Zuckerberg's Chan Zuckerberg Initiative-funded[30] anti-prison group Alliance for Safety and Justice. According to the Washington Free Beacon,[31] Anderson "cowrote the 2014 law that loosened punishment for drug offenses and theft in California." Additionally, Anderson "pushed a law that has freed violent felons who went on to commit murder and other crimes."

From her childhood gatherings with the Afro-American Association, to her staff as California Attorney General to the Riots of 2020 and her advocacy of the George Floyd Justice in Policing Act of 2020, anti-police activism is a thread in Kamala Harris's life.

Kamala Harris marked Dellums's July 2018 death with an X post.

Vice President Kamala Harris ✓
@VP

Follow   ...

Deeply saddened by the loss of former Congressman and Mayor of Oakland, Ron Dellums. His years of service to both the Bay Area and California will continue to serve as a beacon for change and progress. Sending my condolences to his family and loved ones.

1:14 PM · Jul 30, 2018

When the Rainbow Sign opened, BWOPA moved in, using the venue as the headquarters until it closed.

BWOPA was very radical in its early days, very much on the left. At one point they organized a black-only political conference.

Says Dezie Woods-Jones:

> *And so, we would meet. And we decided we wanted an all-Black conference, and we wouldn't let even the white media in. And of course, they thought we were meeting and sabotaging, planning to, you know, have a revolution.*
>
> *The movement was a part of your total essence. It wasn't just words or verbiage. It became a part of who you were and your determination to act. We were really committed to die.*[32]

Kamala Harris remembers the Rainbow Sign fondly:

I loved the powerful orations from the stage and the witty, some-times unruly, audience banter. It was where I learned that artistic expression, ambition, and intelligence were cool. It was where I came to understand that there was no better way to feed someone's brain than by bringing together food, poetry, politics, music, dance, and art.[33]

Young Kamala was particularly impressed by the first Black woman to run for US President – New York Congresswoman Shirley Chisholm.

In 1971, Congresswoman Shirley Chisholm paid a visit while she was exploring a run for president. Talk about strength, 'Unbought and unbossed,' just as her campaign slogan promised.[34]

Shirley Chisholm was involved in several communist front operations and was endorsed by the cop-killing[35] Black Panther Party.

Representative Chisholm's last years in Congress were spent agitating for the repeal of the McCarren Act, which had been used to "crack down on Communist Party members". [36]

Those who are sympathetic to communism tend to resist efforts to dismantle it.

BWOPA - Black Women Organized for Polit ✔ @BWOP · Nov 30, 2019 ···
Celebrating Shirley Chisolm's Birthday at @Kamala's campaign office.

Dezie Woods-Jones remembers the young Kamala Harris fondly:

> *When I see Kamala, it's always a hug and a, 'How are you doing?'*
> *And 'Mother Dezie,' and you know, 'Are you okay, and do you*
> *need?' I mean, and it's authentic. It's outside of the politics...* [37]

And with a great deal of pride at selection as Joe Biden's running
mate:

> *I was trying to jump up and down and holler at the same time. I*
> *was streaming with tears, with joy, and certainly thinking of the*
> *women who I've had the opportunity over my 79 years, 60 plus*
> *years of activism, to stand on their shoulders and watch them do*
> *that.*
>
>   *To know that they made sacrifices so we can continue to make*
> *this progress. I'm happy, glad. But besides being happy, glad about*
> *her success, I am proud. But in addition to being proud, I am*
> *grateful that we are finally seeing the results, or we're seeing some*
> *results of the many, many years and the many, many individuals,*
> *and the result of many African American women who made this*
> *moment possible.* [38]

 Black Women Organized for Political Action · Follow
December 1, 2020 · ⊙

Kamala, Dezie, BWOPA & The Rainbow Sign
Kamala Harris' history with BWOPA goes way back. || This audio clip is from a recent podcast episode released on 11/19 with BWOPA's founder, Dezie Woods-Jones and MSNBC's 'into America' podcast. Dezie talks about the connection with Kamala Harris, BWOPA and the now closed Black Cultural Center, The 'Rainbow Sign' in Berkeley founded in 1971.
· · ·
Listen to the full episode where ever you get your podcasts! It's a great listen. 🎙 🎧 🎶 See Less

Kamala Harris and Dezie Woods-Jones

Dezie Woods-Jones remains president of Black Women Organized for Political Action, the organization she founded at Rainbow Sign.

And Kamala Harris remains a BWOPA supporter to this day.

TEENAGE YEARS, MARXIST DAD

Donald Harris was teaching at Northwestern University in Illinois and when he was hired at the University of Wisconsin, Shyamala moved back to Northern California with their two children before the couple divorced in 1972. The Wisconsin job didn't last long.

Don Harris soon returned to sunny California to take up a visiting professorship of economics at Stanford University, where he was eventually recruited full-time as an open Marxist.

Kamala and her younger sister Maya regularly visited their father during school holidays.

When she was twelve, Kamala Harris and her sister moved with their mother to Montreal, Quebec, where Shyamala had accepted a research and teaching position at the Jewish General Hospital as a breast cancer researcher. Kamala Harris attended a French-speaking primary school before graduating from Westmount High School in Westmount, Quebec, in 1981.

Beginning circa 1974, the Stanford branch of the Union for Radical Political Economics (URPE) began a campaign to recruit a Marxist professor, specifically Don Harris, to Stanford's economics department.

After a long campaign by URPE, Don Harris was offered, and accepted, a permanent professorship at Stanford.[39]

Marxist Offered Economics Post

By KEN McLAUGHLIN

Don Harris, a prominent Marxist professor, has been offered a full professorship in the Economics Department here, Department Chairman James Rosse confirmed yesterday.

Rosse said Harris has not yet accepted the offer, but he "expects to hear from him this week."

Harris, who still holds a tenured position at the University of Wisconsin, has served as a visiting professor here, and is currently teaching at the University of the West Indies in Kingston, Jamaica.

The appointment is the direct result of student pressure in recent years to hire more faculty who favor an "alternative approach" to economics, said Economics Prof. John Gurley, who now teaches the only undergraduate course in Marxist economics.

Gurley said the appointment of

Harris was the culmination of a six-month "round-the-world" search for the most qualified Marxist professor available.

'Exceptionally Good'

Gurley called Harris "an exceptionally good teacher, outstanding researcher and one of the leading young people in Marxist economics."

One knowledgeable source told the Daily that some senior faculty members were very hesitant about hiring Harris, but that they gradually yielded to student pressure.

A conservative economics faculty member, who wished to remain anonymous, said he was "not part of the decision and it would thus be fair not to say anything."

He also added that "as far as I'm concerned, [Harris] is not in the same field I'm in."

Stanford Daily, May 13, 1975, page 1

On November 12, 1976, a letter appeared in the Stanford Daily headed "Faculty column misstates record" signed by members of the Stanford branch of the URPE, claiming full credit for Harris's appointment:

> The program in Marxian economics would be much weaker than it is today if had it not been for massive student efforts in the form of petitions, open meetings ...
> [It] was only after a divisive one and a one-half year struggle that the opposing elements in the department gave into student pressure and conceded to 'the appointment of Prof. Donald Harris. Thus, the presence of Marxian economists here simply indicates the success of the student struggle. ... The recent addition of course offerings in Marxian economics is again a direct result of student pressure, not departmental benevolence.[40]

Signatories were Bill Dittenhofer, Ari Cohen, Eric Berg, David O'Connor, Arthur Slepian, Sandy Thompson, and Tracy Mott.[41]

The URPE was born in 1968 as a spinoff of the radical Students for a Democratic Society (SDS).[42] URPE and another SDS descendant, the Democratic Socialists of America (DSA) have overlapped considerably since DSA's founding in 1982.

For example, one of Professor Harris's Stanford URPE supporters, the late[43] Tracy Mott, became a professor at the University of Denver, where he worked closely with Colorado DSA activists.

During the summer and fall of 2006, the DSA's Political Action Committee helped DSA activists around the country host house parties to raise funds that helped Bernie Sanders become the "sole socialist in the US Senate."

According to DSA magazine Democratic Left:

> Boulder, Colorado, guests braved a downpour to attend the party at the home of Leslie Lomas and hear a talk about giving money by economics professor and socialist Tracy Mott.[44]

Don Harris regularly churned out papers with titles such as "The Black Ghetto as Colony: A Theoretical Critique" (1972) and "Capitalist Exploitation and Black Labor: Some Conceptual Issues" (1978).

URPE had a close relationship with the Institute for Policy Studies (IPS), a preeminent far-left policy organization based in Washington DC. Since its founding in 1963, the IPS has consistently followed a pro-Marxist line on foreign policy, defense, and economic issues.

To put its policy recommendations into action, the IPS "built networks of contacts among congressional legislators and their staffs, academics, government officials, and the national media."[45]

The IPS also was on very close terms with representatives of communist-run Cuba and the former Soviet Union.

In 1978, Brian Crozier, director of the London-based Institute for the Study of Conflict, described IPS at the National Review as the "perfect intellectual front for Soviet activities which would be resisted if they were to originate openly from the KGB."[46]

In the 1988 book: "Winning America: Ideas and Leadership for the 1990s", edited by IPS leaders Marcus Raskin (father of current United States Representative Jamie Raskin) and Chester Hartman, IPS visiting fellow[47] and DSA affiliate[48] Sean Gervasi recommended a slate of radical colleagues as potential appointees in a hoped-for new Democratic administration after the 1988 election.[49]

Gervasi's wish list including the following potential appointees and hires:

+ **Barry Bluestone:** a former SDS leader,[50] and URPE founder member.[51] Bluestone later served as a senior policy staffer for Speaker of the House Dick Gephardt (D-MO).[52]

+ **Gar Alperovitz:** IPS fellow,[53] Long time DSA affiliate.[54]

+ **Robert Browne:** DSA affiliate,[55] IPS affiliate,[56] former SDS supporter.[57]

+ **Jeff Faux:** Long time DSA affiliate.[58] Faux has worked as an economist with the US Office of Economic Opportunity and the US Departments of State, Commerce, and Labor.[59]

+ **Carol O'Cleireacain:** DSA member,[60] Brookings Institute. In 2014, O'Cleireacain was appointed Detroit deputy mayor for economic policy, planning, and strategy.[61]

+ **Howard Wachtel:** DSA affiliate,[62] IPS affiliate,[63] URPE founding member.[64]

+ **Art MacEwan:** URPE founding member,[65] DSA affiliate.[66]

Also on the list was Don Harris, Marxist professor, Stanford University.[67]

However, Republican George H.W. Bush won the 1988 election, so Professor Harris ended up lecturing at Stanford until his retirement.

Interestingly, DSA comrade Carol O'Cleireacain and a "Don Harris" were listed as speakers at DSA's third annual Socialist Scholars Conference, held in April 1985 at the Borough of Manhattan Community College.

April 4, 5, 6   The 3rd Annual

Socialist Scholars Conference

"The Left in Crisis"

Boro of Manhattan Community College,
CUNY 199 Chambers St. (near Trade Center),
New York City

Join . . . Ellen Willis ● Bogdan Denitch ●
Luciana Castellina ● David Gordon ● Harry Magdoff ●
Cornel West ● Carol O'Cleireacain ● Allan Hershkovitz
● Ray Franklin ● Stanley Aronowitz ● Judith Stein ● Jan
Rosenberg ● Cynthia Epstein ● Michael Walzer ● Ira
Katznelson ● Erwin Knoll ● Stanley Greenberg ● Frances
Fox Piven ● Paul Sweezy ● Yair Tzaban ● Saskia Sassen-
Koob ● Michael Harrington ● Amy Clampitt ● John Hy-
land ● Chester Feurstein ● Joan Barkan ● Joan Cohen ●
Dorothy Healey ● Irving Howe ● Barbara Ehrenreich ●
Robert Engler ● Jennifer Hunt ● Judith Lorber ● Jewel
Bellush ● Bernard Bellush ● R.L. Norman ● Jo Ann Mort
● Vern Mogensen ● Don Harris ● William Kornblum ●
John Rantz ● John Trinkl ● Ruth Spitz ● Patricia Mann ●
Barbara Epstein ● Deborah Meier ● Gordon Adams ●
Rosanna Giamanco ● Dave Garrow ● Paulette Pierce ●
Robert Lekachman ● Paul Piccone ● Patrick Hughes ●
James Weinstein ● James Aronson ● Jeff Escoffier

This year's conference is on the theme of "The Left in
Crisis." Last year's conference brought more than 2000
participants together. This year the conference is being expanded to over 80 panels. There will be panel sequences
on feminist, labor, theoretical, economic, cultural, third
world, and American political topics.

Sponsors/Participants (in formation)
CUNY Ph.D. Program in Sociology, and Dissent, Nation, Institute for
Democratic Socialism, Mid-Atlantic Radical Historians Organization,
Monthly Review, Social Policy, Social Text, Socialist Review, Telos,
CUNY Democratic Socialist Society Club, CUNY Democratic Socialist
Graduate Student Club, South End Press, and The Fabian Society

Pre-registration:
$15.00 Regular
$7.50 Student

Make checks payable to "Socialist Scholars Conference"
and mail to: CUNY Democratic Socialist Club
33 West 42nd St. Rm. 901, New York, NY 10036
For more information, call 212-790-4320

Democratic Left, January-February 1985, page 16

Incidentally, a young Barack Obama had attended DSA's first and second annual Socialist Scholars Conference, in 1983 and 1984.[68]

Ironically, Kamala Harris was soundly defeated in the 2020 Democratic Presidential primary, by among others, Bernie Sanders - a favorite of Professor Don Harris's old URPE and DSA colleagues.

COLLEGE AND A PRO-COMMUNIST BOSS

After high school, Kamala Harris attended Howard University, a historically black university in Washington DC. At Howard, Harris was active in the left's campaign against Apartheid South Africa. The *real* goal of this Soviet-directed effort - which was at the time a cause popular with all shades of the left - was not racial justice but rather the destruction of an anti-communist government.

Kamala Harris protesting in the National Mall, 1982

Kamala Harris was active at university, where she chaired the economics society, led the debate team, and joined the Alpha Kappa Alpha sorority. Harris graduated from Howard in 1986 with a degree in political science and economics.[69]

In 1984, Kamala Harris served an internship during her sophomore year for Alan Cranston, a Democrat who represented California in the US Senate for several terms.

"I loved going to work — it felt like the epicenter of change, even as an intern sorting mail," Harris, once said — later touting how she "believed the Senate was a place to turn activism into action."

Cranston reportedly advised Kamala Harris to "make as many friends as you can on the way up" since "you'll need them on the way down."[70]

 **Kamala Harris** ☑
@KamalaHarris

The summer of my second year at Howard, I interned for Sen. Alan Cranston in the mailroom. I loved going to the Capitol every day to learn how our government worked. All young women interested in politics and government deserve the same opportunity to get their foot in the door.

Like almost everyone else of significance around Kamala Harris, Alan Cranston was close to communism. This may have been purely coincidental, but it was consistent with Kamala Harris's life trajectory.

Foe of Aid to Anti-Communist Forces

Senator Cranston had a consistent record of voting against almost all aid to countries fighting Communist aggression or insurgencies, including South Vietnam and El Salvador, and for refusing to support anti-communist movements fighting for democracy in Communist dictatorships like Nicaragua, Angola, Mozambique, etc.

Senator Cranston's work in the interests of revolution began in his college years at Stanford University. In July 1935, Alan Cranston and his Stanford track team friend John Atkinson joined a group of students from the University of Mexico to dislodge Tomas Garrido Canabal, "dictator" of the state of Tabasco.[71]

Following the alleged killing of five students who had gone to Tabasco to vote against Canabal, an organization was formed at the university to enter the state "to observe a militia campaign to expel Tabasco Governor Tomas Garrido Canabal". Cranston and Atkinson, who were attending summer school in Mexico City, joined the movement. It was a bit anti-climactic, however, "as the Governor was deposed before Cranston and the militia reached their destination".[72]

Office of War Information

During World War II, Cranston was Chief of the Foreign Language Division of the Office of War Information (OWI), the US information and propaganda organization – and a hotbed of communist influence.

Cranston recommended that the OWI hire David Karr, as "a senior liaison officer working with other Federal agencies." Karr had been writing for the Communist Party USA newspaper, The Daily Worker, as well

David Karr

as for Albert Kahn, an author who was later revealed in Congressional testimony to be a Soviet agent.

In spite of this record, Cranston recommended Karr for employment, claiming "that he knew he had worked for The Daily Worker but did not know he was a communist".

After the war, Karr launched a successful career in international finance, which included extensive dealings with the former Soviet

Union. In 1975, for example, Karr arranged a $250 million credit for the Soviet Foreign Trade Bank.

His main contact in Moscow was reported to be Djerman Gvishiani, deputy chairman of the Soviet State Committee for Science and Technology and son-in-law of Soviet Premier Alexei Kosygin.[73]

Karr frequently boasted of having close ties with prominent US senators and presidential candidates and that he transmitted information between the Soviet and American governments on such issues as détente, trade, and strategic-arms negotiations.

Karr, then living in Paris, also headed a Franco-American firm called Finatech. According to KGB files, Karr arranged meetings between Senator Ted Kennedy (D-MA) and Soviet leaders. A KGB file describes Kennedy in 1978 trying to help a close friend, former Senator John V. Tunney (D-CA), get some business in the Soviet Union.

In 1992, Yevgenia Albats, a Russian journalist assigned by the Russian Parliament to examine the archives after the aborted Soviet coup attempt of 1991, quoted "an extremely top secret KGB memo to Soviet leaders:"[74]

> In 1978, American Senator Edward Kennedy appealed to the KGB to assist in establishing cooperation between Soviet organizations and the California firm Agritech, headed by former Senator J. Tunney.
>
> This firm in turn was connected to a French American company, Finatech S.A., which was run by a competent KGB source, the prominent Western financier D. Karr, through whom opinions had been confidentially exchanged for several years between the General Secretary of the Communist Party and Sen. Kennedy. D. Karr provided the KGB with technical information on conditions in the US and other capitalist countries which were regularly reported to the Central Committee.[75]

Karr also provided his Soviet employers with inside information on the presidential or vice-presidential campaigns of several leftist Democratic candidates, including Sargent Shriver, Jerry Brown, and Jimmy Carter and the anti-communist Democrat Henry "Scoop" Jackson of Washington.[76]

Cranston remained a longtime friend of Karr because the Soviet agent "had a strong social conscience that made him an intense promoter of Detente" (with the Soviet Union).[77]

Weakening Taiwan

Senator Cranston also worked to aid the long-term strategic goal of the People's Republic of China to weaken US support for America's ally Taiwan.

In January 1978, then Senate Majority Whip Cranston urged the US to "normalize" relations with the People's Republic of China "as soon as possible" on terms favorable to Beijing.

Cranston had just returned from leading a 10-member congressional delegation on a four-city tour of China.

Senator Cranston said he "doesn't believe that Peking will try to take Taiwan by force if the United States renounces a mutual defense treaty in effect since 1954."[78]

Cranston declared that he felt more urgent about the need to set up diplomatic ties with China because of his trip.

> I feel we should do so swiftly, that we should recognize the absurdity of maintaining our relationship with Taiwan on the grounds it is the government of all China. Clearly, it is not...[79]

Cranston approved of the terms outlined by the Chinese communists for "normalized" relations: an end to US-Taiwanese diplomatic relations; an end to the mutual US-Taiwanese defense treaty and withdrawal of US military personnel from free Taiwan.[80]

Promoting Disarmament

The non-profit organization American Security Council, which supports a United States foreign policy of "Promoting Peace Through Strength", gave Cranston a "0%" rating in 1988.[81] In fact, Cranston founded the "Global Security Institute" (GSI), which pushes disarmament,[82] a strategy that would embolden potential adversaries and weaken America's global standing in the world. It is not surprising that Cranston became close to the Soviet leader and lifelong unrepentant socialist Mikhail Gorbachev.

From an interview with Cranston in 1997:

In the Senate, I focused on arms reduction efforts with the Soviet Union and that led to a friendship with Mikhail Gorbachev. He left office about the same time I did. He set up a foundation as a base of operations, of which I became Chairman in the United States. I'm now working with Gorbachev and other world leaders on trying to find ways to promote a more orderly world in the wake of the Cold War. One of our projects involves global security and an effort to lead the world toward the abolition of nuclear weapons, which I think can be accomplished.[83]

Kamala Harris chose to intern with probably the most pro-communist US Senator of that time.

After graduating from Howard, with a degree in political science and economics, Kamala Harris returned to California to attend law school at the University of California, Hastings College of the Law through its Legal Education Opportunity Program.

While at UC Hastings, she served as president of its chapter of the Black Law Students Association.[84] She graduated with a Juris Doctor in 1989 and was admitted to the California Bar in June 1990.[85,86]

One step closer to Senator Cranston's old job.

CHAPTER 2

BAY AREA REDS

SAN FRANCISCO HAS long been hijacked politically by those with deep communist connections. This section seeks to illustrate the evolution of San Francisco politics, highlighting the powerful players that have molded and shaped those who are in Kamala Harris's orbit and those who came before her.

KAMALA HARRIS MEETS WILLIE BROWN

When Kamala Harris moved back to the Bay Area, she walked into an incredibly incestuous rat's nest of communist-affiliated activists and politicians.

Kamala Harris's relationships and political appointments were not just personal or career advancements, but part of a broader ideological and political network deeply rooted in communist sympathies within the Bay Area's political landscape.

Brown and Harris circa 1994

Bay Area political culture is heavily communist and has been for many decades. Most leading Bay Area Democrats have a communist skeleton or two in their closets.

Kamala Harris fit right in.

Kamala Harris met San Francisco Democratic Party heavyweight Willie Brown in 1994 when he was speaker of the California State Assembly.

ABC News profile of Mayor Willie Brown: Kamala Harris on Right (Screenshot)

Their short relationship set tongues wagging, but Harris fails to mention her former boyfriend even once in her 2019 biography The Truths We Hold.

According to Patrick Byrne of SF Weekly:

> *She was 29, he was 60. Their May/December affair was the talk of the town during the year before Brown's successful 1995 bid to become mayor. But shortly after he was inaugurated, Harris dumped Brown, a notorious womanizer.*
>
> *Brown appointed her to two patronage positions in state government that paid handsomely — more than $400,000 over five years.*
>
> *In 1994, she took a six-month leave of absence from her Alameda County job to join the Unemployment Insurance Appeals Board. Brown then appointed her to the California Medical Assistance Commission, where she served until 1998, attending two meetings a month for a $99,000 annual salary.*[1]

Most commentators have focused on these payments and that fact Willie Brown was still technically married (though long separated from his wife Blanche) while dating Harris.

The real scandal should have been, given Harris' own radical background, that Willie Brown has been - for the bulk of his colorful life - a communist sympathizer, deeply embedded in Bay Area Marxism-Leninism.

San Francisco and the Bay Area have been communist hotbeds since the 1920s. The Communist Party USA (CPUSA) was strong in the International Longshore Workers Union and had a strong following in other unions at Stanford University, UC Berkeley and other colleges. By the 1940s, the CPUSA had heavily infiltrated the local Democratic Party.

When 17-year-old Willie Brown moved from small-town Texas to San Francisco in 1951, he was perfectly timed to ride the communist wave that was well on the way to dominating Bay Area politics.

THE BURTON BROTHERS

Willie Brown's enduring association with communism was catalyzed by his connections with the influential Bay Area political figures, the Burton brothers, Phillip and John.

According to CalMatters columnist James Richardson:

> *Those who can trace their political lineage directly, or indirectly, to (Phillip) Burton include House Speaker Nancy Pelosi, Gov. Gavin Newsom, former Assembly Speaker and San Francisco Mayor Willie Brown, former state Senate Pro Tem John Burton (Phil's younger brother) – and now vice presidential nominee Kamala Harris...*
>
> *Pelosi owes her Congressional seat to Burton who had close ties to Bobby Kennedy. After Burton died, his wife Sala took his seat. When she lay dying in 1987, Sala recruited Pelosi to run for the seat. Pelosi had long been an organizer and money-raiser in San Francisco politics.*
>
> *While Pelosi inherited Burton's seat in Congress, Willie Brown inherited Burton's role as a powerbroker in California politics. Brown has been part of the Burton circle since befriending John Burton when they were students at San Francisco State.*
>
> *Harris, too young to have known Phil Burton, dated Brown when he was Assembly Speaker...Harris was by his side when he ran for mayor. On election night, she handed him a blue cap emblazoned with 'Da Mayor' Their relationship ended soon after, but her career took off.[2]*

In 1947, newly-minted lawyer Phillip Burton moved back to the San Francisco Bay Area where he met a young Democratic activist and former Communist Party USA member named Bert Coffey. Burton, Coffey, Jack K. Berman (first husband of the late Dianne Goldman aka Senator Dianne Feinstein), and communist Dr. Carlton Goodlett formed the nucleus of the San Francisco Democratic Party machine which still dominates the city today.[3]

In the 1960s, Phillip Burton spearheaded the formation of a leftist coalition in San Francisco, uniting labor unions with activists from the black and gay communities, thereby steering the city to the far-left.

From University of San Francisco political science professor James Taylor:

> *Although Burton's name does not get mentioned as regularly as it used to. It hangs over the city because it set the foundation for what the power establishment in the city is right now, which is main-stream liberalism...*[4]

Willie Brown met Phillip through his brother John.
Says Willie Brown:

> *I was not an observer of what was going on politically in San Francisco, although I instantly became a member of the youth group of the NAACP... They talked about things like Black people becoming police officers, Black people driving busses, Black people becoming deputy sheriffs, Black people overing becoming firemen. I heard all those things in the NAACP.*[5]

Brown enrolled at what is now San Francisco State University-where he met John Burton:

> *And I heard things about politics from Burton. As a matter of fact, I joined the Young Democrats because Burton encouraged me and invited me to join.*[6]

When John Burton stood unsuccessfully for the California State Senate in 1967, Willie Brown was on his team.

Both Burton brothers and Willie Brown were up to their eyeballs in communism.

Willie Brown admits that his friend and mentor John Burton was close to the Bay Area far-left including with the legendary communist labor leader Harry Bridges:

> *Through the labor movement they knew him... Through the left wing socialist, communist movement they knew him. Longshoremen and Harry Bridges' crowd. So, John was very much exposed in every way*[7]

How many people do you know who have been mentored by communists?

World Youth Festival

Organized by the Soviet-controlled World Federation of Democratic Youth, the World Youth Festival has been held every three or four years since 1946 as a rallying point for international communist youth.

From July 29 - August 6, 1962, the Eighth World Youth Festival was held in Helsinki, Finland. In fact, the US House Committee on Un-American Activities conducted hearings on "Communist Youth Activities", specifically examining the World Youth Festival held in Helsinki.

COMMUNIST YOUTH ACTIVITIES
(Eighth World Youth Festival, Helsinki, Finland, 1962)

HEARINGS
BEFORE THE

COMMITTEE ON UN-AMERICAN ACTIVITIES
HOUSE OF REPRESENTATIVES
EIGHTY-SEVENTH CONGRESS
SECOND SESSION

APRIL 25 AND 27 AND OCTOBER 4, 1962

Committee on Un-American Activities on the World Youth Festival in Helsinki, 1962

Communist folk singer Pete Seeger joined with musicians Phil Ochs, Tom Paxton, Judy Collins, Odetta and Bob Dylan to raise funds at the City University of New York to pay young Americans to attend the Soviet-run gathering in Finland.[8]

Many young American radicals travelled to Helsinki including young communists Bobbie Rabinowitz, Michael Myerson and Harold Supriano. Michele Hall, daughter of communist Hawaiian union leader Jack Hall and future wife of John Burton also made the pilgrimage.[9]

World Peace Council

Various American political figures, including members of Congress Phillip Burton, John Burton, and others, were involved or showed interest in the activities of the World Peace Council (WPC), a Soviet propaganda tool. This involvement included attending luncheons, receptions, and meetings with WPC delegates, some of whom were high-ranking Soviet officials or KGB operatives.

1975 Delegation

From September 29 - October 12, 1975, the Soviet-controlled WPC sent a delegation on a ten-day tour of the United States, where they were "warmly and enthusiastically received". In six of the ten cities visited, the delegation was officially welcomed by the mayors' offices and presented with "keys to the city", medals and proclamations.

The delegation included Romesh Chandra, Indian communist leader and Secretary General of the World Peace Council; Josef Cyrankiewicz, former Premier of communist Poland and Chairman of the Polish Peace Committee; Yacov Lomko, Editor-in-Chief of the Moscow News, leading member of the Soviet Peace Committee, and CPUSA member Karen Talbot, a US member of the WPC Secretariat.

The WPC delegates were guests of several members of Congress at a luncheon in the House of Representatives' dining room, and at a reception. Among those present were several members of the Congressional Black Caucus, including Congressman John Conyers (D-MI), and Congressman Ron Dellums (D-CA).

Congressman Phillip Burton, by then House Majority leader, hosted the luncheon, "expressing interest in the work of the WPC" and a Soviet propaganda operation called the New Stockholm Campaign.[10]

1978 Delegation

In 1978, Congressmen John Burton, Ted Weiss, Ron Dellums, John Conyers, Don Edwards, Charles Rangel and others... attended a World Peace Council-organized meeting on Capitol Hill.

WPC delegation members included President Romesh Chandra, KGB Colonel Radomir Bogdanov and Oleg Kharkhardin of the Communist Party of the Soviet Union International Department.

Institute for Policy Studies

The Institute for Policy Studies (IPS) celebrated its 20th anniversary with an April 5, 1983, reception at the National Building Museum attended by approximately 1,000 IPS staffers and former staff.

The Congressional IPS committee members included Phillip Burton and Ron Dellums as well as Leon Panetta (D-CA)[11] a future Obama Secretary of Defense and head of the CIA.

John Burton would go to become was a Democratic Party Congressman from California, a California state Assemblyman, chair of the California Democratic Party and a mentor to former California Senator Barbara Boxer.[12]

This network of influence illustrates that American political figures such as the Burton Brothers were not just passively involved but actively engaged with international communist movements, laying a radical foundation and ultimately affecting both American foreign policy and domestic politics.

Willie Brown and the Communist Party

Willie Brown was elected to the California Assembly in 1964 as a left-wing Democrat with the backing of the local W.E.B. Du Bois Club, the youth wing of the Communist Party USA.[13]

The national W.E.B. Du Bois Clubs network at the time was headed by local boy Terence Hallinan, a member of a notorious San Francisco communist family.

Hallinan was a student radical at Berkeley in the sixties, teaching seminars on Marxism-Leninism in his father Vincent Hallinan's law offices - rechristened the "San Francisco School for Social Science." The Du Bois Clubs identified and nurtured the young lawyer, Willie Brown.

According to Brown biographer James Richardson:

> The key to Brown's 1964 campaign was voter registration in the black neighborhoods. Brown's registration drive in the Eighteenth Assembly District netted 5,577 new Democratic voters in three months, a staggering number for the era. Many of the frontline troops registering voters had been among those arrested in the civil rights demonstrations. Terence Hallinan organized his radical friends from the W.E.B. Du Bois Club into the 'Youth Committee for Assemblyman Brown', which worked primarily on voter registration.
>
> Hallinan kept the youth committee active for two years, helping Brown to permanently harden his base of support in his district. In later years, registration drives underpinned Brown's campaigns for favored Assembly candidates when he became Speaker. His first effort in the science was impressive.[14]

Terence Hallinan gained the nickname "Kayo" from his prowess as a boxer.

Ironically, Kayo Hallinan was himself knocked out in 2003 when Kamala Harris defeated him to become San Francisco District Attorney.

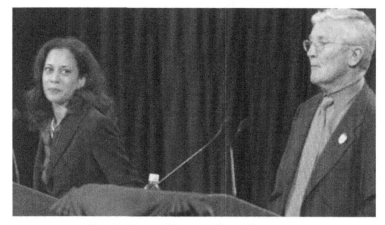

Kamala Harris and Terence Hallinan debate in 2003

Two years later, Willie Brown and iconic Bay Area radical Robert Scheer apparently got behind ex-communist lawyer Robert Treuhaft's 1966 campaign for Alameda County District Attorney.

Campaign for Alameda County District Attorney, 1966.
Left to right, Bobb Scheer, Bob Treuhaft, and Willie Brown

Robert Scheer was editor of the famous radical journal Ramparts – and a veteran of the Fair Play for Cuba Committee,[15] which was referred to by the Senate Judiciary Committee as part of "Castro's Network in the United States".[16]

1969 Ramparts cover: child holds a Vietcong flag

In 1970, Scheer led - with Black Panther Party leader Eldridge Cleaver - the US People's Anti-Imperialist Delegation, a two-and-a-half month tour of North Korea, North Vietnam, and China.

In China: Eldridge Cleaver back center, Robert Scheer, back row, 3rd from right

Robert Treuhaft and his wife Jessica Mitford (of the famous English aristocratic family) joined the Communist Party USA in 1943 and remained members until 1958. Robert Mitford remained a radical however, active in the National Lawyers Guild, a "legal action front operated by the Communist Party USA"[17] and the Soviet-controlled International Association of Democratic Lawyers.[18]

In 1963, Treuhaft and Doris Brin Walker, who kept up her Communist Party USA membership until her death in 2009,[19] founded their own law firm, which employed many young radical associates and interns, including future US Secretary of State, Senator and First Lady, Hillary Rodham [Clinton] during the summer of 1971.[20]

Walker famously represented iconic communist Angela Davis against murder and kidnapping charges, leading to her acquittal.[21]

Doris Walker with her client Angela Davis on May 25, 1972, via NY Times

As an aside, the Communist Party USA's "People's World" reported on September 17, 2024 that Angela Davis stated during a festival of l'Humanité, the newspaper of the French Communist Party, that she would be voting for Kamala Harris in the 2024 Election.

In the article titled "Angela Davis: Electing Harris will open space for more radical struggles", Davis stated that the election of Kamala Harris would result in a climate more conducive for ultimately pushing "anti-capitalist and anti-racist programs forward". Speaking of Harris, Angela Davis said that there is "no question about who progressive people and people who identify with radical change will vote for" in the US election.[22]

'TAKING APARTHEID APART'

On April 28, 1991, eight hundred people filled the ballroom of the Hyatt
Regency Embarcadero Hotel, to greet South African Communist Party
leader Chris Hani in an event billed as "Taking Apartheid Apart". The
crowd contributed more than $12,000 towards the Communist Party
USA's formerly-titled "People's Weekly World" newspaper fundraiser
and to promote the work of the South African Communist Party.

Comrade Hani was greeted with resolutions of support from
California Assembly speaker Willie Brown, San Francisco mayor
Art Agnos, Oakland mayor Elihu Harris, Richmond mayor George
Livingston, Berkeley mayor Loni Hancock, and Doris Ward, chair of
the San Francisco Board of Supervisors.

Co-chairs of the banquet were and Ignacio de la Fuente of
the Moulders Union and iconic communist Angela Davis.[23] The
Welcoming Committee included[24] Dr. Carlton Goodlett, in addi-
tion to communists Southern Organizing Committee for Economic
and Social Justice co-chair Anne Braden, singer Pete Seeger, Young
Communist League member John Bachtell and others.

Screenshot of 'Taking Apartheid Apart' Invitation

People's Weekly World Gala Banquet

In September 1999, several years after the end of his relationship
with Kamala Harris, Willie L. Brown, Jr., Mayor of San Francisco,
co-sponsored a Communist Party USA fund raising event in Berkeley.
Several Communist Party USA members including Arnold

Becchetti, Marilyn Bechtel, Libero Della Piana, as well as Oakland based Democratic Congresswoman Barbara Lee co-sponsored the same event.[25]

Communist Party USA Publication, Peoples Weekly World, September 11, 1999

Co-sponsors of the October 8, 2000, Bay Area People's Weekly World banquet included San Francisco Mayor Willie L. Brown, plus the vice mayors of Berkeley and Oakland.[26]

Honorees included Los Angeles-based Communist Party USA vice chair Evelina Alarcon.[27]

CARLTON GOODLETT'S WIDE NET

According to Terence Hallinan, an endorsement from Bay Area physician and newspaper owner Carlton Goodlett was important to the election of many political leaders. Goodlett helped to inspire and promote the political careers the late Representatives Phillip Burton, John Burton, Ron Dellums and Willie Brown.[28]

Carlton Goodlett

On February 11, 1997, Congresswoman Nancy Pelosi addressed Congress, paying a tribute to Carlton Goodlett, who died of Parkinson's disease at the age of 82:

> *In 1950 he joined with my predecessor, the great Representative Phillip Burton, in founding the San Francisco Young Democrats. He put his heart into supporting the campaigns of candidates he believed in, like Phillip Burton, John Burton and Willie Brown, our current mayor of San Francisco.*
>
> *Dr. Goodlett's presence was deeply felt. His absence will be felt equally. He was a man who did many things, all of them well. As we celebrate Black History Month, we need look no further for inspiration than Dr. Carlton Goodlett. He was a renaissance man who mobilized the intellectual resources of his area to fight for civil rights. He was a healer, a mentor, a courageous leader, an activist and advocate and truly a citizen of the world. As the world will mourn his loss, we must remember that he is an inspiration to us all.*[29]

Nancy Pelosi forgot to mention Carlton Goodlett's deep communist ties.

FOREST KNOLLS

In May 1961, Willie Brown used his NAACP connections as well as those with Carlton Goodlett's the Sun-Reporter newspaper (which targeted black Americans[30] in the San Francisco Bay Area) to protest the exclusive Forest Knolls housing development. Brown claimed that the real estate group refused to sell him and his wife Blanche a home due to his race.

Willie Brown was ready for a very public fight. He even "brought with him a photographer from the Sun-Reporter" when visiting the "housing tract before his wife".[31]

The Communist Party USA had been organizing similar "incidents" in several parts of the country for years. Without fail, communists exploit righteous causes to create division and chaos.

Seattle Communist Party newspaper, January 1948

Among those who joined Willie Brown's picket line was Dianne Berman, the wife of a prominent attorney. Years later, Dianne Berman (later Dianne Feinstein), would become mayor of San Francisco and then a United States senator from California from 1992 until her death in 2023 at age 90.

Throughout her career, Feinstein enjoyed a mutually beneficial political friendship with Willie Brown, and it all began on the "Forest Knolls picket line."[32]

Willie Brown's 1962 California Assembly Campaign

Willie Brown's 1962 election platform was "I will seek to end racial and religious segregation in schools, housing and employment. I am dedicated to the principles set forth in the Constitution of the United States of America and the State of California."[33] The Forest Knolls protests certainly gave his campaign a boost, as well as some publicity.

Carlton Goodlett supported Willie L. Brown's campaign for California Assembly in 1962, donating $7,500, and naming Brown The Sun-Reporter Man of the Year. Although he lost his first Assembly race, Willie Brown would end up winning in 1964 with the support of the black community that Dr. Goodlett helped galvanize.[34]

That support was ongoing through Willie Brown's political career.

A Covert Connection: Goodlett's Communist Circles

Carlton Goodlett commenced his 38-year career as a family physician in San Francisco in 1945 but in 1948 he became the joint publisher of the Reporter Publishing Company which eventually controlled several black weekly newspapers. As both publisher and editor of the flagship Sun-Reporter, Goodlett had a vehicle to press for the social and economic betterment of African Americans in the Bay Area.

A crusading newspaper under his direction, the Sun-Reporter's motto was, "That no good cause shall lack a champion, evil shall not thrive unopposed."[35]

In the late 1940s, Goodlett, taught at the Communist Party USA-controlled California Labor School:

> *In Goodlett's first year and a half in the city, he was asked by Dave Jenkins, the head of the California Labor School, to join the faculty. He accepted. The school was established by the International Longshoremen's and Warehousemen's Union. The longshoremen were regarded by many conservatives as being communists, or at least a communist front organization. So red-baiters of all hues in San Francisco started whispering that Goodlett was also a red, or if not, at least a fellow traveler.*[36]

That suspicion was well founded.

Carlton Goodlet, as a member of the World Peace Council's Presidium, was a prominent anti-nuclear activist, heading delegations around the globe including Moscow and "formulat[ing] a world disarmament plan".[37]

Carlton Goodlett traveled many times to the Soviet Union and other socialist countries including a visit to hostile North Vietnam in 1975.[38]

In 1970, Goodlett attended a World Peace Conference in Stockholm where he was awarded the most "prestigious" communist award in the world, the Lenin Peace Prize.[39]

Goodlett also served on the "American Committee for the Presentation of the Lenin International Peace Prize."

W. E. B. DU BOIS PEACE AWARD

AMERICAN COMMITTEE FOR PRESENTATION of the Lenin International Peace Prize

POST OFFICE BOX 392 • SAN FRANCISCO 1, CALIFORNIA

Co-Chairmen
HOLLAND ROBERTS
Member of the Bureau
of the World Peace Council
CARLTON GOODLETT, M.D.
Publisher of the SUN REPORTER

Dear

As you know, Dr. W. E. B. DuBois, leading peace
worker in the United States and noted scholar, is
one of the five world figures – and the only
American – given the International Peace Award in
1959 for his life-long contributions to peace.
He is the third American to receive it. The others
were the Right Reverend Arthur W. Moulton, Episcopal Bishop from Utah,
and Paul Robeson.

Alice Palmer: A Conduit for Subversive Influence in American Politics

In 1987, Carlton Goodlett served on the Board of Directors of the Chicago-based Black Press Institute.[40] Alice Palmer and her husband Buzz Palmer established the Black Press Institute (BPI) in Chicago circa 1982.

In a 1986 interview with the Communist Party USA paper People's Daily World, Alice Palmer explained BPI's role in influencing decision makers such as the Congressional Black Caucus:

> *After the 1960s some of us looked around and observed there was no national Black newspaper...So we started the Black Press Review. We received the Black newspapers from around the country, reprinted articles and editorials that gave a sense of the dynamics and the lives of Black people and sent them out to the Congressional Black Caucus and other opinion leaders, saying 'Look, here is what black America is thinking and doing....*
>
> *Since then, we have moved into organizing forums and dialogues...*[41]

The BPI was basically a Soviet propaganda operation targeting black Americans.

In 1980, Alice Palmer was invited by the revolutionary Maurice Bishop-led government of the Caribbean island of Grenada to attend celebrations marking the first anniversary of the country's Marxist-Leninist "revolution".

1ST FESTIVAL OF THE GRENADA
REVOLUTION

MARCH 1ST—13TH

OFFICIAL GUEST

Name..ALICE PALMER.....................No............

FESTIVAL OF THE REVOLUTION

In 1985, Alice Palmer led a delegation of 16 far-left black journalists to the Soviet Union, German Democratic Republic and Czechoslovakia.[42]

Alice Palmer told the People's Daily World:

> The trip was extraordinary because we were able to sit down with our counterparts and with the seats of power in three major capitals- Prague, Berlin and Moscow. We visited with foreign ministers, we talked with the editors of the major newspapers in these three cities...
>
> It was a very unusual trip because we were given access... Every effort was made to give us as much as we asked for... We came back feeling that we could speak very well about the interest of the socialist countries in promoting peace.
>
> This was before the (Soviet nuclear test ban) moratorium, this was before the Reykjavik offers... It was very clear to us in our conversations and interviews with people at that time, that this was already something of concern and, something that would be promoted when the opportunity arose, as we can see that it has been.[43]

In March 1986, Alice Palmer covered the Communist Party of the Soviet Union Congress in Moscow for the Black Press Institute.

LIFE UNDER SOCIALISM

An Afro-American journalist in the USSR

Alice Palmer of the Black Press Institute, editor of the Black Press Review, was the only Afro-American to cover the 27th Congress of the Communist Party of the Soviet Union. Following are some of her impressions of the Soviet Union's plans for economic and social development, and affirmative action Soviet-style.

Alice Palmer told the People's Daily World

> *I spent a great deal of time with a woman from the Novosti (Press Agency) and she and I had a lot in common...I had a chance to go shopping, just as I would if were back in Chicago...It is useful to those people who would like to demonize the Soviet people. When I stood in line, it was the same kind of line I stand in in the Jewel grocery store in Chicago. It was merely because the place was crowded, not because at the end of the line there was nothing for me to purchase.*[44]

Alice Palmer was elected International Organization of Journalists (IOJ) vice president for North America at the organization's 10th Congress, October 20-23 1986, in Prague Czechoslovakia. She also traveled to the Soviet Union and Bulgaria during the same trip.[45] Alice Palmer's IOJ duties were to include coordinating the activities of IOJ chapters in the US, Canada, Mexico and the Caribbean.[46]

The IOJ was a Soviet front operation, based in Prague until its expulsion by the Czech government in 1995.[47]

A summary of a paper by Bob Nowell entitled "The Role of the International Organization of Journalists in the Debate about the 'New International Information Order,' 1958-1978" states:

> *This paper examines the International Organization of Journalists (IOJ), which it identifies as a Soviet-dominated organization. The paper suggests that the IOJ has capitalized on "Third World" countries' discontent with Western news media by offering itself as the ideological leader and trainer of anti-Western journalists.*
>
> *It then examines the function and methods of the IOJ in the*

context of post-World War II communist international front orga-
nizations; reviews the IOJ's structure, publications, and training
centers; and explores its role in shaping 'Third World' arguments
in the debate about the New Information Order. The paper argues
that the IOJ's efforts generally have served Soviet foreign policy on
international communications.[48]

During her time as IOJ vice president, Alice Palmer worked with highest levels of the Soviet international propaganda machine.

The IOJ's main job was to promote "peace" - which meant, in Soviet terms, US disarmament and eventual destruction or subjugation by Moscow.

Alice Palmer, like Carlton Goodlett and many others featured in this book, was effectively an agent of Soviet foreign policy goals.

In 1995, Illinois State Senator Alice Palmer decided on a run for the US Congress from South Chicago. At a gathering in the Hyde Park home of former Weather Underground terrorists Bill Ayers and Bernardine Dohrn, Alice Palmer introduced her chosen successor, Barack Obama.

"I can remember being one of a small group of people who came to Bill Ayers' house to learn that Alice Palmer was stepping down from the senate and running for Congress," said Dr. Quentin Young, a prominent Chicago physician, referring to the informal gathering at the home of Bill Ayers and Bernardine Dohrn. "[Palmer] identified [Obama] as her successor," Young explained.

Barack Obama and Palmer "were both there," he said.[49]

Quentin Young was a leading Democratic Socialists of America comrade, an advocate for a socialist single-payer healthcare system in America, and the Obama family's personal physician.[50]

FULL CIRCLE

While Kamala Harris was no longer on great terms with Willie Brown, the Communist Party USA still took a strong interest in her career.

When Harris was confirmed as California's new Attorney General in 2016, the People's World news site celebrated her victory.

California's new top cop, San Francisco's progressive District Attorney Kamala Harris, vowed to insure "the law of this state is on the side of the people."

According to the CPUSA article, Kamala Harris "pledged to crack down on fraudulent mortgage lenders, cut down on the state's high prison recidivism rate, and aggressively enforce environmental and civil rights laws."[51]

Meanwhile, Willie Brown was moving in tandem with his old communist friends - from a pro-Soviet position to a more China-friendly stance.

Until her death in 2016, the late San Francisco "power broker" Rose Pak, was regarded as a "likely agent of influence for Beijing"[52] and China's "enforcer" in the Bay Area Chinese community.

From San Francisco Magazine:

> *Pak continues that tradition today by entertaining newly elected Asian-American politicians... at sumptuous dinner parties at the official residence of the Chinese consul in Forest Hill... She also organizes trips to China for favored politicians and developers... to meet a raft of Chinese government officials whom she has courted to foster business ties.*[53]

On December 24, 2014, the Consulate General of China in San Francisco posted an image of Rose Pak with Consul General Luo Linquan. The post reads in part:

> *Consul General Luo spoke highly of the devotion by Rose to the promotion of the Sino-US friendship and her selfless service to the local Chinese community, and expressed his hope to further enhance cooperation with the Chinese Chamber of Commerce and to establish personal friendship with Rose, so as to further promote friendly exchanges Between China and San Francisco and improve the welfare of the local Chinese Community.*

Rose Pak at the Chinese Consulate in December, 2014

Rose Pak was very close to the late Senator Dianne Feinstein and her old friend from the 1960s, Willie Brown.

The San Francisco Examiner put it this way in an article tellingly entitled "Willie and Rose: How an alliance for the ages shaped SF":

> *Rose Pak wanted all roads to lead to Chinatown, benefiting her core constituency. Willie Brown helped her make it happen, leveraging that same constituency to consolidate political power. It was an alliance that shaped San Francisco in many ways, then and now.*[54]

Willie Brown has long cultivated deep ties to China, including with Senator Dianne Feinstein's old friend, Chinese Communist Party boss Jiang Zemin.

From an October, 2002 article from SFGate:

> *In his final visit to the United States as Chinese president, Jiang Zemin stopped over in the Bay Area Monday to cement long-standing ties with San Francisco Mayor Willie Brown and the city's influential Chinese American community.*
>
> *At a private luncheon hosted by Brown at San Francisco International Airport, the 76-year-old Jiang spoke warmly about his relationship with San Francisco. Two decades back, as mayor of Shanghai, he cultivated the sister- city relationship with then-Mayor Dianne Feinstein…*
>
> *'I was impressed every visit with the rapid development of your city and the creativity of your people,' he said. The growing ties 'between San Francisco and cities in China have become an important part of US-China relations,' he added.*
>
> *Jiang chose to make the farewell stop in the Bay Area because 'he's an old friend of Mayor Brown,' said Wang Ling, a press attache at San Francisco's Chinese Consulate. 'You know Mayor Brown has been (on trade missions) to China three times, and each time he's met with President Jiang. So, they have a very good relationship.'*
>
> *Chinese leaders also have cultivated political ties with San Francisco's powerful Asian community. 'One of the strongest characteristics that the Chinese have is loyalty and friendship,' said Rose Pak, a Chinatown power broker and Brown supporter.*[55]

The Feinstein, Brown and Pak triad could have been accurately described as the Chinese Communist Party's best friend in the Bay Area.

When the cigar smoking Rose Pak passed in September 2016, Senator Feinstein issued the following statement:

> *I am deeply saddened by the passing of Rose Pak, one of Chinatown's and San Francisco's leading public figures.*
>
> *I have known Rose for decades and observed with great admiration her tireless efforts to improve the lives of San Francisco's Chinese community.*
>
> *No one could question Rose's unparalleled devotion to her community—she gave every ounce of her being to serving others.*[56]

In October 2016, Senator Feinstein and Willie Brown (center, rear) celebrated Rose Pak's life together at an event in San Francisco:

> Senator Dianne Feinstein ✓
> @SenFeinstein   ...
>
> Celebrating the life of Rose Pak on Friday. It was wonderful to be surrounded by so many friends to tell stories of her courage & devotion.
>
> 3:46 PM · Oct 11, 2016 · Twitter Web Client

San Francisco District Attorney Kamala Harris also issued a statement:

> *San Francisco has lost a fearless advocate of the Chinese community with the passing of Rose Pak. She led an unwavering fight that stretched four decades to secure housing and vital services for poor and vulnerable immigrants.*
>
> *Rose never backed away from speaking truth to power, and she was a San Francisco icon. Her spirit will live on in the countless*

lives she touched and the many she inspired to continue to serve vulnerable communities.[57]

One friend of communism honoring another?

Kamala Harris is not the only San Francisco politician mired in communism. But she has undoubtedly fit right into the mold of the San Francisco far-left and will carry her destructive ideology into the presidency, if elected.

CHAPTER 3

A RAINBOW BLUEPRINT FOR A ONE-PARTY STATE

IT IS IMPOSSIBLE to fully understand modern US politics, the rise of Barack Obama, Kamala Harris and others, or the divided state of the nation without a firm grasp on the following:

- The pro-China Maoist sects of the 1970s and 1980s, particularly the League of Revolutionary Struggle (Marxist-Leninist),
- Jesse Jackson's "Rainbow Coalition" of the 1980s, and
- San Francisco lawyer and political power broker Steve Phillips and his network's "New American Majority".

These seemingly different eras and individuals are interconnected and have a profound impact on Democratic politics today.

The goal: Demographically engineer a permanent socialist electoral advantage, smashing conservatism in America forever.

Kamala Harris is deeply embedded in the movement.

STEVE PHILLIPS AND THE STANFORD MAOISTS

The League of Revolutionary Struggle (LRS) was founded in Oakland, California in September 1978 by a coalition of Asian-American, black, Chicano and white pro-China / Maoist activists.

At its peak, the LRS had chapters in over a dozen cities with nearly 3,000 cadres and thousands of followers. The LRS newspaper, Unity/La Unidad, was published bi-monthly in three languages: English, Spanish and Chinese.[1]

The LRS had a novel feature for communist organizations of the era, in that most of its membership was black, Asian or Hispanic, and women played strong leadership roles.[2] Keep in mind the significant role of women in the LRS, as we will explore how this relates to Kamala Harris's involvement with the 'Emerge' organization later in this chapter.

The LRS was truly a "rainbow" organization.

The San Francisco Bay Area was always the LRS's main stronghold, with branches at several local colleges, particularly Stanford University.

Typical of Maoist organizations, the LRS was deeply secretive. The LRS had considerable influence in local and student politics but was always careful to maintain the lowest possible public profile.

However, on May 23, 1990, the LRS was very publicly outed at Stanford University.

After months of investigation, The Stanford Daily senior staff writer Michael Friedly began to blow the lid off LRS activity at the university.

The ripples of that exposé are still being felt today.

Wrote Michael Friedly:

> Over the past three months, The Daily has interviewed dozens of students who have some familiarity with the League. These interviews were part of an investigation of the League which included more than 100 interviews with students, administration officials and nationwide experts. Many students interviewed by The Daily asked not to be identified because they said they are afraid of harassment by League members.[3]

The bombshell article went on to detail the LRS's history of highly secretive political manipulation of certain student groups and its wider influence on student politics:

> A secretive nationwide organization called the League of Revolutionary Struggle (Marxist-Leninist) has been a little-known factor in student politics at Stanford for several years, a Daily investigation has found:
>
> Through the selective recruitment of Stanford students into its organization, the League has been able to influence aspects of progressive politics on campus by trying to place its members in leadership positions within the ASSU (Association of Students at Stanford University, the student government), the communities of color and in staff positions.
>
> The total number of Stanford students and staff members who are League members is apparently fewer than 30, but these individuals are in positions that allow them to shape student government

policies, according to a number of sources who said they have either been recruited by the League or have worked with League members in the ASSU or student of color organizations.

The presence of the League has been in part responsible for dramatic effects at Stanford, ranging from divisions within the communities of color to the pressured resignation of an administrator to parts of the planning of last spring's takeover of University President Donald Kennedy's office.[4]

The LRS used students as strategic assets, placed with precision. With fewer than 30 members, their impact was magnified by their tactical positions. This subversion allowed for a Marxist-Leninist agenda to be promoted at Stanford under the guise of progressive politics.

While many saw student activism at Stanford as spontaneous, this was a calculated effort to steer those movements towards the LRS's own ideological goals, creating a false narrative of student-led change.

Friedly went on to expose the LRS's cultish secrecy and hunger for power:

> *The League, based in the Bay Area but with membership across the country, has been able to recruit Stanford students into its organization in a manner secret enough so that students are not initially told they are being recruited by the League, according to several Stanford students who said they were recruited but did not join the League.*
>
> *Recruitment of individuals by the League is generally conducted over a long period of time, several years in some cases, according to students who were recruited. Students who are successfully recruited by the League are then able to further the League's goals by running for student offices and helping to determine policies in the ASSU.*[5]

The LRS tactics were not confined to student politics, but a broader strategy of infiltration, where a small, dedicated group swayed the direction of a university's entire political landscape.

In typical Maoist fashion, the LRS focused heavily on racial politics and agitation.

From Unity newspaper

Explained Friedly:

> According to League theory, the United States is composed of
> various 'oppressed nations,' such as the Afro-American nation in
> the South, the Chicano nation in the Southwest and the Asian
> American nation.
>
> The overall goal of the League has been the liberation of these
> nationalities under a socialist state, according to a League publication
> called 'Peace, Justice, Equality and Socialism' that explains its goals.
>
> Until it can gain enough support to stage a revolution, the
> League attempts to 'organize, agitate and educate the masses' by
> working with more mainstream groups, according to the publica-
> tion. By making mass organizations more radical, the League can
> gain enough support for its 'protracted revolution' in the United
> States, the publication states. Unlike the
> Communist Party USA, which is a pre-
> dominantly white organization, the League
> focuses on mass organizations dealing with
> people of color for its support within stu-
> dent and labor movements.
>
> At Stanford, the League has tried to
> work toward its goals with varying degrees
> of success in MEChA, a Chicano/Latino
> student group; AASA; the Black Student
> Union and the ASSU through the People's
> Platform.[6]

Enter Steve Phillips and Jesse Jackson's 'Rainbow Coalition'

Steve Phillips with Jesse Jackson during the 1987 'March on Sacramento'

The LRS's racial tactics would find wider application when the League became one of several Maoist organizations to join Jesse Jackson's "Rainbow Coalition" during his presidential campaigns of 1984 and 1988.

Stanford law student and Maoist activist Steve Phillips was a delegate to Jackson's 1984 and 1988 campaign conferences and took a year off from college to serve as the California student coordinator of Jackson's 1988 campaign.[7]

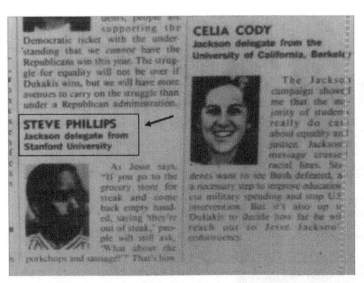

League of Revolutionary Struggle newspaper Unity, October 10, 1988

Michael Friedly went on to name several alleged LRS activists, including two staffers of his own newspaper. Friedly quoted student activist Richard Suh, who was courted by the League, but eventually balked at full membership:

> *Former Asian American Student Association chair Richard Suh said he was heavily recruited by Elsa Tsutaoka the office manager of the Asian American Activities Center.*
>
> *According to Suh, when Tsutaoka asked him to apply for membership in the League, Suh asked her which Stanford students were members of the League. 'You shouldn't ask that question,' was the reply, he said.[8]*

When questioned by the Stanford Daily, Tsutaoka "denied having any knowledge of the League or that she had ever recruited for the League."[9]

Added Friedly:

> *Because the recruitment process is secretive and individuals refuse to acknowledge that they are members of the League, it is difficult to prove whether anyone is a League member.*
>
> *Council of Presidents member David Brown and former COP member Stacey Leyton are both believed to be members of the League, according to a number of sources. Brown refused to comment. Leyton denied that she was a member or that she had any knowledge of the League's membership at Stanford.*
>
> *Although there is no indication that she joined the League, COP member Ingrid Nava, who was recently re-elected to a second term, was heavily recruited by the League beginning at the end of last summer, according to a number of students. Nava refused to return numerous phone calls.*
>
> *At the end of last summer, Nava lived briefly at a house on Bryant Street in Palo Alto known sarcastically by some progressive students as the 'Revolutionary Hotel', where recruitment for the League has occurred, according to sources who say they have been recruited.*
>
> *Tsutaoka and Steven Phillips, a former BSU chair and current Daily multicultural editor who has allegedly recruited for the League, currently live in the house. Phillips recruited Nava*

beginning in September, according to a student who was also recruited by the League. Phillips said he had no knowledge of the League's involvement at Stanford and has not recruited for the organization.[10]

Such evasions were standard Maoist practice. The flat-out denials were almost certainly flat-out lies.

Elsa Tsutaoka contributed to the LRS's newspaper "Unity" on May 4, 1987. She authored another article for the April 11, 1988 edition and worked in electoral politics with Steve Phillips.

Note the following 1990 election campaign photo, taken from Steve Phillips's Facebook page. Phillips is center left wearing his "Students for Jesse Jackson" T-shirt, with Elsa Tsutsaoka at front right:

Steve Phillips is center left; Elsa Tsutaoka is front right

Steve Phillips & 'Marx, Mao, and Lenin'

Phillips and Tsutaoka were campaigning for LRS comrade Mabel Teng,[11] who was a Jesse Jackson co-chair and the "first Chinese American elected to the San Francisco board of supervisors".[12]

In May 1985, the LRS's Unity published a supplement featuring Stanford University's "South African divestment" movement.

The article profiled the activities of several Stanford Out of South Africa (SOSA) activists including Steve Phillips – Black Student

Union chair, SOSA liaison committee with the Administration and Stacey Leyton of Students Against Reaganism.

In the interview, Steve Phillips proudly stated:

> *...some of the people who have played roles in organizing SOSA have been folks who've worked with UNITY and take a Marxist-Leninist perspective...It's really exciting to see the principles of Marxism-Leninism being successful and making a difference...*

Unity Supplement May 1985

In 1990, "Steven C. Phillips, 1984 – 1986 chair of Stanford University's Black Student Union and co-chair of the California Black/African Student Statewide Alliance 1987 – 1990," contributed an article on Nelson Mandela to the July 9, 1990 issue of Unity.

He authored another article "Keeping hope alive in 1990" in the November 26 issue.

In a December 20, 2012, post on his PowerPAC+ blog, Steve Phillips proudly confirmed his revolutionary Maoist background:

> First, let me make clear that I come out of the Left. I've studied Marx, Mao, and Lenin. In college, I organized solidarity efforts for freedom struggles in South Africa and Nicaragua, and I palled around with folks who considered themselves communists and revolutionaries. and I did my research paper on the Black Panther Party. ... My political baptism was the Jesse Jackson 1984 Presidential campaign...[13]

The League of Revolutionary Struggle Splits

Communist organizations often face internal power struggles and ideological battles, resulting in splits. In September 1990, the LRS split, with the majority group (including most of the Asian comrades) dropping traditional Maoism, while maintaining control of the Unity newspaper.

Many members of this faction - the Unity Organizing Committee (UOC) - began to rise through the ranks of the Democratic Party.[14]

The minority faction maintained a more traditional Marxist-Leninist-Maoist outlook, rebranding as Socialist Organizing Network (SON). The SON later merged with the Freedom Road Socialist Organization, which in recent times changed its name to Liberation Road – while maintaining its traditional pro-China orientation. For clarity, Liberation Road will be referred to as FRSO/Liberation Road going forward.

On January 28, 1991, the Unity newspaper carried a statement: "A call to build an organization for the 1990s and beyond" formalizing the former LRS's new majority faction.

The statement listed more than 150 activists working to build the new Unity Organizing Committee (UOC). The LRS wasn't dying. It was reincarnating.

Among those committed to building the UOC were several Stanford University comrades previously accused of LRS membership. They included:

+ David Brown - former student body co-president, Stanford University
+ Stacey Leyton - West Coast organizer United States Students Association
+ Ingrid Nava - student body co-president, Stanford University
+ Steven C. Phillips - writer, education activist, San Francisco

David Brown went on to work in education and later became chief of staff at the office of Democratic Party leader and Alameda County Supervisor Wilma Chan[15] – herself a former leading LRS comrade.[16]

Ingrid Nava is now labor lawyer, specifically the associate general counsel at SEIU Local 32BJ, New York.[17]

Stacey Leyton went on to serve as an appellate representative to the Ninth Circuit Judicial Conference from 2010 until 2013 and currently serves as a Lawyer Representative to the Northern District of California. She worked for a time for left-leaning Supreme Court Justice Stephen Breyer.[18]

Steve Phillips once argued a "racial discrimination" case before Justice Breyer, when still a working lawyer.

Years later, Steve Phillips still fondly remembered some of his old comrades.

Steve Phillips
April 18, 2014 · San Francisco, CA · 🌐

I've progressed financially to where I no longer have to borrow rent money from Stacey Leyton or steal bus fare from Elsa Tsutaoka's coin jar (sorry Elsa), so why am I so resistant to paying even $0.99 for an app? Any app.

👍 34   5 Comments

👍 Like   ↗ Share

Steve Phillips works with many of his revolutionary comrades, to this day.

Like many political projects on the left, the UOC started off with enthusiasm, but seems to have quickly run out of momentum. The group published Unity through 1992 and a couple of issues of a magazine of the same name in 1993-94. While UOC faded from view, many of its former members would go on to prominence in social movements and electoral politics.

In 1992, during the dying days of UOC, Steve Phillips stood for San Francisco Board of Education as a Democrat. He served for eight years as the favored candidate of Willie Brown.[19]

During his time on the board, Steve Phillips also got to rub shoulders with the "likes of Nancy Pelosi, Dianne Feinstein, Gavin Newsom and Kamala Harris."[20]

Enter the Sandlers

Today, Steve Phillips's website states that he is a "national political leader, civil rights lawyer, and senior fellow at the Center for American Progress…Phillips has appeared on multiple national radio and television networks including NBC, CNN, MSNBC, Fox News and TV One. He is a columnist for The Nation and a regular opinion contributor to The New York Times."[21]

In 2014, Steve Phillips was named one of "America's Top 50 Influencers" by Campaigns & Elections magazine.[22]

So how did an old Stanford Maoist manage to achieve so much influence so quickly?

Part of it no doubt comes down to Phillips's affability and intelligence. Steve Phillips comes across as a genuine and likable man – there is very little of the Maoist fanatic about him. As Phillips's

friend. Van Jones famously said: "I'm willing to forgo the cheap satisfaction of the radical pose for the deep satisfaction of radical ends".[23]

Part of his success may also come from marrying the right person.

Steve Phillips married his Stanford University girlfriend, the late
Susan Sandler. This marriage unified Phillips' revolutionary zeal and
strategic vision with a very, very significant fortune.

Susan Sandler, Steve Phillips, and a friend

Susan Sandler was the daughter of the late "progressives" Herb
and Marion Sandler of San Francisco, who "pocketed $2.3 billion
when they sold their bank to Wachovia in 2006".[24]

In 1963, Marion and Herb Sandler bought Golden West Financial
Corporation, a two-branch California savings and loan company,
with a $3.8 million loan from Marion's brother, businessman Bernard
Osher – once ranked the 584th richest man in the world.[25]

Golden West was sold in 2006 for $24 billion. The Sandlers'
approximate 10% shareholding in the company netted them billions.[26] Of this amount, the Sandlers donated $1.3 billion to their
political vehicle, the Sandler Foundation.[27]

This money has financed several major "progressive" organizations,
such as the Center for American Progress and ProPublica.[28] Some of
it has also directly helped to give Steve Phillips the wherewithal and
political influence to pursue his socialist dreams.

According to New York Times reporter Matt Bai, the Sandlers', along with Progressive Insurance magnate Peter Lewis and leftist financier George Soros, additionally established the organization America Votes "to coordinate various get-out-the-vote drives during the 2004 election."[29]

DEMOCRACY ALLIANCE

Herb and Marion Sandler also sent their son-in-law Steve Phillips as their representative to the October 2005 founding meeting of the "Democracy Alliance" at the Chateau Elan near Atlanta.[30]

The super-secretive Democracy Alliance has since recruited more than a hundred and fifty rich leftist donors and labor unions to fund "progressive" Democratic candidates across America.

Both Steve Phillips[31] and Susan Sandler[32] have served on the board of the Democracy Alliance.

According to a January 2024 profile in "Inside Philanthropy", Steve Phillips is intent on using his wealthy contacts to carry forward his youthful revolutionary vison:

> Back in his Stanford days as a student activist, Phillips looked at revolutions in Africa, Central America and China. 'But how do you apply these lessons learned in what's going on in this country? And how do you leverage this relationship to this constellation of wealthy people?'
>
> Phillips dove in and tried to identify people who had particular racial justice priorities. He traveled around the country, racking up frequent flyer miles. He became a DA board member and chair of the investment committee.
>
> He also started to learn just how powerful these donor circles could be in getting things done in the government. He recalls that the regional Colorado Democracy Alliance (CODA), steered by a handful of donors, among them Tim Gill and Pat Stryker, leveraged philanthropy and political donations to flip the state legislature in Colorado.
>
> Back in California, Phillips applied these lessons to create the California Donor Table (CDT), a statewide community of donors who pool their funds to make investments in communities of color. The majority of CDT's donors are from the Bay Area, including

*real estate mogul Wayne Jordan and his wife, lawyer Quinn
Delaney, founders of the Akonadi Foundation.*

*'Steve, Susan, Quinn and Wayne set us on a great path to help
us both programmatically, in terms of spending the money, and in
doing donor education... So I think Steve's work has been key in
combining racial justice, equity and realism,' said Ludovic Blain, a
founding donor of CDT.*[33]

Ludovic Blain is a former member of Steve Phillips's PowerPAC+.[34]
Later in this chapter, we'll explore how Wayne Jordan, Quinn Delaney,
and their Akonadi Foundation have significantly shaped Kamala
Harris's career trajectory.

Steve Phillips was very influential inside the Democracy Alliance,
perhaps due to his unique race-based strategic vision that many of the
more business-focused members lacked.

Steve Phillips Book Signing at 2016 Democracy Alliance Investment Conference

Moving forward, it will become evident to readers how the
Democracy Alliance intertwines with numerous figures in Kamala
Harris's orbit.

KAMALA HARRIS IN THE DEMOCRACY ALLIANCE ORBIT

In 2017, a "Private and Confidential" program from the Democracy
Alliance was obtained by the Washington Free Beacon.[35] The program revealed that Kamala Harris, a Senator at the time, addressed

the exclusive audience on video. Harris's presentation came directly before a discussion by militant left "philanthropist" George Soros.

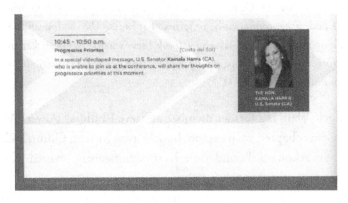

Screenshot from the 2017 Democracy Alliance Program

Quinn Delaney and her husband Wayne Jordan were also featured at the 2017 Democracy Alliance Conference. They were part of a "Partner-Hosted Caucus Meeting" titled "Building a Progressive Narrative in a Trump Bubble - Yes, It Can Be Done!"

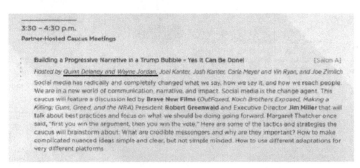

Screenshot from 2017 Democracy Alliance Program

It is not a random connection. "Longtime supporters" Quinn Delaney and Wayne Jordan hosted a fundraiser at their home for Kamala Harris in 2023.[36]

Quinn Delaney also serves on the Board of Advisers at Emerge America, an organization that recruits and trains Democratic women for elected office.

Kamala Harris co-founded Emerge California - Emerge America's launchpad – in the early-2000s. There are now chapters across America.

From an Emerge Facebook Post dated January 20, 2021:[37]

Kamala Harris founded Emerge with her comrade Andrea Dew Steele, who was *also* a "featured guest" at the 2017 Democracy Alliance meeting.

Steele participated in a panel discussion titled "The NEXT Majority: How Virginia's Women Candidates, Activists, and Voters Provide a Playbook for the 2018 Elections". "Progressives were horrified and perplexed when most white women voters chose Donald Trump over Hillary Clinton," the description said in part. "However, the anger over the election inspired many women to become first-time candidates and activists," it continued.

The NEXT Majority: How Virginia's Women Candidates, Activists,   [Salon F]
and Voters Provide a Playbook for the 2018 Elections

Hosted by Fran Rodgers, Marcy Carsey, Shelley Rubin, the Tioga Fund, and the Women Donors Network

Progressives were horrified and perplexed when most white women voters chose Donald Trump over Hillary Clinton. But anger over the election inspired many women to become first time candidates and activists. The first electoral test of the "gender resistance" is in Virginia 2017. Join this caucus to hear from the **Women Effect Action Fund's** team—**Civix Strategy Group** Founder and CEO **Karen Hicks** and **Analyst Institute** Executive Director **Aaron Strauss**—about their fascinating test on mobilizing and persuading women voters now. Here from **Emerge America** President **Andrea Dew Steele** about Virginia's unprecedented success in training and fielding women candidates. Join the conversation on translating the recent surge in grassroots women's activism into policy and electoral wins for all progressives—and how those lessons can be applied in 2018.

Screenshot from 2017 Democracy Alliance Program

It makes sense that Kamala Harris is deeply connected to those in Steve Phillips's orbit at the Democracy Alliance. After all, he and his late wife Susan Sandler have been supporting Harris for many years.[38, 39] During a 2020 podcast, Phillips bragged that "few people know her [Kamala Harris] like we do."

Steve Phillips   ...
@StevePtweets

Many are just getting to know @KamalaHarris but few people know her like we do. In our latest @DemocracyColor podcast, we sit down with @lateefahsimon & share stories about the Kamala we've come to know over the past 20 years. Check it out & please share! democracyincolor.com/podepisodes/20...

11:45 AM · Aug 20, 2020

Steve Phillips Post Dated August 20, 2020

Steve Phillips's vision of a "New American Majority" aligns completely with Kamala Harris's goals.

Back to the Rainbow

To understand Steve Phillips's modern political vision, we need to go back to Jesse Jackson's Rainbow Coalition of the 1980s.

Before the split and demise of the League of Revolutionary Struggle, Steve Phillips and many of his comrades already held influential positions in the Democratic Party.

Most of Phillips's comrades came to the Democratic Party through the Jesse Jackson movement. Others came through the successful 1983 socialist driven "Rainbow" campaign to elect leftist Congressmember Harold Washington to the Chicago mayoralty.

It was Harold Washington's success that reportedly inspired a young Barack Obama to move from New York to Chicago.[40]

Some Maoists also joined the Democratic Party through the campaign of Democratic Socialists of America comrade David Dinkins, who was elected to the New York mayoralty in 1990, on the coattails of the Rainbow Coalition.

League of Revolutionary Struggle "Unity", October 1990

In the early 1980s - after the election of Ronald Reagan - the Democratic Party was in serious decline.

In 1984, the left wing of the Democratic Party and its satellite organizations attempted a comeback through the Rainbow Coalition, headed by Jesse Jackson. The goals of the campaign were to "oppose Reaganomics and gain support from Blacks, working-class people, immigrants, women, and the LGBT community."[41]

The pro-Soviet Communist Party USA, and the "communist lite" Democratic Socialists of America endorsed and supported the Jackson campaign.

In 1988, Communist Party USA chairman Gus Hall, when asked who the Communist Party would support for President in the 1988 election, said:

> *I think our members will work for the candidates they think have the most progressive, most advanced positions. At this stage most members of the Party will be working for Jesse Jackson on the basis that he does have an advanced position.*[42]

One Communist Party USA supporter - San Francisco Democratic Party operative Willie Brown - was Jesse Jackson's campaign manager in 1988.[43]

However, it was the Maoist groups: Line of March, the Communist Workers Party and Steve Phillips's LRS comrades who joined the "Rainbow" en masse,[44] taking up many of the key leadership roles in Jackson's campaigns.

The Rainbow Coalition's goal, which coincided perfectly with that of the LRS and other the Maoist groups, was to unite "progressive" white voters with leftist black, Latino, Asian-American, Native American, and gay activists into a multi-colored electoral coalition.

In 1988, Jesse Jackson got 6.9 million votes with this strategy and won several states.[45]

Today, "minorities" make up a much larger proportion of the population, and some, particularly Asian-Americans, have trended even more Democratic since the mid-1990s. Steve Phillips has been working hard to convince leading Democrats and his Democracy Alliance "partners" to stop wasting money on white "swing voters" and court minority voters instead.

PERMANENT SOCIALIST POWER

In May 2016, Steve Phillips wrote in Medium:

> *The way to win for Democrats is to go all in investing in, inspiring, and mobilizing voters of color. The Obama formula — the only formula that has worked in national elections over the past decade — consists of mobilizing people of color so that at least 28% of all voters are of color and then winning at least 81% of the support of all voters of color while holding at 36.5% of the white vote.*[46]

According to Steve Phillips and his allies, the way to permanent socialist power in America is the mass-mobilization of the progressive white vote coupled with a growing "progressive" minority vote uniting behind an increasingly radicalized Democratic Party.

Steve Phillips is a champion of relentless and strategically targeted voter registration and Get Out the Vote drives, financed by his deep-pocketed allies from the Democracy Alliance.

Phillips wrote about his updated version of the LRS/Rainbow Coalition strategy in his 2016 New York Times Best seller "Brown is the New White."

Notably, his latest "How We Win the Civil War" builds on the same race-obsessed strategy, focusing on the so-called demographic shift towards a more racially diverse electorate representing a "New American Majority". In his books, Phillips emphasizes that this demographic change should be leveraged to secure a multiracial one-party state.[47]

New American Majority

Steve Phillips's argument is simple. A growing minority population, coupled with a stable base of "white progressives" *already* has the majority – the "New American Majority."

According to Steve Phillips, this is how the New American Majority breaks down:

> As Obama's elections showed, the country's demographic revolution over the past fifty years has given birth to a New American Majority. Progressive people of color now comprise 23 percent of all the eligible voters in America, and progressive Whites account for 28 percent of all eligible voters. Together, these constituencies make up 51 percent of the country's citizen voting age population, and that majority is getting bigger every single day.[48]

Here is a handy graphic illustrating the concept:

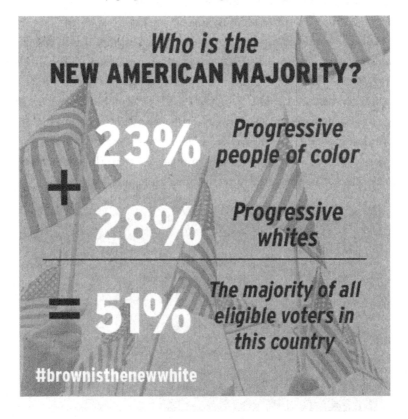

Who is the NEW AMERICAN MAJORITY?

23% Progressive people of color

+ 28% Progressive whites

= 51% The majority of all eligible voters in this country

#brownisthenewwhite

Steve Phillips believes that if this base can be sufficiently mobilized by running "progressive" "candidates of color" like Barack Obama, Stacey Abrams or Kamala Harris, the far-left of the Democratic Party will be able to rule America in perpetuity.

The New American Majority has the political power to:

Win the White House
33 states have 398 electoral votes, 128 more than the 270 need to win

Elect 331 members of Congress
218 votes to control the chamber

Elect 64 Senators
4 more than the 60 votes needed to overcome filibusters

#brownisthenewwhite

According to Phillips, Democrats are wasting their time on white "swing voters". Instead, he urges his party to spend their money on turning out minority voters, especially in Georgia and the Sunbelt states and in the northern cities in "swing states" like Michigan, Wisconsin and Pennsylvania.

According to Phillips's own figures, "minorities" have increased from 12 percent to 38 percent of the population in the last quarter century. This makes the "Rainbow Coalition" strategy much more viable.

THE COMMON THREAD

Compare Steve Phillips's "New American Majority" thesis with the argument put forth in the League of Revolutionary Struggle's theoretical journal Forward, Spring 1989 edition:

> *The Jackson campaign also pointed the way towards a progressive electoral strategy, which the left needs to develop as part of its immediate political program. Concretely, this means developing strategies to expand and shift the electorate, and breaking the so-called conservative electoral 'lock' in the South and Southwest, which has upheld the right-wing edge in the last four presidential elections.*
>
> *People of color now approach 30% of the US population. The changing demographics in the US will make oppressed nationalities the majority in California and Texas by the turn of the century, and they will comprise a steadily increasing proportion of the population as a whole.*
>
> *With increased voter registration and participation, Black, Latino, Asian, poor white and other historically disenfranchised voters can constitute a new, progressive electoral majority. This new electoral majority, with its base in the South and Southwest and key Northern industrial areas, can make the critical difference in future elections. It provides the electoral basis for reversing the right-wing direction of American politics.*
>
> *Electoral work is thus an important aspect of our work to build the mass movement against the right, and for democracy and social progress.*[49]

According to the League of Revolutionary Struggle, Jesse Jackson's campaign focused on expanding the electorate and breaking the conservative hold in the South and Southwest. By mobilizing black, Latino, Asian, and poor white voters, a "new, progressive electoral majority" could be formed, capable of reversing right-wing politics, forever.

LRS believed that achieving the persistent left majority would take an obsessive focus on voter registration.

Likewise, PowerPAC+'s preceding organization PAC+ made the goal clear on the cover of their 2012 report.

This is all about a "PERMANENT progressive majority" – that is the exploitation of changing demographics to create an electorally unchallengeable one-party socialist state.

Steve Phillips's concept is not new; He has simply brought the LRS/Jesse Jackson vision into the modern era.

Democratic support for the 'Rainbow' strategy

Steve Phillips's New American Majority as outlined in his bestseller "Brown is the New White" has considerable support in Democratic Party circles, including Stacey Abrams, Cory Booker, Nancy Pelosi, Van Jones and Barack Obama.

And of course, Kamala Harris.

From Steve PHillip' Facebook page

Ben Davis
@bdaviskc · Follow   X

Sen. @CoryBooker and Steve Phillips discuss
#BrownIsTheNewWhite and how to pave the path to a
more equitable America

7:36 PM · Apr 25, 2018   ⓘ

♥ 4   💬 Reply   ↑ Share

Read more on X

Kumar Rao
@KumarRaoNYC · Follow   X

.@VanJones68 starting off event at @FordFoundation
Demographic Revolution: New American Majority
#BrownIsTheNewWhite

6:28 PM · Apr 6, 2016   ⓘ

♥ 2   💬 Reply   ↑ Share

Barack Obama certainly is on board. The former president used the "Rainbow Coalition" strategy to win the presidency twice.

EMERGE AND THE NEW AMERICAN MAJORITY

The New American Majority concept has been eagerly embraced by the organization founded by Kamala Harris.

The Emerge movement started 22 years ago in CA with Kamala Harris as a founder.

Today Emerge California, we stand proud; 900 alumni strong, with over 220 women serving in office, and excited to send our own Kamala Harris to the White House. #ElectWomen

👍 19   👎 1   ↗ 23

"Now is the time to get involved and help us change this nation for the better," Emerge declares on their website.[50] "Our country is changing—from our demographics to the way we live our lives—and our government must reflect this new reality and a progressive vision of the future."

Screenshot from the Emerge Website: The New American Majority

Emerge president A'shanti Gholar wrote an article published at Ms. dated July 23, 2024, titled "The Kamala Harris I Know, and What It Could Mean for America".[51]

Gholar is clearly not interested in meritocracy.

She writes in part:

> Over two decades ago, [Kamala Harris] co-founded Emerge, the nation's largest network of Democratic women elected officials and candidates that I have the honor of leading today. In those two decades, Kamala Harris has gone from being the first Black and South Asian woman to serve as San Francisco district attorney, to the first Black and South Asian woman to serve as vice president of the United States. Now, she's earned enough delegate support to become a presidential nominee—another first for a woman of color—and could become the first woman president of the United States. The significance of this moment cannot be overstated.

Gholar made it clear that Emerge is fully on board with the New American Majority strategy and in fact uses the term specifically:

> At Emerge, we elect women of the New American Majority: Black, Brown and Indigenous women and women of color, as well as young, LGBTQ+ and unmarried women—a growing force in American politics. And it is happening. Nevada is the first state in the country to have a majority-woman legislature, because of Emerge alums. Across the way in Michigan, Emerge helped flip the House of Representatives in 2022, and now Democrats control both chambers of the Michigan legislature for the first time since 2008. And we have done the same in Colorado, Maine, New Mexico, Virginia and other states.

Emerge president A'shanti Gholar, Hillary Clinton, Andrea Dew Steele

Notably, Hillary Clinton's PAC Onward Together lists Emerge as a partner and has provided them with financial support.[52]

The modern Rainbow Coalition/New American Majority strategy, coupled with boots-on-the-ground support from the Democratic Socialists of America and the China-focused Communist Party USA and FRSO/Liberation Road is fast turning Steve Phillips's neo-Maoist vision into a reality.

BACKING OBAMA

Steve Phillips played a major role in putting Barack Obama ahead of Hillary Clinton in the battle for the Democratic Party presidential nomination in 2008.

His late wife Susan Sandler was "the first and largest donor behind the independent efforts to support Barack Obama's 2008 presidential campaign."[53]

In early 2008, Steve Phillips, along with his old college radical friends Andy Wong and Ben Jealous - both former Jesse Jackson supporters - raised $10 million to back the long-shot campaign for Barack Obama.[54]

They applied the "Rainbow Coalition" strategy by initiating

"minority" voter registration campaigns in 18 states, in a project called Vote Hope "that increased communities of color participation in state primaries and the federal general election in 2008."[55]

This was the impetus needed to get ahead of the then-widely favored Hillary Clinton.

In 2013, Steve Phillips served on a panel at San Francisco's Chinese Historical Society in commemoration of Martin Luther King Jr.'s 1963 March on Washington, alongside former LRS comrades Francis Wong[56] and Jon Jang.[57]

Jon Jang wrote a comment the following Steve Phillips Facebook post about the event:

> *Steve, you and I were one of the few I know that share how the Jesse Jackson Rainbow Coalition had an impact on the election of President Obama.*

In "Brown is the New White", Steve Phillips convincingly argues that Jesse Jackson's Rainbow Coalition strategy set the stage for Obama's victories:

> *Before Obama went to law school ... a forty-two-year-old Black civil rights leader shook up the political system by running for president of the United States of America. To get from Martin in 1968 to Barack in 2008, we needed Jesse in 1984 and 1988.*
>
> *It was during the presidential elections of the 1980s that the seeds planted in the 1960s began to sprout and become visible in national politics. Jackson was fond of saying, 'When the old minorities come together, they form a new majority.'*
>
> *The potential of this prophecy came into sharp focus in the 1988 campaign as Jackson won the presidential primaries in eleven states, led the race for the Democratic nomination near the halfway point, and finished as the Democratic runner-up with the most votes in history up to that time.*
>
> *The key to Jackson's success—and Obama's electoral victories twenty years later—was the power of connecting the energy of people of color and progressive Whites seeking justice, equality, and social change to a political campaign for elected office.*[58]

It is unlikely that Barack Obama would have become President without Steve Phillips, Jesse Jackson, and the League of Revolutionary Struggle.

PowerPAC+

To further apply the LRS/Rainbow Coalition strategy to modern American conditions, Steve Phillips created PAC+ (later PowerPAC+), PowerPAC.org, and Democracy in Color specifically to fund and campaign for leftist "candidates of color."

According to his Netroots bio:

> *He [Steve Phillips] is co-founder of PowerPAC+ a social justice organization dedicated to building a multiracial political coalition.* **PowerPAC+ conducted the largest independent voter mobilization efforts backing Barack Obama, Cory Booker, and Kamala Harris.** *[emphasis added]*[59]

Many of PowerPAC+'s board members were Phillips's former student Maoist friends from Stanford, including both Stacey Peyton and Ingrid Nava.[60]

Steve Phillips's key lieutenant in PowerPAC+ was Aimee Allison.[61]

Yet another old Stanford radical, Aimee Allison ran successfully in 1989 for the Stanford Council of Presidents (student government), on the "Slate of the Times" ticket.

Allison's fellow slate members included alleged former League of Revolutionary Struggle comrades David Brown and Ingrid Nava.

Members of the "State of the Times" for Council of Presidents: Chin-Chin Chen, David Brown, Aimee Allison and Ingrid Nava.

Keeping up with the Times

Stanford Daily, April 13, 1989, page 1

In June 2014, PowerPAC+ sponsored a "Race Will Win the Race" conference at the National Press Club in Washington DC to publicize Steve Phillips's LRS/Rainbow Coalition race-based political theories.

Participants included Steve Phillips, Aimee Allison, Stacey Abrams, Senator Cory Booker, Congressmembers Marcia Fudge (D-OH) and Mark Takano (D-CA), former Stanford activist and PowerPAC+ board member Julie Martinez Ortega,[62] Ingrid Nava and Steve Phillips's old student comrade,[63] LRS supporter[64] and PowerPAC.org president Andy Wong.[65]

PowerPAC+ endorsed and supported more than forty "social justice" candidates on several slates between 2012 and 2016.

Almost every candidate was a "person of color".

Meanwhile, PowerPAC+'s sister data gathering organization
PowerPAC.org worked on "researching where votes of color can make
a difference in races, how demographic trends can affect [sic] change
in public policy and leadership, and how civic engagement method-
ologies can change how campaigns are run."[66]

PowerPAC.org endorsed five gubernatorial "candidates of color" in
the 2018 election cycle - Steve Phillips's personal friend Ben Jealous
(Maryland), David Garcia (Arizona), John Chiang (California), and
two PowerPAC+ board members Andrew Gillum (Florida) and
Stacey Abrams (Georgia).[67]

Backed with tons of Steve Phillips and Democracy Alliance money
and working the "Rainbow" strategy, John Chiang's campaign was a
bust, but Ben Jealous, David Garcia, Stacey Abrams and Andrew
Gillum all convincingly won their primaries.

All four lost in the general election, but Abrams and Gillum came
both agonizingly close in Georgia and Florida, respectively.

Andrew Gillum in particular owed his near success to Steve
Phillips and company.

Steve Phillips, Andrew Gillum, Susan Sander, 2015

Democracy Alliance members George Soros, Tom Steyer, Norman Lear, Susan Sandler, and Steve Phillips contributed significant sums especially in the closing weeks of the primaries.[68] Steyer topped the list with $1 million,[69] with the Soros family coming in second with $450,000.[70]

As a bonus, the "black candidates only" Collective PAC chipped in $231,000.

As a 501 (c) (4), Collective Future (an arm of Collective PAC) is not legally required to disclose its donors. However, Collective PAC founder Quentin James did serve on the board of "movement" staff recruiting organization Inclusv,[71] alongside Steve Phillips, PowerPAC+ board member Gregory Cendana,[72] and long-time PowerPAC+ affiliate Alida Garcia.[73]

In July 2016, Steve Phillips launched "Democracy in Color", "a media organization dedicated to race, politics and the multicultural progressive New American Majority."

Aimee Allison served as resident of Democracy in Color and hosted the organization's regular podcast.

Steve Phillips and Aimee Allison (wearing Kamala tee shirt) August, 2024

As Steve Phillips wrote in The Nation in April 2016: "the rainbow revolution…propelled Obama into office."[74]

Will Kamala Harris complete that revolution?

Kamala Harris for VP

Kamala Harris - a female of color, far-left but not publicly so - is, on paper, the ideal modern Rainbow Coalition candidate.

And she certainly understands that the modern version of the Rainbow Coalition strategy is the way to win.

Kamala Harris ✔
@KamalaHarris

· · ·

We need a leader who has the experience of working with all folks—including women, people of color, the LGBTQ+ community, and working families.

Rebuilding the Obama coalition is the only way we can beat Trump. That's how I intend to win.

9:35 PM · Nov 22, 2019

◯ 778   ⟲ 1.1K   ♡ 5.6K   ◻ 6   ↥

In 2020, while the nation was preoccupied with the Covid-19 virus, Steve Phillips and his "former" Maoist friends were trying to choose Democratic presidential candidates Joe Biden's and Bernie Sanders's running mates for them.

Steve Phillips and long-time collaborator Aimee Allison pushed hard for a "woman of color" to round out Biden's presidential ticket.

More than that, Phillips and Allison promoted a short list that consisted entirely of radicals with direct ties to their own socialist clique.

Initially, Steve Phillips supported his old friend Senator Cory Booker for the Democratic presidential nomination, but his campaign flamed out – though not as spectacularly as Kamala Harris's did.

Defying Steve Phillips's race-based political math, neither candidate resonated with voters.

Undeterred, while Joe Biden was still battling Bernie Sanders in the Democratic primary, Steve Phillips and Aimee Allison came back for a second bite at the cherry.

Phillips and Allison promoted the line that Biden or Sanders must choose a "woman of color" for his running mate. More importantly, that candidate had to be either Kamala Harris, or former PowerPAC+ board member Stacey Abrams of Georgia.

Aimee Allison, Stacey Abrams, Steve Phillips, "Race will win the race conference", 2014

Steve Phillips's Democracy in Color website featured an "Open Letter to Democratic Presidential Candidates: A Call for Committing to Choosing a Woman of Color as Candidate for Vice President:"

> *Dear Vice President Joe Biden and Senator Bernie Sanders.*
>
> *Here is a fact: the Democratic Party needs the leadership, vision, and expertise of women and people of color now more than ever. While you cannot change who you are, you can show us who you value by committing to choose a woman of color as your running mate for Vice President.*
>
> *The majority of Democratic voters are women, and nearly half of all Democratic voters are people of color. At the intersection of those communities—which make up 77% of all Democratic voters in the last two presidential elections—women of color have a unique and critical role to play in galvanizing the entire progressive coalition. ...*
>
> *We strongly urge you to show the leadership this moment demands by publicly committing today to picking a woman of color to serve as your Vice President.*[75]

The letter was co-signed by Phillips-affiliated groups She the People, PowerPAC+, Southern Elections Fund, and The Collective PAC, and the Stacey Abrams-linked New Georgia Project Action Fund.[76]

Other groups signing on were Higher Heights for America, Indivisible, Latino Victory Project, and two fronts for the pro-China communist group FRSO/Liberation Road - the New Florida Majority and the New Virginia Majority - plus the Communist Party USA-influenced Texas Organizing Project.[77]

Kamala Harris knew many of those organizations.

In August 2018, she had addressed a "She the People" forum "Hidden figures: how women of color are making history in the midterms" at that years "Netroots" conference.

Kamala Harris Addresses Netroots, August 2018.

At the event, Kamala Harris posed for a photo op with Aimee Allison, former PowerPAC+ board member Crystal Zermeno[78] from the Texas Organizing Project and Tram Nguyen from the New Virginia Majority.

L-R: Aimee Allison, Kamala Harris, LaTosha Brown, Crystal Zermeno, Tram Nguyen

Steve Phillips also contributed an op-ed to The Nation, in which he dictated his instructions to Biden and Sanders:

> *After months of dancing around the issue of diversifying the Democratic ticket, the remaining viable candidates finally got more specific on Sunday, with Joe Biden firmly pledging to choose a woman as his running mate, and Bernie Sanders saying that 'in all likelihood' he would follow suit.*
>
> *What neither of these septuagenarian white men could bring themselves to do, however, was to say that that woman would be a person of color...* [79]

Steve Phillips, of course, knows exactly what "people of color" wanted - because his friend and colleague Aimee Allison and her She the People group told him so.

Steve Phillips continues:

> *People of color are also eager to see a Democratic ticket that reflects electoral reality. As my research has found, nearly half of Democratic voters are people of color; it is certainly relevant that the last time the Democrats won the White House was when an African American topped the ticket. Groups such as She the People, a national network of women of color in politics, have crystallized the demands for gender and racial diversity into a call for a woman of color as the vice presidential nominee.* [80]

Then Steve Phillips rolled out the "stats" to bolster his argument:

> *The math of the moment lends empirical support to choosing a woman of color. The 2008 exit polls showed that it was women who made Barack Obama president, with 56 percent voting for him. My research has found that 46 percent of his coalition consisted of people of color; just 23 percent of Obama voters that year were white men.*
>
> *Clinton was defeated in 2016 in part because of two key shortcomings: a dramatic drop-off in black voter turnout (the first decline in 20 years) and the fact that a meaningful number of white women decided to give Trump a chance. As the Democrats seek to unseat Trump, a running mate who appeals to women and inspires voters of color seems like the obvious electoral strategy to pursue.* [81]

Then Steve Phillips gives Biden and Bernie his list of approved candidates - with his proteges Stacey Abrams and Kamala Harris right at the top:

> *The list of women of color who could strengthen a Biden or Sanders ticket is long and impressive. Stacey Abrams received more votes statewide than any Democrat had before during her gubernatorial run in Georgia, and was popular with young voters. As a 40-something leader tapped into popular culture, she could help Biden with the youth vote that he has failed to excite. Kamala Harris, Massachusetts Representative Ayanna Pressley, Illinois Senator Tammy Duckworth, and New Mexico Governor Michelle Lujan Grisham are some of the other talented women of color who could significantly enhance the Democratic ticket this year.[82]*

Ayanna Pressley is an extreme leftist with close ties to Democratic Socialists of America[83] and the Maoist-initiated, Beijing-friendly, Chinese Progressive Association of Boston.

Chinese Progressive Association - CPA Boston
March 31, 2010

Honorary Chair Suzanne Lee with Boston City Councilors Ayanna Pressley and Felix Arroyo who read an Official Resolution from Boston City Councilors congratulating CPA

Michelle Lujan Grisham benefited from PowerPAC+ endorsement and support in the 2014 election cycle.[84]

But really, Phillips is just using Pressley, Lujan Grisham, and Duckworth for camouflage. It's Abrams or Harris that he really wants.

Aimee Allison was even more explicit in a March 11 article in Newsweek:

Only a historic increase in the number of voters of color, especially women of color, will deliver the swing states that Democrats must carry to win. This is what we saw in 2018, when Democrats took back the House of Representatives with a 37 percent rise in turnout among women of color from the 2014 midterms. This is what we are hoping for in 2020.

So how do we get there? How do we motivate voters of color and ensure that 2020 can still be a year of positive political transformation? We get there with a woman of color vice president on the Democratic ticket. ...

Women of color have the numbers to generate a Democratic victory—if we show up at the polls. In swing states across the country, women of color dominate Democratic voter rolls. We are a third of Democratic voters in Florida, North Carolina and Texas. In Georgia, we're 44 percent. For us to show up like we did in 2018, we need Democrats to prove that they still care about us, see us and value us. ...

Women of color are already leaders in statewide and local organizations that register and turn out communities of color and white progressives alike. In 2018, high turnout from women of color flipped seats and secured the House for Democrats. Candidates like Lucy McBath in Georgia's 6th Congressional District flipped seats that white male Democrats previously spent millions to lose.

Meanwhile, candidates like Ayanna Pressley, Rashida Tlaib and Alexandria Ocasio-Cortez inspired millions of voters beyond the borders of their own districts—even crossing over into pop culture—with their history-making races and bold leadership.

Let's keep the strategy that led us to victory in 2018. A short-list of vice presidential candidates can begin with Stacey Abrams, Kamala Harris and Deb Haaland. Any one of these extraordinary leaders would genuinely excite women of color voters.[85]

When Kamala Harris officially became Joe Biden's vice president elect in November 2020, Aimee Allison's She the People was quick to take full credit for the success.

"Kamala Harris is our Madam Vice President! WE DID THIS. We mobilized and rallied behind Kamala and showed her we have what it takes to make history," declared the post at the She the People Facebook page, which continued: "At the beginning of this year, we told Biden his path to the white house was with a woman of color, look at us now! Today, WE CELEBRATE!"

The She the People post, unfortunately, was correct.

Deb Haaland

Deb Haaland, previously a Native American congresswoman from New Mexico, is now Secretary of the Interior. Her career closely aligns with Aimee Allison's "She the People," focusing on "progressive women of color".

Deb Haaland is also very close to one of the key organizers of the 2016 "Dakota Access Pipeline" protests, Judith LeBlanc of the Native Organizers Alliance.

Judith LeBlanc Second from left, Deb Haaland center

Judith LeBlanc is also a 50-year veteran leader of the pro-China Communist Party USA.

Judith LeBlanc

After President Joe Bien shut down the Keystone Pipeline on his first day of office, Judith LeBlanc made it her mission to ensure that her good friend Deb Haaland - though missing out on the VP spot - would become the next US Secretary of the Interior.

Deb Haaland had little name recognition. Almost straight after the election, Judith LeBlanc mounted a "Deb for Interior" drive with badges, buses, social media campaigns, etc.

LeBlanc and friends also rounded up some celebrity left endorsements including Leonardo DiCaprio, Mark Ruffalo, Kerry Washington,[86] Sarah Silverman, Cher, Rosario Dawson, America Ferrera, Chelsea Handler, Alyssa Milano, Julianne Moore, Mandy Moore, Zoe Saldana, Marisa Tomei, Jane Fonda, Gloria Steinem and Sarah Silverman.[87]

Gloria Steinem was a former Democratic Socialists of America co-chair.[88] Sarah Silverman is a "lifetime DSA member".[89]

The following graphic shows several "Deb for Interior" supporters. The communist Judith LeBlanc is bottom, second from left.

Here are Aimee Allison, Deb Haaland and Judith LeBlanc together for a 2020 webinar entitled "The Power of Native Women":

Deb Haaland was confirmed as US Secretary of the Interior after some contentious Senate Hearings in March 2021.[90]

She now has authority over all the public lands in America – approximately 20% of the land area of the country. She is openly hostile to the fossil fuels industry and is busily using "climate change" as an excuse to shut as much energy extraction on public lands as she possibly can.

Within days of taking office, Secretary Haaland "revoked a series of Trump administration orders that promoted fossil fuel development on public lands and waters, and issued a separate directive that prioritizes climate change in agency decisions."[91]

Secretary Haaland is putting the US economy and national military preparedness at grave risk. This no doubt pleases Judith LeBlanc, her comrades in the Communist Party USA and their masters in the Communist Party of China.

Deb Haaland is a huge fan of Kamala Harris and "wholeheartedly" endorsed her "in a personal capacity" for her presidential campaign in 2024.[92]

The Phillips/Harris connection

The Harris family and the Phillips-Sandler partnership go way back.

Steve Phillips has known Kamala Harris and "her circle of people" for well over twenty years.[93]

He considers her a "friend".

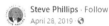

Steve Phillips · Follow
April 28, 2019 · 🌐

I'm with Cory, also friends with Kamala, and increasingly impressed with Warren, so make of that what you will, but I'm not letting go of holding Biden to account for the Thomas hearings and what happened to Anita Hill.

Steve Phillips has certainly helped to fund and guide Harris's political career every step of the way.

From a PowerPAC+ blog post:

> Once named the 'female Barack Obama,' Kamala ran for Attorney General of California in 2010 on a progressive platform…
>
> PowerPAC.org and PowerPAC+ have been Kamala supporters since 2010. In our efforts to support Kamala, PowerPAC.org produced a political ad outlining Kamala's promise to protect the most vulnerable working-class neighborhoods by holding California polluters accountable to their environmental crimes.

This short biography of Susan Sandler from the Sandler Phillips Center ties together several threads:

> Susan Sandler is a philanthropist and political donor. She was the first and largest donor behind the independent efforts to support Barack Obama's 2008 presidential campaign.
>
> She was also the **lead investor in the independent activities supporting Kamala Harris' 2010 campaign for California Attorney General** and Cory Booker's 2013 election to the United States Senate. [emphasis added]
>
> She has served as a board member of several progressive nonprofit organizations including the Democracy Alliance.[94]

PowerPAC+'s support for Kamala Harris cut both ways.

In March 2013, California Attorney General Kamala Harris appointed her old friend, Oakland lawyer and PowerPAC+ board member Eric Casher"[95] to serve a four-year term as Commissioner on the California Fair Political Practices Commission (FPPC). The FPPC enforces "political campaign, lobbying and conflict of interest laws."[96]

Today, Eric Casher is fully on board with the Kamala Harris candidacy.

In 2014, PowerPAC+ supported Cory Booker in his US Senate re-election campaign in New Jersey, and also backed Kamala Harris for California Attorney General.

In December 2014, PowerPAC+ released a tribute video marking the 10th anniversary of the organization.

PowerPac+ beneficiaries Stacey Abrams, Senator Cory Booker, Congressmembers Mark Takano (D-CA) and Marcia Fudge (D-OH), Stockton California councilmember Michael Tubbs and NAACP leader Ben Jealous all contributed.[97]

Then California Attorney General Kamala Harris also chipped in, saying:

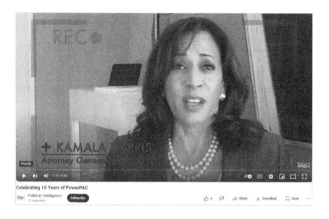

I have seen the work of PowerPAC around the country…it really is the work that inspires a lot of people to really consider the fact that they could be leaders…and if they chose to take that step there will be support for them and the support will be broad and it will be deep and it will be significant…[98]

When Kamala Harris announced her 2016 US Senate bid, Steve Phillips brought a PowerPAC+ party (including Aimee Allison, Amy Chen and Michael Tubbs) to one of the kick-off events.

Also mentioned in the Facebook post is Jill Habig, who would serve as deputy campaign manager and policy director for "Kamala Harris for US Senate", and as policy director for her transition team. Prior to joining the campaign, Habig served as special counsel to then-Attorney General Harris, advising her on "key legal issues and policy initiatives".[99]

Habig's work emphasized "consumer fraud, health, education, human trafficking, and civil rights, including issues related to gender and LGBT rights."

Addisu Demissie, married to Habig, is an activist lawyer known for his political campaign work. He has also been involved with Steve Phillips's initiatives, notably serving on the board of Inclusv,[100] an organization focused on training and recruiting progressive political staffers.

Aimee Allison, Steve Phillips's deputy at PowerPAC+ and Democracy in Color, also chimed in on the Harris's Senate run:

> *This Tuesday, California Attorney General Kamala Harris announced her US Senate bid to replace Senator Barbara Boxer, who is retiring next year. We are thrilled at the opportunity to support a progressive that represents California and the nation.*
>
> *The PowerPAC+ family has supported Kamala Harris since before she ran for statewide office in 2010, and her record in leadership has been stellar. She took on banks responsible for the mortgage crisis, she stood up for marriage equality and she supported criminal justice reform. She is the right leader for the multiracial majority.*

Notice a theme? Kamala Harris is the "right leader for the multiracial majority" or the "New American Majority". PowerPAC+, of course, helped Kamala Harris in that successful race as well.

Home / Media / Political Intelligence

Kamala Harris announces 2016 U.S. Senate Bid

Posted by Aimee Allison on January 13, 2015

This Tuesday, California Attorney General Kamala Harris announced her U.S. Senate bid to replace Senator Barbara Boxer who is retiring next year. We are thrilled at the opportunity to support a progressive that represents California and the nation.

The PowerPAC+ family has supported Kamala Harris since before she ran for statewide office in 2010, and her record in leadership has been stellar. She took on banks responsible for the mortgage crisis, she stood up for marriage equality and she supported criminal justice reform. She is the right leader for the multiracial majority.

We need her in the Senate now more than ever. Now's our chance to get her campaign off to a strong start. Donate what you can today.

2016 starts now.

MAYA HARRIS

Kamala's younger sister Maya Harris was a young student radical at Stanford in the early 1990s. She started at Stanford as Steve Phillips was winding down his near decade of campus activism.

Maya Harris was close to many of Steve Phillips's Black Student Union friends, while organizing protests against the acquittal of police involved in the beating of Rodney King in Los Angeles.[101]

Maya Harris would go on to become a senior fellow at the Sandler-funded Center for American Progress.[102] Steve Phillips also helped Maya Harris's husband, Tony West (another Stanford alumni), get hired at the Obama Justice Department – number three under Barack Obama's "wingman",[103] former United States Attorney General Eric Holder.

According to PowerPAC+:

> *We set up a D.C. office and worked closely with the administra-*
> *tion's personnel staff to build a Diversity Talent Bank that the*
> *White House used to identify and hire more than 60 people,*
> *including Associate Attorney General Tony West.*[104]

It should be noted here that Eric Holder is actively involved in
Kamala Harris's 2024 presidential campaign. As reported at Politico,
Holder "was in charge of vetting of running mates for Vice President
Kamala Harris..."[105]

The former Attorney General currently chairs the National
Democratic Redistricting Committee, which seeks to "build a comprehensive plan to favorably position Democrats for the redistricting
process..." and was reported as former President Barack Obama's
"main post-presidency political focus."[106]

Eric Holder and Steve Phillips share an interest in racial politics. In
October 2020, they shared billing on a panel for the blandly named,
but far-left San Francisco Foundation titled "Philanthropy Can Build
Power and Bolster Democracy". During the discussion, attendees
provided a list of organizations that they believe deserve funding for
their "impactful work to advance racial equity and democracy".[107]

In April 2015, Maya Harris was appointed to be one of three senior
policy advisers to lead the development of an agenda for Hillary
Clinton's 2016 presidential campaign.[108]

Just before the 2016 election, Steve Phillips said that Maya Harris
would be a "social justice ally" in the Hillary Clinton White House.[109]

In her book published after the 2016 election titled "What
Happened", Hillary Clinton described meeting with Black Lives
Matter activists, and her request to her senior policy advisor Maya
Harris to "work closely with them":

> *I took seriously the policies some of the Black Lives Matter activ-*
> *ists later put forward to reform the criminal justice system and*
> *invest in communities of color. I asked Maya and our team to work*
> *closely with them.*
> *We incorporated the best of their ideas into our plans, along*

with input from civil rights organizations that had been in the trenches for decades.[110]

After her experience in Hillary Clinton's 2016 campaign, Maya Harris transferred her skills to manage her sister's short-lived 2020 presidential campaign.[111]

Despite investing heavily in Kamala Harris's career, Susan Sandler would not live to see her efforts come to full fruition.

After a very long battle with cancer, Susan Sandler died, aged 58 in December 2022, after 30 years of marriage to Steve Phillips.[112]

Understandably, Steve Phillips was overjoyed when Kamala Harris finally got the message that Joe Biden was abandoning his re-election run.

Steve Phillips has used his political and financial capital to rally the Democratic Party behind Kamala Harris.

According to the New York Times:

> *Steve Phillips, a Democratic donor and longtime supporter of Ms. Harris, said that he was encouraging donors and groups with whom he worked to publicly back Ms. Harris 'and to demand*

that Whitmer, Newsom and anybody else fully endorse Harris immediately.'[113]

On July 23, 2024, Steve Phillips had an OpEd published in the left-leaning Guardian news site.

In it, Phillips laid out the reasons why though Biden was likely to win anyway, running Kamala Harris would make the victory easier.

Steve Phillips @StevePtweets · Jul 23
I'm getting 2008 vibes (and the data bears this out).

My latest for the @guardian on how #Kamala2024 looks very, very strong

Running Kamala Harris may actually be a political masterstroke for the Democra...

Here are some excerpts from Steve Phillips's article – cold, hard race-based math, with a little emotive delusion mixed in:

Kamala Harris will likely be the next president of the United States – and that's overall good news if you care about democracy, justice and equality…

Even though the electoral fundamentals for this year's election have always favored the Democrats – despite what numerous misleading polls have been showing…Harris's selection will largely shore up the weaknesses that were dragging down Biden's poll numbers.

Since 2020, 16 million young people have become eligible to vote, and 12 million people, most of them older, have died. Biden beat Trump by 30 points among young people, according to the exit polls, and he lost among the oldest voters (52% for Trump, 47% for Biden). So the fundamental composition of our nation's electorate is more progressive, more diverse and more favorable to Democrats right now than it was in 2020...

Lastly, a reality that historians will certainly puzzle over in future years when they try to understand why Biden was forced out less than three and a half months before election day is that the economy is actually going like gangbusters. Fifteen million jobs have been created under the Biden administration and the stock market is at an all-time high, swelling 401k retirement coffers by an average of $10,000 according to Fidelity investments.

An 18 July CBS poll showed Trump leading Biden by 51% to 47%...

The top line weakness came from the results for voters of color, which showed just 52% of Latinos and 73% percent of African Americans currently supporting the president (with drop-off primarily among men from these groups).

If, in fact, support for Democrats among people of color is the principal problem, then putting Harris at the top of the ticket is a master stroke. The enthusiasm for electing the first woman of color as president will likely be a thunderclap across the country that consolidates the support of voters of color, and, equally important, motivates them to turn out in large numbers at the polls, much as they did for Barack Obama in 2008...

All of this adds up to the likelihood that the 47th president of the United States will be Kamala Devi Harris.[114]

As a Marxist, Steve Phillips naturally assumes that America's black and Latino voters will consider race, rather than the issues when going to the polls in November.

There is little doubt that Steve Phillips is still a revolutionary at heart.

In a Democracy in Color podcast recorded very soon after Kamala Harris had chosen Tim Walz as her running mate, Phillips debated the merits of Walz over Pennsylvania Governor Josh Shapiro in terms of what each candidate would bring to a winning coalition.

In classic Maoist terminology Steve Phillips stated:

But then it gets back to – what's the role of progressives? So there's this concept of a united front, in that in any kind of revolution or

> *social change…you bring together as broad a coalition as you possibly can and you focus on the goal at hand…*[115]

And that goal is building a permanent New American Majority. In the chapter on Tim Walz, readers will discover why Steve Phillips's use of the phrase "united front" is so significant.

CHAPTER 4

MAOIST FRIENDS AND BLACK LIVES MATTER

LATEEFAH MEETS KAMALA AND STEVE

WHILE SERVING AS San Francisco district attorney, Kamala Harris took under her wing a young San Francisco activist named Lateefah Simon.

Lateefah was primed for activism. According to her personal bio, her aunt "was a Black Panther and instrumental in shaping its Free Breakfast for Children Program." Her own journey into activism was marked by an early arrest during an Iraq War protest while in seventh grade, an event she credits with awakening her to the "power" she held as an activist.[1]

After hiring her and helping Simon get through college, Harris introduced her young friend to many influential San Franciscans.

Lateefah Simon, who is running for Congress, currently serves as President of the Meadow Fund, which was founded by Patty Quillin, the wife of Netflix co-founder Reed Hastings. The Meadow Fund describes itself as "a donor-advised fund...[whose] grantmaking program is driven by our intersectional approach to racial, gender, and criminal justice reform."[2] Simon also serves on the Board of Trustees of the San Francisco Foundation,[3] a grantmaking organization that "prioritize[s] race and socioeconomic status..."[4]

Distributing funds to race-obsessed leftist organizations appears to be quite lucrative. According to Simon's Financial Disclosure Report to run for Congress, Patty Quillin doled out $557k To Simon in 2023, which was reported as "earned income".[5]

In recent years, Simon has served as president (now board member)[6] of "one of the leading funders in the movement for racial justice", the Akonadi Foundation (founded by longtime Kamala Harris supporters and donors Quinn Delaney and Wayne Jordan in

2000)[7]. Simon also chairs the Bay Area Rapid Transit (BART) board and is a member of the Board of Trustees for the California State University.[8]

Steve Phillips has actively endorsed[9] and funded Lateefah Simon's political campaigns.[10]

Influence of Oscar Grant's Death

Oscar Grant III, a troubled[11] 22-year-old black man, was fatally shot by Bay Area Rapid Transit (BART) police officer Johannes Mehserle in the early morning hours of January 1, 2009, at the Fruitvale BART station in Oakland, California. At the time, Grant was involved in a disturbance on a BART train with his friends. Mehserle was convicted of involuntary manslaughter.

Like in many similar cases, Oscar Grant became a cause célèbre, exploited by communist organizations such as the Workers World Party,[12] the ANSWER Coalition[13] and the Freedom Road Socialist Organization[14,15] as an opportunity to condemn police for supposed brutality and racism.

Unsurprisingly, mass rioting took place in Oakland in the wake of Oscar Grant's death. Hundreds were involved in the riots, which included widespread destruction of property, with businesses being looted and vandalized. Charges were dropped against most of the rioters.[16]

Lateefah's friend, Black Lives Matter co-founder Alicia Garza, stated that Oscar Grant was a springboard for Black Lives Matter:

> *When people tell the story of Black Lives Matter, they either start it in 2014 with Mike Brown, or they start it in 2013 with Trayvon Martin. But for us, right, for those of us who created Black Lives Matter, it really does kind of start with Oscar Grant.*[17]

Lateefah was deeply moved by the death of Oscar Grant. In April 2024, Steve Phillips hosted Lateefah Simon on a "Democracy in Color" broadcast titled "Lateefah Simon is taking up the baton".[18]

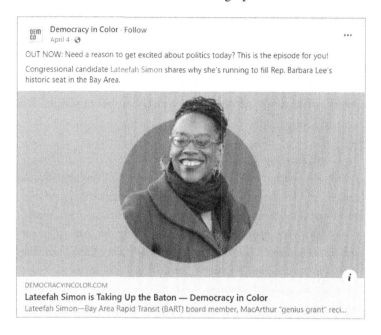

> **DEM CO** Democracy in Color · Follow
> April 4 · 🌐
>
> OUT NOW: Need a reason to get excited about politics today? This is the episode for you!
>
> Congressional candidate Lateefah Simon shares why she's running to fill Rep. Barbara Lee's historic seat in the Bay Area.
>
> DEMOCRACYINCOLOR.COM
> **Lateefah Simon is Taking Up the Baton — Democracy in Color**
> Lateefah Simon—Bay Area Rapid Transit (BART) board member, MacArthur "genius grant" reci...

According to Phillips, Simon was "driven by the death of Oscar Grant" in her successful run for the Bay Area Rapid Transit (BART) Board of Directors. Like her mentor Kamala Harris, anti-police sentiment runs deep for Simon. She describes how "organizers" like herself fought for charges to be brought against the police officers involved in Oscar Grant's death:

> *Every institution that I have entered, I've wanted to shift it to meet really the needs of folks who deserve material conditions to be shifted in community. So the idea to run for the BART board, you know, and it was a position that only kind of political knew about after the death, murder of Oscar Grant, you know, us as organizers*

*being in that BART board meeting every other week demanding
that the BART do something about these officers, the chief, we had
no oversight commission with BART Rapid Transit that has its
own Police Department, by the way.*

With Lateefah Simon on the BART board, police officers would
be better off moving to Florida.

'Uncle Steve' and 'Miss Lee'

During the discussion, Lateefah Simon makes it clear that she has
a personal relationship with Steve Phillips and Barbara Lee, both of
whom are very close to Kamala Harris, as well.

Simon refers to Phillips as "Uncle" and explains she would call him
"like, every other week" after she began her campaign to take Barbara
Lee's seat in Congress:

> *...I launched my campaign on February 28th, and I think I
> called you February 27th saying like, 'Uncle, I'm running, this is
> crazy.' And for those of you who don't know, Steve was trained and
> mentored a lot of young people to get into politics, and you would
> always say, even after people give, keep calling. So that's, I'm not
> asking for nothing, I just want to let you know I'm calling Steve like
> every other week like, 'Hey Steve,' because you also say in your text
> that politics cannot be transactional, that we are building not only
> coalitions, we are building another way of being by saying we are
> doing this thing to take everyone with us, and I believe that, and a
> lot of that came from you...*

Lateefah Simon also references her close personal relationship with
Representative Barbara Lee, who was one of Lateefah Simon's professors at Mills College. During one of these classes, Simon describes an
exchange with Barbara Lee, who posed a hypothetical question about
running for Congress:

> *So when Miss Lee called me and just told me she was running for
> the United States Senate and reminded me that when I was in
> her class, uh, she was my professor at Mills where I used to bring
> my oldest daughter on the weekends to that five-hour class that
> Barbara would fly out too every Friday night so she could teach on*

Saturdays, she reminded me. She said, 'Te, you remember that?' Well, I said one day I would retire from the house, and I asked the students in the class who would run for Congress. She reminded me that I raised my hand while it was a factious conversation. She just, she didn't endorse me at that time, didn't say you need to run. She said, 'I think you need to talk to your family. That these positions don't come by, you're a fighter, they don't come by, but once in a lifetime.'

Lateefah Simon's journey into politics reflects an intricate web of political mentorship by militant left activists.

Barbara Lee

During the podcast Steve Phillips explained that one of his "political heroes" was the openly socialist congressman Ron Dellums. Phillips continues to state that it was Dellums's seat that was filled by Barbara Lee. "During the 1980s, I met and got to know Barbara Lee as we both worked on Jesse Jackson's presidential campaign before she succeeded Dellums in Congress, representing that seat", he said.[19]

And now Lateefah Simon is running in California's Oakland-based District 12 to replace Barbara Lee.

Barbara Lee is also very close to Kamala Harris. In November 2023, Harris described Lee as a "dear friend, and an extraordinary leader, and a courageous leader, and in so many ways, for so many of us, a conscience of our country."[20]

Like many Bay Area congressmembers, Barbara Lee is a lifelong Marxist.

In the early 1970s, Lee was a confidential aide to Black Panther Party "Minister of Defense" Huey Newton,[21] and a member of the Afro-American Association with Kamala Harris's parents.

Lee also worked as a staffer for the Congressmember Ron Dellums.[22]

Representative Lee was a huge supporter of Grenada's Marxist Prime Minister, the late Maurice Bishop, and has been a decades-long ally of communist Cuba.[23]

As Steve Phillips alluded to, Barbara Lee was prominent in Jesse Jackson's Rainbow Coalition. While serving as a Democratic California Assembly member, Lee ran unsuccessfully for the National Coordinating Committee of the Communist Party USA splinter group Committees of Correspondence.

tian Leadership Conference, later becoming its assistant director. A long-time member of the D.C. Statehood Party, he was elected as a delegate to the D.C. Statehood Convention in 1981. He serves presently as an Advisory Neighborhood Commissioner. A member of the Communist Party, USA, for 20 years, he served as chair of its D.C., Maryland and Virginia districts, as its Legislative Director, and on the National Committee and National Board. He left the party following its support for the coup in the former Soviet Union.

GEOFFREY JACQUES is a poet, journalist, essayist, curator, editor, activist and critic. Born in Detroit, he moved to New York in 1983. He has been active in the peace, trade union and social justice movements for over 20 years, and

HON. BARBARA LEE represents the 13th Assembly District (which includes Oakland, Alameda and Emeryville) in the California State Assembly. She serves on five standing legislative committees and a wide range of commissions. Lee founded a community health center while working on her graduate degree in Social Work in the mid-'70s. She served as a senior advisor and administrative assistant to Rep. Ronald V. Dellums from 1975-87. She is a member of the Rainbow Coalition, Black Women Organized for Political Action, and many other organizations.
                                    Continued on next page

Committees of Correspondence Newsletter – Page 11

Committees of Correspondence NCC profiles, Corresponder Volume 2, number 1, 1993

With Marxist heavy hitters Kamala Harris, Steve Phillips and Barbara Lee's enthusiastic support, is it any wonder Lateefah Simon is a rising star in the "Democratic" party?

Center for Young Women's Development

As a high-school dropout, Lateefah Simon was working full time at Taco Bell. She was a teenaged parent and on probation for shoplifting. But her life would soon change.

While on probation, Simon was referred to the blandly-named non-profit, the "Center for Young Women's Development", which ostensibly provided job training and other services for troubled young women.[24] Later renamed the Young Women's Freedom Center, the organization's Board Chair was Ayoka Turner while Simon was Board President.[25] Turner is deeply tied to the Freedom Road Socialist Organization,[26] that is known for racial agitation.

Currently, Democracy Alliance president Pamela Shifman sits on the board.[27] Funny how all roads seem to lead back to Steve Phillips.

Banko Brown

As an aside and keeping with the theme of anti-police sentiment and racial agitation, Lateefah Simon addressed a crowd protesting the shooting of Banko Brown, a black female-to-male trans activist who was killed by a security guard while attempting to rob a Walgreens in San Francisco, California in April 2023.

Lateefah Simon at Banko Brown Protest

The protest was organized by Simon's friends at the Young Women's Freedom Center.[28] Banko Brown had been "involved" with the Young Women's Freedom Center since she was 12 years old, according to the Bay Area Reporter, a local publication that reported on the protest.

That report also mentioned Lateefah:

> Lateefah Simon, a straight ally who is on the BART board of directors and is running for Congress in the East Bay to replace

Congressmember Barbara Lee (D-Oakland), who is running for US Senate, led the vigil in prayer.

'Creator, I ask you to hold this man who was shot because of what he looked like and who we are,' said Simon, who is also Black.

Like bees to honey, the Party for Socialism and Liberation also attended the gathering.

The local article noted that "[Banko] Brown's pastor", the Reverend Amos C. Brown, leader of a local NAACP chapter, was also at the event. Brown, who has referred to America as a "racist country"[29] is coincidentally very close to Kamala Harris. Brown also "blamed America for 9/11 *at a memorial service for one of the victims*" [emphasis added].[30]

Kamala Harris with Amos Brown (L) from her Facebook dated August 30, 2008

A San Francisco Chronicle article from August 2024 quoted Steve Phillips disparaging those who compare the relationship between Kamala Harris and Amos Brown to that of former President Barack Obama's relationship with his Marxist[31] pastor Rev. Jeremiah Wright:

> 'It's old, it's tired, it's ineffective,' said Steve Phillips, a San Francisco attorney, author and top Democratic donor who was an early supporter of both Obama and Harris. 'It didn't work on Obama, so that might give them a little pause to start with.'[32]

As one takes the time to examine Kamala Harris's foundational relationships, the same trends repeat themselves time and again: Leftist activism, racial agitation, anti-police and anti-America sentiment.

Kamala passed this militant ideology directly to her young charge, Lateefah Simon.

Lateefah, Activist

At the formerly-named Center for Young Women's Development, Lateefah Simon doubled down on her leftist activism. She started attending San Francisco Board of Supervisors meetings regularly. She questioned authorities on their responsibilities to young women like herself. Her "passion and intelligence" caught the attention of then-Supervisor Tom Ammiano and a young city attorney named Kamala Harris.[33]

Event featuring "free" Preschool in 2005. L-R Kamala Harris, Rob Reiner and Tom Ammiano

Tom Ammiano was also close to the communist movement.

Ammiano was first elected to the San Francisco Board of Supervisors with the active help of the Gay & Lesbian Taskforce of the Committees of Correspondence.[34]

In 1996, as a City Supervisor, Ammiano sponsored the Communist Party USA's annual Bay Area People's Weekly World fundraising banquet, at a now-closed restaurant called His Lordships in the Berkeley Marina.[35]

The leadership at the Center for Young Women's Development was also impressed by Lateefah Simon's political efforts. By the time she was 19, Simon was named executive director, with a staff of 10 and a $750,000 annual budget.

A true mentor

Kamala Harris helped guide her through those years, Lateefah Simon has said.

"She just changed my life. She was tough as nails. She said to me, 'You need to be excellent. ... So first off, you need to go to college.'"

Simon enrolled at Mills College in Oakland, eventually graduating with a bachelor's degree in public policy. As previously mentioned, Barbara Lee was one of Simon's professors at Mills College.

Kamala Harris, by then San Francisco's district attorney, enlisted Simon to help start a program "Back on Track" to help first-time, low-level drug offenders stay out the criminal justice system.

Kamala Harris ✔
@KamalaHarris
⋯

Fourteen years ago today, when I was DA of San Francisco, Lateefah and I started Back on Track—a program that provided opportunities for young people involved in the criminal justice system to get them out of the system for good. It's time we take this program nationwide.

5:38 PM · Oct 11, 2019

"Our goal was to get people off the street. How do you do that? Turned out it was easy — you just ask them what they need," says Simon. "Housing? A bank account? A job? therapy? A gym membership, so you can take better care of yourself. We could help them get those things."[36]

Lateefah and Kamala Harris developed a close friendship that endures to this day.

Kamala Harris continued to boost Lateefah Simon's activist/political career in any way she could, including endorsing her protégé in her 2016 run for the Bay Area Rapid Transit board - even neglecting her own campaign for US Senate to support her race.[37]

Rubbing Elbows with Radical Influencers

In June 2024, Lateefah Simon met up again with her old sponsor Steve Phillips when she moderated a panel in Berkeley entitled "We the People: Building a Resilient Multiracial Democracy in 2024 and Beyond".

Steve Phillips's co-panelists were Ash-Lee Henderson, co-executive Director of the Highlander Research and Education Center in Tennessee and Maurice Mitchell, the New York-based national director of the Working Families Party (WFP).[38]

The Working Families Party supports and cross-endorses far-left Democratic candidates in several states, including California.

The WFP is very much in the orbit of the pro-China communist group FRSO/Liberation Road (formerly known as Freedom Road Socialist Organization).

Unsurprisingly, the WFP is supporting Lateefah Simon in her Congressional race.[39]

The Highlander Center (formerly the famous Highlander Folk School) was run by pro-Soviet communists for many decades, but is now dominated by Maoist groups, particularly FRSO/Liberation Road.

Ash-Lee Henderson wears Freedom Road Socialist Organization shirt

Highlander Center-trained activists are currently busy engaging in Maoist-influenced race-based agitation in Tennessee, Virginia, the Carolinas, Georgia, Alabama, Georgia, Mississippi and many other states.

Ash-Lee Henderson is a confirmed long time Freedom Road Socialist Organization comrade.

She is pictured here wearing her favorite Freedom Road Socialist Organization T-shirt.

YEC/STORM

When Kamala Harris first met Lateefah Simon, the younger woman was serving on the board of directors of the Oakland-based Youth Empowerment Center (YEC).

This organization was funded by the Levi Strauss Foundation, the Zellerbach Family Foundation, the James Irvine Foundation, the San Francisco Foundation, the Charles Stewart Mott Foundation, Surdna Foundation, Inc. and others.[40]

YEC in turn distributed this money to the four main radical groups: C-Beyond, Youth Force Coalition, Underground Railroad and the School of Unity and Liberation (SOUL) – funded by YEC in 2001 to the tune of $250,000.[41]

The last group was founded in 1996 by Harmony Goldberg and Rona Fernandez out of the 1995 student movement at the University of California - Berkeley to support affirmative action, which gives preferential treatment to certain individuals based on skin color.[42]

Says Goldberg:

> I became revolutionized through the course of my experience of trying to change things electorally, trying to change embedded racism. I concluded that to build power we needed to liberate our own people, instead of trying to convince people in power to do it.
>
> We studied the Third World movements of the 1960s and 1970s, here and abroad: South Africa, Cuba, China, Chile. We studied the [revolutionary] classics, the histories. We decided to commit to an organizing method, not just direct action or ideological organizing.
>
> I am not an 'ist,' merely a revolutionary, with identity as a socialist.[43]

SOUL board members included Maria Poblet,[44] Adam Gold and future Black Lives Matter founder Alicia Garza.[45]

By 2001, the YEC board consisted of Harmony Goldberg and Adam Gold from SOUL, Cindy Wiesner from the allied People Organized to Win Employment Rights (POWER), Van Jones of the Ella Baker Center for Human Rights and Lateefah Simon.[46]

Youth Empowerment Center Board of Directors
Harmony Goldberg, President   Anthony "Van" Jones, Secretary
Adam Gold, Treasurer   Cindy Weisner, Director
Lateefah Simon, Director

From 'Undue Influence' website

YEC, SOUL, POWER and the Ella Baker Center for Human Rights were all essentially front groups for "Standing Together to Organize a Revolutionary Movement" (STORM) –a revolutionary cadre organization based in the San Francisco Bay Area.

According to the STORM's own history "Reclaiming Revolution":

> *From September 1994 to December 2002, STORM helped to re-invigorate the Left, both locally and nationally. STORM members fought on the frontlines of some of the most important struggles of those eight years. We built organizations and institutions that continue to fight. And we supported the development of a new generation of revolutionary internationalists in the Bay Area and across the country.*
>
> *We studied philosophy, wage exploitation, capitalism, imperialism and globalization, Lenin's theories of the state, revolution and the party, and the political ideas of Mao Tse-tung and Antonio Gramsci.*[47]

Every YEC board member: Harmony Goldberg,[48] Cindy Weisner,[49] Adam Gold,[50] Van Jones,[51] were documented STORM comrades except Lateefah Simon.

Van Jones became the most famous former STORM comrade of all when he was appointed as President Obama's "Green Jobs Czar" in 2009. After this author exposed his communist background,[52] Fox News host Glenn Beck and others mounted a major campaign to force Van Jones out of the White House. Jones eventually resigned in disgrace but has since managed to re-invent himself as a political pundit and CNN commentator.

Van Janes is also a friend of Steve Phillips. Jones has known Phillips as an activist in the 1980s and when he served on the San Francisco Education Board in the early 1990s.[53]

Here are Steve Phillips and Van Jones pictured at an April 2016 Ford Foundation sponsored discussion themed "Brown is the New White: Changing Demographics and a New American Majority":

Brown is the New White: Changing Demographics and a New American Majority

Van Jones, a key Democratic Party insider, credits three black Democratic women with ensuring that Kamala Harris took over when Joe Biden renounced his presidential candidacy, rather than allow any other rivals for the position.

Donna Brazile, Karen Finney, and Jotaka Eaddy

Jones specifically named Donna Brazile, Karen Finney, and Jotaka Eaddy "orchestrated and engineered" Kamala Harris's victory.[54]

Van Jones told CNN:

> "...and first of all... when you talk about Donna Brazile, Karen Finney, Jotaka Eaddy: these are African-American women who are the pillars of the democratic party. They do the hard work... and they orchestrated and engineered this outcome [emphasis added] not because Kamala Harris is a black woman but because they could not see the Democratic party in disarray and they wanted to make sure that if there was going to be a loose ball it landed in the most capable hands; someone who won as district attorney, someone who's won as attorney general, someone who's won as Senator, someone who's won as vice president. A winner who has delivered over and over again so they engineered the football getting into their right hands...[55]

Karen Finney is a CNN political commentator and high-level Democratic Party strategist with close ties to Hillary Clinton.[56]

Donna Brazile is a former student radical who gained access to the highest reaches of the Democratic Party through her "mentor and friend"[57] Jesse Jackson. Brazile posted on X in August 2018: "I was with Jesse Jackson in 1984: An Outsider, a trouble maker & a believer in the Rainbow Coalition."[58]

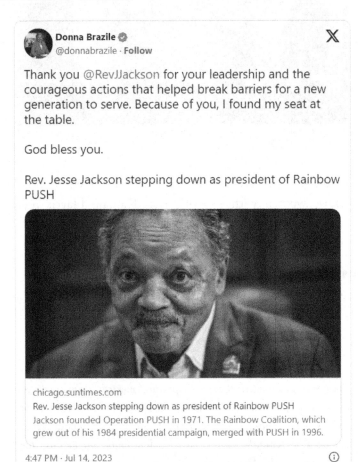

In 2014, Donna Brazile worked with Steve Phillips to pressure the Democratic Congressional Campaign Committee to contract with more minority-owned consulting firms.[59]

Jotaka Eaddy, a former student activist turned Silicon Vally business-woman/influencer, founded the movement #WinWithBlackWomen, which raised more than a million dollars for Kamala Harris's first presidential campaign.[60]

Jotaka Eaddy also serves as one of five members of the board of the Southern Elections Foundation, which was founded to "fight[ing] massive voter suppression with massive voter registration."[61]

The other members are PowerPAC+ activists Steve Phillips, Andy Wong, Ben Jealous, plus Mississippi NAACP activist Derrick Johnson.[62]

Alicia Garza and the Maoists

Lateefah Simon has another very close friend, a "sis" - Alicia Garza, of Black Lives Matter fame, who has formally endorsed her old friend's run for Congress.[63]

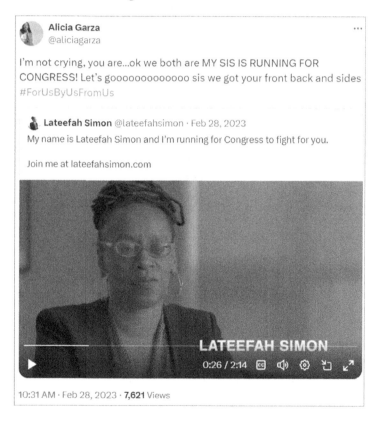

The Simon/Garza relationship goes back many years.

The pair have moved in the same circles since at least the early 2000s when Alicia Garza was part of SOUL and Lateefah Simon was hanging around with her STORM comrades.

This "comradeship" has endured up until recent times.

Alicia Garza (L) with Lateefah Simon

Here's a photo of Lateefah Simon, Alicia Garza and Van Jones at a San Francisco school board meeting in August 2016:

As Alicia Garza was close with Lateefah Simon, and Lateefah Simon was close with Kamala Harris, it's likely that Kamala Harris and Alicia Garza got to know each other over the years.

In February 2018, Kamala Harris gave a shout out[64] to Alicia Garza's on the launch of her new organization "Black Futures Lab."

Kamala Harris ✔ @KamalaHarris · Feb 27, 2018 ···
⚑ United States government official
"For too long, people have spoken for us and perpetuated false representations of the issues that drive our votes." Congratulations @AliciaGarza on the launch of @blackfutureslab!

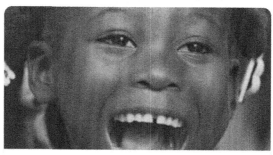

colorlines.com
Alicia Garza Launches New Organization to Harness Black Political Po...
"Black folks drive the progressive political power in this country, but rarely benefit from the fruits of our labor. We are launching the Black ...

In August 2020, Alicia Garza published an article in Glamour magazine "With Kamala Harris in the VP Slot, We Just Made History—Let's Do It Again in November" praising Joe Biden for giving Kamala Harris the vice-presidential spot.[65]

Garza was writing in her capacity as principal of the Black to the Future Action Fund, which she founded to "make Black communities powerful in politics:"

> For the first time in history, a Black woman, as vice president, will be charged with being the top advisor to the president of the United States, presiding over the Senate, and breaking any tie as it relates to legislation being passed in Congress.
>
> This is a role that ostensibly could help to set policy and practice in the White House, and as such, could ensure what we've pushed for at the Black to the Future Action Fund—a government of the people, for the people, and by the people.
>
> The most important part of this choice is what it can do to energize the strongest base of the Democratic Party: Black women…
>
> We want to know that a campaign has its finger on the pulse of how issues like health care, housing, criminal system reform, and the economy will be addressed—not just in general, but in terms of how racial and gender disparities built into each of these issues will be specifically addressed and resolved.[66]

Many on the far-left were still angry over some of Harris's allegedly overharsh treatment of black and Latino defendants during her time as a prosecutor in San Francisco.

From the Washington Post:

> As speculation mounted in recent months about her chances of being tapped as Joe Biden's running mate, Sen. Kamala D. Harris (D-Calif.) began introducing some eye-catching legislation.
>
> One measure boosted research for uterine fibroids, a condition that threatens pregnancies and disproportionately affects Black women. Another toughened a measure to ban police chokeholds following the killing of George Floyd. In the same stretch, she used her Senate perch to push for greater voting access.
>
> All those issues are of deep concern to the Black activists whose skepticism of Harris helped doom her own presidential campaign but who were gaining influence in the Democratic Party amid a season of racial reckoning. Harris turned to some of those activists, meeting with them repeatedly as she crafted the Senate provisions. And by the time Biden was in the final throes of his arduous selection process, many of the same critics who had looked with suspicion at Harris's past work as a prosecutor were suddenly pulling for her as a fellow Black woman.[67]

In August 2020, Alicia Garza had a private meeting with Kamala Harris to hash out some issues.

Garza said she discussed "some of the challenges of this moment, some of the policy that we needed to see her champion in this moment, and it was an important and a good meeting," Garza said.

It helps, she added, that Harris suggested she might not embrace the same policies today.

Garza said her support for Harris is conditional.

"Now that there is this level of representation on the ticket, that is expected to translate into substance," Garza said. "I can already tell you that there are going to be some fights."[68]

In recent years, Alicia Garza has served as a special projects director for the Bay Area branch of the Washington DC-based National Domestic Workers Alliance (NDWA)[69] – a labor union for mainly migrant hotel, hospital and cleaning workers.

The NDWA is largely led by old Maoists and some newer recruits to the China-aligned FRSO/Liberation Road.

In August 2012, another Maoist-led organization, the Chinese Progressive Association-San Francisco (CPA-SF), celebrated the 40th anniversary of their founding.

The NDWA sent a significant delegation to mark the auspicious occasion.

Yes, these are genuine Maoists. Note that the Freedom Road Socialist Organization extended comradely greetings to the very same event.

They also chipped in $150 towards the costs, as did their front group Right to the City Alliance.[70]

Congratulations to all of you at CPA for 40 years of organizing, transformation, and leadership in San Francisco!

Freedom Road Socialist Organization

Domestic Workers Bill of Rights

For several years, the NDWA has been promoting its "Domestic Workers Bill of Rights", a heavily socialist document aimed at more unionizing and exploiting the political muscle of millions of legal and illegal immigrants.

Kamala Harris is of course right behind Alicia Garza and the "domestic workers" cause.

 **Kamala Harris** ✔   **X**
@KamalaHarris · **Follow**

Oakland-based organizer and Black Lives Matter co-founder Alicia Garza is a powerful voice against police injustice. She created Black Futures Lab to mobilize Black political power and is fighting for millions of domestic workers that live in the U.S. #BlackHistoryMonth

"We are clear that all lives matter, but we live in a world where that's not actually happening in practice. So if we want to get to the place where all lives matter, then we have to make sure that Black lives matter, too."

ALICIA GARZA

‖ GIF

7:30 PM · Feb 21, 2019   ⓘ

In November 2018, Kamala Harris got fully behind the NDWA's Domestic Bill of Rights.

Pramila Jayapal, Kamala Harris and Ai-jen Poo at Domestic Workers
'Bill of Rights' press conference, January 17, 2019

In fact, she later claimed credit for helping to write the Senate version of the bill.

Kamala Harris ✔
@KamalaHarris

Follow   ...

From working with unions as San Francisco's District Attorney, to helping author the Domestic Workers' Bill of Rights in the U.S. Senate, I've always fought for workers.

And so will the economic team we announced today.

10:03 PM · Jan 8, 2021

The NDWA, Senator Harris and far-left Congresswoman Pramila Jayapal (D-WA) announced they would be "introducing groundbreaking new legislation to improve the lives of domestic workers and transform the way people work in America."

According to the NDWA press release:

> *The first ever national Domestic Workers Bill of Rights, which will be officially introduced early in the 116th Congress, will provide basic labor protections to more than two million nannies, house cleaners, and care workers across the country, while developing innovations for the future of one of the fastest growing occupations in the country.*
>
> *'The work of domestic workers is so incredibly important, both as caregivers and as organizers. This is the work that our economy is built on, yet too often, it's undervalued and underappreciated,' said*

Senator Kamala Harris. 'In America, we all deserve basic rights,
safety, and dignity in the workplace. By fighting for fairness and equal
treatment, we are fighting for the best of who we are as a country.'[71]

Alicia Garza, of course, approved:

Thanks to the powerful leadership of
@domesticworkers leaders, Senator
@KamalaHarris and @RepJayapal will introduce a
national #DomesticWorkersBillOfRights. Black
and Brown women are fighting for fair wages, a
chance to care for our families, health care, and
protection from sexual assault -- and we are
WINNING!

Representative Pramila Jayapal and Ai-jen Poo attended a year
long course together at the FRSO/Liberation Road-Linked radical
training school Rockwood Leadership Institute in 2010.[72]

Alicia Garza also attended the Rockwood Leadership Institute.[73]

On July 22, 2024, Ai-jen Poo posted about her connection with
Kamala Harris on Instagram. "I have known our Vice President
Kamala Harris for many years now," she began. Poo explained that
Kamala Harris was the "lead sponsor" in the Senate for the Domestic
Workers Bill of Rights. Harris "gathered women labor leaders" as
VP, Poo explained, in order to "hear about how women were being
impacted economically by pandemic closures…"

Cementing their bond, Poo continues to gush that Kamala Harris
"championed affordable child care, paid leave and aging and disability
care in the Biden-Harris economic agenda and personally called me
as she prepared to elevate these policies as essential priorities…"[74]

The Domestic Workers Bill of Rights was initiated and promoted
by graduates of a militant training school, supported by their comrade Kamala Harris. When researching Kamala, the same radical
groups and individuals continually appear.[75]

THE CHINESE PROGRESSIVE ASSOCIATION AND BLM

Alicia Garza is very close to the Chinese Progressive Association-San Francisco (CPA-SF), a very influential "community organization" based in San Francisco's Chinatown.

The connection was probably made by longtime CPA-SF leader Alex Tom, who recruited the then-Alicia Schwartz to activism at UC San Diego in the very early 2000s. Alex Tom is a diehard pro-China Marxist. He has traveled to the "People's Republic" on multiple occasions including for a period studying Chinese language at Sun Yat-sen University in Guangzhou.[76]

Alex Tom also indoctrinated Alicia Schwartz/Garcia into the "Rainbow Coalition" strategy.[77]

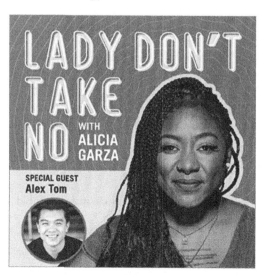

Founded in the 1970s by young Maoist activists from the I Wor Kuen, the CPA-SF became a front for the League of Revolutionary Struggle (LRS).

At the time, most of Chinatown's leaders were anti-communist and supported Taiwan. The young Maoists set out to change that position and they have largely succeeded. The CPA-SF has significantly influenced the city's political landscape, pushing it towards the far-left. Consequently, securing an election victory in San Francisco has become nearly impossible without the endorsement or support from the CPA-SF.

From the start, the CPA-SF Maoists sought to build strong ties to their Chinese counterparts.

According to Stanford University History Comparative Studies in Race and Ethnicity Honors graduate Kaori Tsukada:

> The CPA began as a Leftist, pro-People's Republic of China orga-
> nization, promoting awareness of mainland China's revolutionary
> thought and workers' rights, and dedicated to self-determination,
> community control, and 'serving the people'
>   Its activities were independent of the Communist Party of
> China or the US, and instead the organization worked with other
> pro-PRC groups within the US and San Francisco Bay Area...[78]

However, the Chinese Communist Party soon began to take notice of its Bay Area acolytes:

> Although there were no monetary interactions, CPA members were
> invited to visit the People's Republic of China a number of times, as
> an opportunity to visit their ancestors' homes and to see socialism
> in action. Although the visiting members were aware that much of
> what they were shown was too perfect, this was also an opportunity
> to see the country where they found a viable alternative to capi-
> talism in an age of restricted information.[79]

Early CPA-SF activist[80] and LRS comrade Mabel Teng[81] put it this way:

> In the early '70s, the People's Republic of China (PRC) inspired
> the world as a leading third world country struggling for self

determination. To us, support for China meant self-respect and pride. CPA worked with pro-China organizations in Chinatown and the US-China People's Friendship Association in celebrating October 1, China's national day, and film showings to promote education and friendship. When the two countries normalized diplomatic relations on January 1, 1979, thousands rejoiced in Ports mouth Square.[82]

Former CPA-SF executive director Alex Tom was extremely explicit about his organization's loyalty to China in a May 22, 2020, webinar hosted by the San Francisco-based Center for Political Education, on "US and China Relations."

Speaking to a friendly audience Alex Tom said:

> *...there is a part of the left that has always been really curious and lifting up the role of China so that's and that is like the Chinese Progressive Association was one of the first organizations to even lift up the revolution in Chinatown right our history basically is founded on people's friendship in China...*
>
> *...and we have a relationship with the Chinese embassy like we actually have so you know I've had to have various conversations with them about our positioning...*[83]

Unsurprisingly, the CPA-SF also followed their LRS comrades into Jesse Jackson's Rainbow Coalition.

CPA-SF Director Mabel Teng introduced presidential candidate Jesse Jackson at the 1984 Democratic National Convention.[84]

Comrade Teng would go on to co-chair the San Francisco Rainbow Coalition and the Asian-Pacific Caucus of the Democratic Party.[85]

Alicia Garza served on the Host Committee for the CPA-SF's 40th anniversary celebrations in August 2012.[86]

Garza is also pictured in the following image, (back row center) during one of the many photo-ops after the event, which was largely funded by Steve Phillips's brother-in-law James Sandler and his wife Gretchen, who chipped in a cool $10,000:[87]

Chinese Progressive Association Facebook Post dated August 8, 2012

At the CPA-SF's 45th anniversary in October 2017, Alicia Garza again served on the event Host Committee, alongside San Francisco Supervisors (City Councilors) Sandra Lee Fewer, Aaron Peskin, Hillary Ronen and Norman Yee and several former League of Revolutionary Struggle comrades.[88]

The event honored the "End National Security Scapegoating Coalition", an organization established by pro-China Marxists to defend and campaign for people indicted by the US government for spying for China.

The Coalition received an award for "committing to end the racial profiling of Asian Americans and all people as national security threats; and for challenging the US Department of Justice's scrutiny of Chinese Americans Guoqing Cao, Shuyu Li, Sherry Chen, and Xiaoxing Xi for espionage related crimes."[89]

James & Gretchen Sandler, Sommai LeBron-Cooke of the Sandler Philanthropic Fund, together with SEIU 1021 and UNITE HERE were the biggest donors to this event.

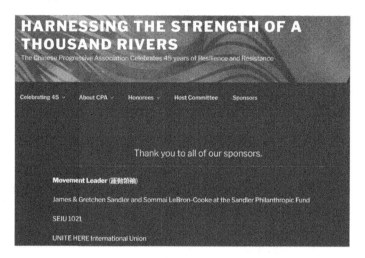

Steve Phillips's PowerPAC organization chipped in an unspecified amount.[90]

Steve Phillips and his family are funding a blatantly pro-Communist Party of China organization.

As recently as 2020, Alicia Garza's "Black Future's Lab" organization was a "fiscally sponsored project of the Chinese Progressive Association."[91]

The Black Futures Lab "seeks to engage advocacy organizations and legislators to advance local-, state- and federal-level policies that make Black communities stronger. It will also craft strategies that harness Black political power to bring those policies to fruition."[92]

Alicia Garza's old friend and comrade Lateefah Simon served as Black Futures Lab "Strategic Advisor".[93]

Interesting also is the fact that the well-known San Francisco FRSO/Liberation Road comrade Michelle Foy[94] has served as CPA-SF's finance and administration director in April 2018.[95]

LEFTROOTS

As it turns out, Steve Phillips funded the birth of another pro-China organization called LeftRoots – a bona fide Marxist activist organization with several branches across the country.

In 2013, Steve Phillips and Susan Sandler were key funders of the "Ear to the Ground Project".[96]

Bay Area activists N'Tanya Lee and Steve Williams, former Standing together to Organize a Revolutionary Movement (STORM) member,[97] were commissioned to tour the US interviewing activists to assess the state of the US left and to come with ideas for a new socialist organization.[98]

Wrote Williams and Lee:

> After more than two decades of on-the-ground organizing in distinct organizations, the two of us have spent the last sixteen months on a unique journey together. We conducted more than 150 interviews with movement activists, read the work of movement intellectuals, and spent a lot of time in conversation with each other— in doing so, we pushed ourselves to imagine the world, and our own work, in new ways.
>
> The Ear to the Ground project became a national research effort and a profoundly transformative process for us as individuals. While the project led to this final report, it's political impact lies less in the words on these pages, but in the relationships and conversations created over the last year, and the ideas for new initiatives that emerged...
>
> Our goals for this report are threefold: that movement activists will see themselves reflected in the report's analysis; that the findings inspire all of us to explore how we might make our work bolder; and that the report can anchor ongoing debates about how

to advance a longterm strategy for social transformation in the United States and beyond.[99]

Of the 158 interviewees, virtually all were socialists.
Or in the words of Williams and Lee:

> *A sampling of the political labels that participants used included: radical, anti-racist, socialist, leftist, non-sectarian left, communist, anti-imperialist, anarchist, progressive, Black feminist, Marxist, revolutionary, rebel, racial justice progressive, revolutionary nationalist, organizer, and activist for human rights.*[100]

They even offered a handy word cloud:

Almost all of those interviewed came from the Maoist community, mostly affiliated with the China aligned Freedom Road Socialist Organization, former STORM and SOUL comrades or ex-League of Revolutionary Struggle cadre.

According to Williams and Lee:

> *We are encouraged by the emergence of several initiatives that seem to be bringing activists together on an ongoing basis to sharpen their individual and collective responses to these critical questions. Projects such as the Organization for a Free Society, Freedom Road Socialist Organization's 'Ask a Socialist' and the many activist study groups that have been popping up across the country make us optimistic that we could soon be developing bold, multi-sectoral strategies that grow out of a deliberate assessment of our current conditions.*[101]

The main recommendation of the report was:

> We need a new Left party. A united party for socialism. Not primarily an electoral vehicle. Should be explicitly anti-capitalist, a bridge between generations, training activists. An eye on the fight for people's power. Without a hard left you have a weak middle. I don't mean dogmatic, but it's clear that capitalism does not have the answer to the world's problems and we need a socialist alternative.[102]

Ex-STORM members Adam Gold, Cindy Wiesner, Harmony Goldberg, Maria Poblet and Van Jones were on the list.[103]

So were former League of Revolutionary Struggle leaders Eric Mann,[104] and Pam Tau Lee, a CPA-SF founder and leader.[105]

Among the many Freedom Road Socialist Organization representatives were Ajamu Dillahunt,[106] Bill Fletcher, Jr.,[107] Bill Gallegos,[108] Fernando Marti,[109] Jon Liss[110] and Scott Kurashige.[111]

Also consulted were Communist Party USA leader Judith LeBlanc, ex-Line of March Maoists Linda Burnham[112] and Max Elbaum[113] and former Communist Workers Party member Makani Themba-Nixon,[114] plus Jerome Scott[115] and Willie Baptist from the League of Revolutionaries for a New America.[116]

Steve Phillips was, of course, also on the list, as were Alex Tom and Alicia Garza and Alex Tom's successor as the executive director of the CPA-SF Shaw San Liu.[117]

The revolutionary nature of LeftRoots is more than apparent in their 2023 document titled: "Making the Impossible Possible: A History of LeftRoots":

> From LeftRoots' founding, we also rooted our organizational identity and thinking in the history of Third World Marxism and left national liberation movements in Africa, Latin America, and Asia. We read Amilcar Cabral and Mao Tse-Tung as well as Lenin and Marx and in our initial membership training we learned about the history of Black Communists organizing the US South.
> We looked to Cuba, Vietnam, and Venezuela for real-world examples of building socialism. We saw these movements and thinkers as a core part of the Marxist tradition, holding

methodological lessons for us on how revolutionaries applied and expanded Marxist ideas to their unique conditions.

We also did this for developmental reasons. The readings and historical examples we looked to helped dispel notions of socialism being a predominantly white or European political project, and it gave us examples of Communist, revolutionary leaders, and movements who looked like us to draw inspiration from.[118]

LeftRoots was launched as a formal organization in 2014, with the first local branch in the San Francisco Bay Area.

Soon LeftRoots was a "national organization of 250 frontline organizers and activists, committed to politically developing their members to lead social movements across the US"[119] The organization grew much bigger in its peak years.

LeftRoots was essentially a front for the CPA-SF and an overlapping sister organization with the Freedom Road Socialist Organization.

Many of its cadre were older former LRS members, and former School of Unity & Liberation (SOUL) and STORM comrades combined with a younger cohort of neo-Maoists, some of whom were also Freedom Road comrades.

The original LeftRoots coordinating committee consisted of:

Alicia Garza (ex-SOUL), Maria Poblet (ex-STORM), Timmy Lu (CPA-SF),[120] Josh Warren-White, Alex Tom (CPA-SF), Cinthya Munoz (ex-SOUL),[121] Steve Williams (ex-STORM), and N'Tanya Lee.

The LeftRoots Coordinating Committee

Alicia Garza, Maria Poblet, Timmy Lu, Josh Warren-White, Alex Tom, Cinthya Munoz, Steve Williams, N'Tanya Lee

left...@leftroots.net

There is no doubt that LeftRoots, (which dissolved in 2023 in preparation for an as yet un-named larger organization) was a pro-communist group.

LeftRoots/CPA-SF comrade Alex Tom formed the China Education and Exposure Program to "build a deeper analysis of China for US progressives and leftists and to the build relationships with the grassroots movement in China."[122]

LeftRoots and CPA-SF leader Lucia Lin[123] led a 2014 tour of young US activists to experience the joys of the Chinese worker's paradise.

In December 2017, LeftRoots cadres - Merle Ratner, N'Tanya Lee, Rose Brewer and Alicia Garza, plus LeftRoots "compas" (financial supporters) Cathy Dang and Juliet Ucelli of the Freedom Road Socialist Organization[124] - spent a few weeks on a women's delegation to Vietnam, one of the "few surviving 20th century socialist experiments."[125]

The delegation included US-based movement leaders from the labor movement, Black Lives Matter and national women's organizations. It was hosted by the Communist Party of Vietnam-controlled Vietnam Women's Union:[126]

Several LeftRoots cadres and compas were part of the delegation and we all returned inspired and moved to share with other US social movement leftists our reflections: on the struggle for socialism, national self-determination and feminism in 21st century Vietnam; the history of the Vietnamese people's fierce & victorious resistance against imperialist exploitation and domination;

and the implications for building the struggle against patriarchy and racial capitalism here in the belly of the beast.[127]

We'll also be sharing specific information about the incredible feminist organizing of Vietnam's Womens Union, reflections on the relationship between Vietnam and the Black struggle...

Pictured in Vietnam: Juliet Ucelli and Rose Brewer back right. Aicia Garza extreme right, N'Tanya Lee front center, Cathy Dang front right.

In June 2014, Steve Williams and N'Tanya Lee made their goal clear:

> "[w]e begin from the standpoint that the **objective of any left strategy must be to topple capitalism** [emphasis added] in order to make way for an economic system that allows for all people around the world to develop their capacities to the greatest extent possible in harmony with the planet."[128]

AKA communism.

The Maoist roots of Black Lives Matter

Alicia Garza has stated that Black Lives Matter (BLM) started with Oscar Grant's death, but BLM emerged in force in 2013 following the acquittal of security guard George Zimmerman in the killing of 17-year-old Trayvon Martin. BLM was not a spontaneous uprising but rather a strategically organized response.

The "movement" was a pre-planned program looking for a spark. If Trayvon Martin had never been killed, BLM would have sprung up in response to the next controversial killing of another young black man by police, or security guards.

The three activists who invented the famous Black Lives Matter hashtag were all deeply connected to the communist and Maoist movements.

As previously noted, Alicia Garza came from SOUL, and the CPA-SF, then went on to join LeftRoots.

In 2011, Alicia Garza was also Chairperson of the Right to the City Alliance steering committee.[129] This organization is closely affiliated to the Freedom Road Socialist Organization.

Patrisse Cullors was mentored by former League of Revolutionary Struggle comrade and Freedom Road Socialist Organization supporter Eric Mann.[130]

Cullors and Mann worked closely for many years in Los Angeles in the Maoist-led Labor/Community Strategy Center, the Bus Riders Union and many other radical groups.

Opal Tometi has been involved for years with the Black Alliance for Peace. She now plays a leading role in the organization–alongside Nnamdi Lumumba, of the far-left Ujima People's Progress Party and Rafiki Morris of the openly communist All-African People's Revolutionary Party.

Opal Tometi hugged Venezuelan pro-China dictator Nicolas Maduro at the 2015 "People of African Descent Leadership Summit" in New York. Several high-ranking officials of the Venezuelan socialist regime also participated.

Opal Tometi, right

During her own speech to the summit, Tometi quoted Joanne Chesimard (aka Assata Shakur), a radical Maoist convicted of murdering a New Jersey state trooper during a 1973 armored car robbery, as saying "you must fight until all black lives matter."

Chesimard lives as a protected fugitive in communist Cuba to this day. Tometi also referred to Chesimard as her "dear exiled sister."[131]

Tometi, Cullors and Garza were all connected through a network called Black Organizing for Leadership and Dignity (BOLD)[132] – which was led by several Freedom Road Socialist Organization aligned comrades, including programs director Sendolo Diaminah of North Carolina.[133]

Sendolo Diaminah right, wearing Freedom Road T-shirt

Black Lives Matter essentially started as a front for LeftRoots, Freedom Road Socialist Organization, the Chinese Progressive Association-San Francisco, and by extension the Communist Party of China.

LeftRoots was openly supportive of and allied to BLM.

On December 19, 2014, Alicia Garza posted a "herstory" of BLM on the Freedom Road Socialist Organization website.

CPA-SF's role in BLM came mainly through another front group Asians 4 Black Lives - which began in Oakland California in late 2014 after the non-indictment of the police officer who killed New Yorker Eric Garner.

Asians 4 Black Lives "began as a response to a call to action from Black Lives Matter organizations in the Bay Area…and the larger Black Lives Matter movement, to put forward these principles and protocols as a model for why and how we, as diverse Asian communities around the country and the world, can show up in solidarity with Black people in this struggle.

Most of the key Asians 4 Black Lives members were Maoists. Pam Tau Lee for example was a founder and leader of the CPA-SF, a member of both the League of Revolutionary Struggle and LeftRoots and an Asians 4 Black Lives pioneer.

Pam Tau Lee, right

Almost all key Asians for Black Lives leaders were from LeftRoots or the CPA-SF or both.

They included former CPA-SF board member Kimi Lee and no surprise here – LeftRoots leader and former CPA-SF boss Alex Tom.

Alex Tom with Kimi Lee, Asians 4 Black Lives

Asians 4 Black Lives also worked with the CPA-SF/LeftRoots comrades Lucia Lin, and Alex Wong to produce the "Asian American Racial Justice Toolkit", a 324 page manual for BLM activists and their Asian American support networks.[134]

Contributors to this "toolkit" included a long list of Maoist and Marxist influenced organizations, including:

+ AAPIs for Civic Empowerment
+ 1Love Movement
+ Asian Pacific Environmental Network
+ AYPAL: Building API Community Power
+ CAAAV: Organizing Asian Communities
+ Chinese Progressive Association SF
+ DRUM - South Asian Organizing Center
+ Filipino Advocates for Justice
+ Freedom, Inc.
+ Khmer Girls in Action
+ Korean American Resource & Cultural Center
+ Korean Resource Center
+ Mekong NYC

+ Providence Youth Student Movement
+ VAYLA New Orleans
+ VietLead[135]

It's not hard to see how BLM and their allies were able to organize "spontaneous" demonstrations all over the country in the Summer of 2020.

THE COMMUNIST STRATEGY IN AMERICAN RACIAL ACTIVISM

For almost a century, the US communist movement has attempted to bring large segments of the country's black population into the revolutionary movement.

One of the main tools to recruit young black activists are the near constant campaigns against alleged police brutality and racism.

These campaigns have been driven since the 1960s, and were mainly driven by Maoist communists. Their goals are to deepen racial divisions, create more embittered, racially motivated activists and to discredit, weaken and even abolish law enforcement – all to create more chaos and facilitate the American socialist revolution.

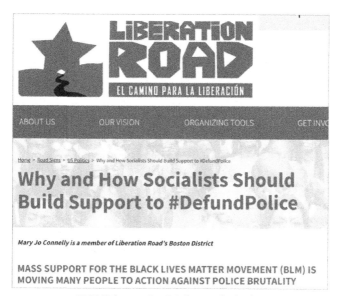

FRSO/Liberation Road Calls to 'Defund Police'

Occasionally based on genuine grievances, but mostly based on gross exaggerations, distortions, propaganda or outright lies, these campaigns were used to spark major race riots across America from Detroit in 1967 to Los Angeles in 1992.

The mass rioting in Ferguson Missouri of August 2014 foreshadowed the Black Lives Matter "mostly peaceful demonstrations" of 2020, and what may lie just around the corner.

The "Ferguson Uprising" began the day after Ferguson Police Officer Darren Wilson shot and killed Michael Brown in self-defense.[136]

The local Maoists were ready for action. They did not necessarily start the protests, but they had the organizational skills and contacts to turn a local tragedy into a nationwide movement.

But let's go back a little.

In 1980, the St. Louis Missouri branch of the League of Revolutionary Struggle formed an activist group called the Organization for Black Struggle (OBS).[137]

One of the key founders of OBS was Jamala Rogers, a committed League of Revolutionary Struggle Maoist[138] who would go on to become a leader of FRSO/Liberation Road.

Jamala Rogers was, with the rest of her comrades, a huge supporter of Jesse Jackson and the Rainbow Coalition.

Jamala Rogers still leads the OBS to this day.

There is no doubt that the OBS Maoists quickly took leadership of Ferguson protests.

With the help from Steve Phillips, Susan Sandler and the Democracy Alliance of course.

According to a November 13, 2015, article in Politico:

> *Some of the biggest donors on the left plan to meet behind closed doors next week in Washington with leaders of the Black Lives Matter movement and their allies to discuss funding the burgeoning protest movement...*
>
>
>
> *The meetings are taking place at the annual winter gathering of the Democracy Alliance major liberal donor club, which... is expected to draw Democratic financial heavyweights, including Tom Steyer and Paul Egerman.*
>
> *The DA, as the club is known in Democratic circles, is recommending its donors step up check writing to a handful of endorsed groups that have supported the Black Lives Matter move-ment. And the club and some of its members also are considering ways to funnel support directly to scrappier* Jamala Rogers *local groups that have utilized confrontational tactics to inject their grievances into the political debate.*
>
> *It's a potential partnership that could elevate the Black Lives Matter movement and heighten its impact. But it's also fraught with tension on both sides...*
>
> *'Major donors are usually not as radical or confrontational as activists most in touch with the pain of oppression,' said Steve Phillips, a Democracy Alliance member and significant contrib-utor to Democratic candidates and causes. He donated to a St. Louis nonprofit group called the Organization for Black Struggle that helped organize 2014 Black Lives Matter-related protests in Ferguson, Missouri, over the police killing of a black teenager named Michael Brown. And Phillips and his wife, Democracy Alliance board member Susan Sandler, are in discussions about funding other groups involved in the movement.*

The movement needs cash to build a self-sustaining infrastructure, Phillips said, arguing 'the progressive donor world should be adding zeroes to their contributions that support this transformative movement.' But he also acknowledged there's a risk for recipient groups. 'Tactics such as shutting down freeways and disrupting rallies can alienate major donors, and if that's your primary source of support, then you're at risk of being blocked from doing what you need to do.'[139]

One OBS and FRSO/Liberation Road comrade Montague Simmons played a major role at Ferguson.

Simmons is pictured below, at left with two of his comrades during a lull in the action.

L-R: Montague Simmons, Jacob Branson, Emma Louise Mutrux

In the Spring of 2015, the New York/New Jersey District of FRSO/Liberation Road sponsored a forum entitled "Ferguson: The Movement So Far and Lessons for Coming Struggles." The first speaker was "our comrade", Montague Simmons, Chair of the "legendary Organization for Black Struggle in St. Louis."

An In-Depth Look at the Ferguson Eruption: Organization for Black Struggle Leader Lays It Out

In Spring 2015, the New York/New Jersey District of Liberation Road sponsored a forum entitled "Ferguson: The Movement So Far and Lessons for Coming Struggles."

The first speaker was our comrade, Montague Simmons, Chair of the legendary Organization for Black Struggle in St. Louis. These five videos,

From the Freedom Road Socialist Organization website

During the session, Montague Simmons thanked comrades from New York who had come in to help – including Maurice Mitchell, now national chairman of the Working Families Party.

Simmons claimed that OBS and their out of state allies are "the most talented organizers in the country" bringing close to 10,000 activists into Ferguson.[140]

Among those activists were Alicia Garza and several of her comrades from LeftRoots, who "sent a delegation to Ferguson, Missouri to support the protests."[141]

From the socialist journal In These Times:

> *Alicia Garza is one of the organizers working on the ground in Ferguson with the wave of new activists who have taken to the streets in the wake of Brown's killing. Based in Oakland, California, Garza is the Special Projects Director for the National Domestic Worker's Alliance (NDWA). Garza is a co-creator of #BlackLivesMatter, a 'political project' and online platform that aims to confront anti-black racism and reaffirm black humanity. Garza is also a member of LeftRoots, a 'national formation of Left social movement organizers and activists' seeking to build socialism in the 21st century.'*

In the aftermath of Brown's killing, Garza recalls feeling 'not only completely horrified, but completely rageful.' She says, 'Just like when any member of your family is hurt in any way, there's a real urge to be there.' She responded to a 'call coming from folks on the ground ... for black folks in particular who were organizers and medics and attorneys and healers to come and support the community of Ferguson and the St. Louis community more broadly.'

With the backing of the NDWA, Garza traveled to Ferguson about three weeks after Brown's death, and spent two weeks working 'to help support capacity building on the ground.' During that time, the Black Lives Matter team organized a Freedom Ride that Garza says 'mobilized more than 500 black people from all over the country to come to Ferguson, to not only stand in solidarity but to lend concrete and material support to organizers who work on the front lines of the Ferguson rebellion.'

Garza says her work in Ferguson was to 'make sure the organizations and activists on the ground had the capacity to really hold this moment and extend it into a movement.'[142]

Alicia Garcia explains her revolutionary motivation to In These Times:

I do think it's important to enter into any space as a leftist...

What Third World liberation movements showed this country was that people make the road by walking—that we need to be guided by strong vision and a strong, disciplined practice...

For me, as someone who wears many hats, I actually see them as one and the same. My work with domestic workers — who are largely women of color and immigrant women, who are poor and low-income — is really similar to my work with Black Lives Matter, which is lifting up the humanity and centrality of black lives in this country as a vision and a portal for the future... which is really similar to my work with LeftRoots, which is about building a strong, vibrant left that's rooted in communities of color and women and queer folks and others who have traditionally been on the margins, and really developing the strategies we need to build effective, long-term, sustained social transformation.[143]

The death of Michael Brown was exploited to spark the Ferguson "Uprising". But even the radicalized Eric Holder Justice Department was unable to charge policeman Darren Wilson with even the most minor of crimes.[144]

Yet, over four years after the release of the Justice Department report exonerating Officer Wilson, California Attorney General Kamala Harris was not about to let the truth trump the Black Lives Matter/Maoist narrative.

Kamala Harris ✔
@KamalaHarris

Michael Brown's murder forever changed Ferguson and America. His tragic death sparked a desperately needed conversation and a nationwide movement. We must fight for stronger accountability and racial equity in our justice system.

2:24 PM · Aug 9, 2019

The communist-led riots of 2020 would give Kamala Harris yet another chance to support Marxist friends.

KAMALA HARRIS AND THE 2020 RIOTS

Despite popular belief fueled by a complicit legacy media, the riots of 2020 were not "grassroots" uprisings sparked by the death of George Floyd in Minneapolis, Minnesota. Floyd, a known criminal who had fentanyl and methamphetamine in his system[145] as he battled police, was exploited by the non-Liberation Road Freedom Road Socialist Organization (FRSO), a pro-China Maoist group that uses race to agitate for communist revolution.

Many other militant organizations jumped on board along with their foot soldiers known broadly as "antifa", spreading the riots across the country right at the height of the Covid-19 pandemic. These groups include America's largest Marxist organization, Democratic Socialists of America (DSA), the Party of Socialism and Liberation (PSL), Workers World Party, Communist Party USA (CPUSA), FRSO/Liberation Road, Black Lives Matter and the Council on American-Islamic Relations (CAIR).

But it started with the Freedom Road Socialist Organization.

Freedom Road Socialist Organization

Jess Sundin is a very influential communist. A self-identified "Marxist-Leninist"[146] and member of "Twin Cities Coalition for Justice 4 Jamar," an anti-police FRSO front group, Sundin could not help but brag about the prominent role her organization played in initiating the 2020 riots, including in the destruction of the Third Precinct and the widespread looting.

Rioters at the Third Precinct in Minneapolis, May 2020

"The first two weeks after George Floyd was killed saw an intense high level of organizing all day and all night, every day," Sundin explained in a video.[147]

"During the day we would have marches and rallies and at night the focus was often at the Third Precinct, which is the police station where George Floyd's killers were working out of," Sundin continued. The Third Precinct was taken over by the rioters in what shockingly appears to have been coordinated[148] with the local officials. Governor Tim Walz admitted[149,150] that he knew in advance that the Third Precinct would be sacrificed to the communist mob.

Tom Hauser
@thauserkstp

Gov. Walz says he was told early yesterday by Mpls Mayor Frey they would likely let the Third Precinct fall. He didn't agree with it, but wasn't his call.

12:24 PM · May 29, 2020

132   298   399   8

X Post from local journalist at Tim Walz Presser Dated May 29, 2020

Allowing the Third Precinct to burn was a symbolic act, inspiring and motivating the police-hating rioters.[151] "I can't tell you the joy it brought all of us to see the third precinct destroyed," Jess Sundin declared.

Sundin explained that violence was always a part of the equation. "There were marches, like I said there were rallies, and lots of the buildings were destroyed, some by fire, you know, some by brute force, sometimes it was golf club, sometimes it was baseball bats."

Jess Sundin

The Freedom Road Socialist Organization was preparing for combat. Note Sundin's use of the phrase "pitched battles", which illustrates the group's *intent* to engage in physical conflict:

> "And a lot of folks wanted to get out to other sites around the cities where there is you know really pitched battles happening, and we support all of that…"

Other Marxist groups quickly jumped onboard. As an aside, Minnesota Representative Ilhan Omar's daughter Isra Hirsi reposted[152,153] a request made by the Twin Cities branch of DSA for riot supplies dated May 27, 2020, including "plywood for shields," "anything else useful for shielding from cops," "tennis rackets" and "hockey sticks".

Hours later, the Third Precinct was torched.

Jess Sundin does not mince words. Not only was her organization promoting, initiating and engaging in violence, FRSO was also very much a part of the rampant looting. "I want to be absolutely clear as an organizer, those night demonstrations, the emptying of the police department, the emptying of the ma…of Target and other major stores is *absolutely tied to, connected to, and part of the movement*," she said.

On May 28, 2020, a local Fox affiliate reported[154] that the local fire department responded to "approximately 30 intentionally set fires". Further, rioters threw "rocks and other projectiles" at the firefighters, damaging equipment.

Enter Kamala Harris

- ✦ On May 28, 2020, the Third Precinct in Minneapolis burned to the ground.

- ✦ On May 29, 2020, Governor Tim Walz admitted that he knew well in advance that the Third Precinct would be sacrificed to the mob.

- ✦ On May 30, 2020, Reuters reported[155] that "[A]t least 13 Biden campaign staff members" expressed on X that they supported the Minnesota Freedom Fund, which posted bail for the rioters.

- ✦ On June 1, 2020, Kamala Harris expressed her support for the rioters, urging her X followers as well as her Facebook followers to donate to the Minnesota Freedom Fund.

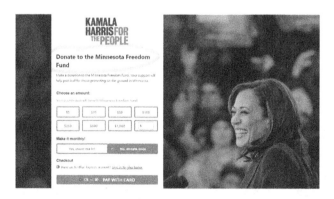

Kamala Harris promoted the radical left Minnesota Freedom Fund, which bailed out Minneapolis rioters. Harris's efforts contributed to the previously-obscure group's unprecedented rush of donations to the tune of $35 million dollars[156] as Minneapolis faced the aftermath of the riots.

The left quickly seized upon the opportunity to spread the riots across the country. This, during lockdowns and school closures brought about by the Covid-19 pandemic.

While mom and pop shops were shuttered, while churches were closed, while citizens were social distancing and wearing masks in the supermarket, while loved ones were being shut out of visiting sick family members in the hospital, while Covid patients were being shoved into nursing homes and while children attended school via computer, rabid leftists rampaged America, ostensibly over the false claim[157] that black Americans were being indiscriminately targeted by police.

But facts do not matter to Kamala Harris, who breathlessly gushed over the rioters on "The Late Show with Stephen Colbert"[158] on June 18, 2020:

> *"They're not going to stop. They're not going to stop. This is a movement. I'm telling you, they're not going to stop. And everyone beware, because they're not going to stop. They're not going to stop before election day in November, and they're not going to stop after election day. And that should be-- everyone should take note of that on both levels, that they're not going to let up, and they should not, and we should not." -Kamala Harris on the 2020 riots, June 18, 2020*

Screenshot: The Late Show with Stephen Colbert, YouTube Clip. "Sen. Kamala Harris: The Nationwide Protests Are A Movement. They're Not Going To Stop", June 18, 2020

During the discussion, Harris reveals that she joined the Washington DC protests (wearing a mask, of course). Harris also gave a shout out to her radical parents, who took her to her first protest in the 1960s, when Harris was "in a stroller". "So it's kind of something I've done my entire life," she told Colbert.

Responding to a question about what Harris learned from her mother, Kamala said in part:

> I learned that-- that the greatest movements that have-- that we have seen in recent history in our country, but probably since the beginning, have been borne out of protest. Have been born out of understanding the power of the people to take to the streets and force their government to-- to become-- to address what is wrong, the inequities, the inequalities, the unfairness, but also the conscience of a government is its people to force the government to-- to be true to the ideals that we say we hold dear. And almost everyone one of those marches has been about one fundamental ideal in our country which is equal justice under law and fighting to make sure we have a government and a country that every, you know, few steps gets closer to achieving that ideal. We've not yet reached it. We've never actually reached it. But these protests I think are the catalyst to getting there.

Harris continued to say that it's "critically important" that the protests continue. A walking advertisement for the rioters, Harris explained:

> ...some of the success that we've been able to achieve around criminal justice reform would not have happened in recent years were it not for Black Lives Matter, and the intensity and the brilliance of that movement, that forced at least that there would be some counter-force to the status quo, which is so reluctant to change if not hostile to change.

It is clear that Kamala is deeply connected to those who rioted in cities across America during the summer of 2020. A "Red Diaper Baby," Kamala Harris's entire life is defined by her allegiance to a radical left ideology that does not remotely resemble the America that most readers experienced.

"That's what these movements do," Harris continued, "that where these systems are so invested and ingrained in what they call 'tradition' but is status quo, often which can be wrong-headed, these movements provide a counter-force to get us to where we need to be."

Harris's dismissal of tradition is reminiscent of the mentality of the "Great Proletarian Cultural Revolution" under Mao Zedong. The goal of Mao was to scrub clean any semblance of history, known as the "four olds"[159] - old ideas, old customs, old culture and old habits. One cannot help but recall former President Barack Obama's pledge[160] to "fundamentally transform" America.

Kamala Harris During Introduction of Justice in Policing Act of 2020

Kamala Harris also used the discussion with Colbert to promote the unconstitutional Democrats' George Floyd Justice in Policing Act of 2020, which violates the Tenth Amendment by threatening to withhold federal funds from states that do not comply with the Act's provisions, which included mandatory bias training and the creation of a national registry of police officers who allegedly abuse their power. These measures were clearly part of a broader effort to appease the mob and undermine law enforcement.

Fortunately, the bill stalled. However, it was reintroduced by the late Rep. Sheila Jackson Lee in May, 2024.[161]

CHAPTER 5

CHINA'S AMERICAN ELECTORAL ARMY

I
T HAS BEEN established that Kamala Harris champions the "New American Majority" strategy, a communist scam to squeeze out conservatives by electorally focusing on "diverse" populations and progressive whites. This tactic evolved from Jesse Jackson's "Rainbow Coalition". This isn't merely about winning elections; it's a calculated power grab aimed at forging a one-party state.

This chapter will allow readers to witness the strategy unfolding through the lens of the "New Virginia Majority" - a case study in political engineering, supported by the same players who promote the New American Majority.

This chapter also uncovers China's strategic playbook to undermine the American Republic, focusing on the Chinese Communist Party's infiltration into every echelon of US electoral politics. Moreover, you'll be introduced to the shadowy figures of pro-China activists within America, working in tandem with the CCP to sway elections, their influence seeping into the very heart of American governance.

Kamala Harris, among other Democratic figures, has not just benefited from but is deeply entwined with this Maoist activism, embodying the New American Majority. The goal is to silence conservatives once and for all.

What would you do if you were Xi Jinping?

If the Chinese Communist Party wanted to manipulate, weaken or even destroy the US Government, wouldn't it make sense to influence US elections, even to help elect candidates willing to cooperate with China?

Would it make sense to risk billions on trade wars, or trillions on a premature shooting war, when politicians and elections could be bought for a fraction of the cost and virtually none of the risk?

China "has been deliberately expanding its influence globally without directly provoking the US." The goal is "to manage and eventually outmaneuver the US through indirect means rather than direct confrontation."[1]

A top advisor to the Chinese Communist Party, Jin Canrong, made this strategy clear in a July 2016 speech delivered during a two-day conference in Guangzhou City, China.

CCP's Top Strategist: We Need To Put the US Under Our Jurisdiction 中共"國師"金燦榮自曝 "邪招" 稱將美國管起來

Currently, Canrong serves as Deputy Dean of the School of International Studies, Deputy Director of the Center for American Studies, Renmin University of China. He has also been a visiting Professor at the University of Michigan according to his World Economic Forum profile,[2] which notes that his "research focus" is "American politics, American foreign policy, Sino-US relations and China's foreign policy."

Jin is widely regarded as the Chinese Communist Party's top strategist, and a "national senior advisor" to the CCP and Xi Jinping.[3] His speech highlights China's overarching strategy under Xi Jinping, which extends beyond mere economic growth to encompass global dominance and influence.

A translation from the Chinese American blog Jennifer's World:

> *So, Mao Zedong solved the problem of survival for the new China. Deng Xiaoping solved the issue of development... Now President Xi wants to solve the issue of respect. After this issue is solved, we will learn from the United States, and enter the fourth stage... In our generation, we need to obtain a status that is equal to the US. The task of our next generation is to put the US under our jurisdiction/management too...*[4]

"We want to squeeze it [the US] out, but we do not dare to fight it," Jin explains. It is crucial to understand that Canrong is *not* relaying a strategy of prosperity for China, but rather a *strategy of world dominance*:

> *The US is very powerful. It is the number one right now, very capable. Frankly speaking, now the United States is still a middle-aged strong man. It has not reached retirement age yet. It is like someone in a workplace who is very good looking, very capable, and basically very popular among coworkers. We are like the number 2 boss who just got promoted. We want to squeeze it (the US) out, but we do not dare to fight it, so it is quite difficult. We in China are trying to come up with various ways.*
>
> + *First, create conditions for it to make mistakes...*
>
> + *Second, we keep it (the US) busy so that it will suffer from depression and want to quit the job itself.*
>
> + *Third, we should get ourselves mixed together with the US, so that it can not fight us. We should create such a situation where you have me inside you, and I have you inside me.*[5]

Have these strategies been successfully implemented? Is the US perhaps faltering in its approach? Are there significant numbers of Americans feeling overwhelmed or losing hope? And, importantly, has China managed to extend its influence within the US itself?

According to Canrong, the Chinese government aspires to influence US politics by strategically investing in every congressional district, aiming to control enough votes to sway elections.

With an understanding that US House races can be decided by

narrow margins, the CCP believes that by controlling a few thousand votes per district, they could effectively dictate the outcomes, thereby manipulating or controlling the US House of Representatives. This strategy envisions turning the US Congress into something akin to China's own legislative body, suggesting a deep infiltration and control over American political processes.

Says Canrong:

> We in the Chinese government hope that in the end, every US Congressman's district will have Chinese investment, and China will be able to control one thousand or several thousand votes, and then we can influence his [the congressman's] attitude.
>
> In fact, the US House of Representatives can be controlled, because the United States has 312 million people, and 435 members of the House of Representatives. On average, a congressional district has about 750,000 people, 750,000 people's voter turnout is only 30%, that is, about 200,000 votes can decide his fate (the fate of the congress candidate).
>
> Generally speaking, the numbers of votes for the two candidates are very close, the gap won't be particularly large. So, in the end, I guess there is only a difference of 10 thousand or several thousand votes. Therefore, if you can have several thousand votes in your hands, you are as good as his father/master.
>
> If China conducts good operations in the US, we may be able to buy it over, and turn the US into our second Standing Committee of National People's Congress.[6]

By achieving economic power in every Congressional district, political influence would naturally be built.

The Chinese, much like the Soviets in their time, have consistently employed the MICE strategy to recruit foreign agents willing to betray their own nation. MICE is shorthand for *Money, Ideology, Compromise, Ego*. Communists long ago figured out that many Western politicians can be seduced by one or more of the MICE factors.

On the ideology front, the Chinese communists have many assets in America, including several influential communist parties, who have decades of experience in exploiting racial difference to create chaos and foment revolution – Black Lives Matter being the latest of many examples.

Jin continues:

> *Of course we can also have other evil tricks, such as throwing the world into further chaos. The United States has a problem. It is really very diverse, and has the highest degree of democracy in the Western countries. Of course, diversity has an advantage, the people have the freedom, have a say. But it also has a disadvantage. It is very difficult to build consensus.*

There you have it. Exploit America's "diversity" to prevent the country ever reaching a national "consensus". Keep working to widen that racial divide. Throw America into further "chaos."

Imagine if China leveraged its network of sympathetic American communists to further manipulate racial divisions, aiming to install politicians favorable to Beijing's interests. This strategy could represent the pinnacle of success for Chinese communists, simultaneously sowing discord and gaining political influence.

CASE STUDY: NEW VIRGINIA MAJORITY

Virginia, once a stronghold for Republican politics, has shifted to reliably voting Democratic, a transformation that began noticeably in 2008. This political evolution, marked by Democratic wins in gubernatorial races and significant gains in the state legislature, is often attributed to demographic changes, particularly in Northern Virginia.

However, deeper analysis reveals that organized efforts by the communist-founded New Virginia Majority, funded by Steve Phillips and his late wife Susan Sandler,[7] played a crucial role in this deliberate shift.

Once a reliably "red" state, Virginia, despite Republican Governor Glenn Youngkin and his team's valiant efforts, now "votes" decidedly "blue."

This conversion was the result of a well-orchestrated, subversive process.

From Real Clear Politics, November 2017:

Obama also was the first Democrat to win Virginia in over four decades, and his party hasn't lost a presidential election there since. But it was Tuesday night's election in the Old Dominion — where Democrats won the governor's mansion for a consecutive time and gained a near-record 15 seats in the House of Delegates — that has politicos wondering whether Old Virginny can now officially be considered a blue state.[8]

Many commentators have blamed demographics – Northern Virginia houses growing numbers of Washington DC bureaucrats for instance, but that is only part of the story. Virginia started drifting noticeably to the left in 2008, as the result of a very disciplined and methodical program implemented by non-Democratic Party actors.

In August 2007, veteran Virginia activist Jon Liss founded what was then called Virginia New Majority (now New Virginia Majority), a mass voter registration organization dedicated to turning the state "blue".

Jon Liss

From the NVM website:

Founded in 2007 in response to the failure of federal comprehensive immigration reform, New Virginia Majority sought to engage 'new Americans' in a more deliberate and strategic way by combining targeted voter organizing with the ideological approach to community organizing that has developed over the last thirty years.

Our organization strives to create a powerful movement to transform Virginia through voter engagement and issue campaigns that develop civic leadership and build public support.

> New Virginia Majority's organizers have knocked on over 1
> million doors, engaging not only immigrant voters, but voters of
> color, women, low-income working people, and youth...New
> Virginia Majority is a multiracial, multi-issue organization that
> uses largescale civic engagement, leadership development, advocacy,
> and strategic communications to advance our goals of creating a
> democratic, just, and sustainable Virginia.[9]

The goals of course are decidedly socialist. That may be because
the NVM founder is a bona fide communist.

Jon Liss, communist

Born in Brooklyn, raised in Falls Church and educated at the
University of Virginia, Jon Liss has been a radical activist his entire
adult life. As a young man, he was involved in multiple leftist orga-
nizations in Virginia, including Northern Virginians Against
Apartheid, Fairfax County Taxi-drivers Association, and with Bernie
Sanders on the Steering Committee of the National Committee for
Independent Political Action (NCIPA)[10] - which overlapped consid-
erably with Jesse Jackson's Rainbow Coalition.

In the early 1980s, Jon Liss was active in the Progressive Student
Network (PSN), a front for the Maoist-leaning Revolutionary Workers
Headquarters (RWHq). When the "Hq" joined with the Proletarian
Unity League to form Freedom Road Socialist Organization (FRSO)
in 1985, Jon Liss was targeted for recruitment into the new revolu-
tionary coalition.

```
2
John Liss (Age 27) Former PSN. Knows FRSO, or at least Hq. Good friend
of John Allocca. Presently a community organizer in Northern Virginia.
National board of NCIPA, also.
     * John Allocca could play a role in contacting. SCn should investi-
gate current student contacts which in turn could be passed on to
PSN. DC area cdes. should also follow up.
Curent address & ph. # available from John Allocca or Bruce
```

From a Freedom Road Socialist Organization potential recruitment list, circa 1988

John Liss has been a confirmed Freedom Road Socialist
Organization comrade since at least 1996.

That year, his name appeared on a list of comrades from
Democratic Socialists of America (DSA), Socialist Party USA

(SPUSA), Committees of Correspondence (CoC), the NCIPA and the Trotskyist group Solidarity who were meeting to work together try to reverse socialist "fragmentation".

Forwarded message:
Subj: Socialists Urge End of Fragmentation
Date: 96-06-26 02:13:53 EDT
From: DavidMcR

The following open letter has been sent to the organizations listed below. Anyone who wants to sign onto the letter, or who seeks further information about the process outlined can get information by sending an email to: Deb...@aol.com

---

Giuliana Milanese COC, Bay Area	Mel Rothenberg COC, Chicago
Eric Vega Larimore-Hall DSA, Sacramento	Daraka DSA, Chicago
Jon Liss FRSO, D.C.	Carl Pinkston FRSO, Sacramento
Sabina Virgo NCIPA, Los Angeles	
David McReynolds SPUSA, New York	Margaret Phair SPUSA, Los Angeles
Tim Marshall Solidarity, Bay Area	Joanna Misnik Solidarity, Nashville

---

In 2010, Jon Liss attended the FRSO/Liberation Road-linked Rockwood Leadership Institute. He still works closely with affiliated comrades and their multiple "front" organizations to this day.[11]

Flipping Virginia...and beyond

Under Jon Liss's steady leadership, NVM has been able to flip one of the most conservative states in the union into an almost reliable Democratic pickup.

While technically "non-partisan", NVM unashamedly targets voters for the left – starting with Barack Obama in 2008.

Jon Liss explains:

We created the organization in 2007. We knock on, probably 400,000 doors—I mean many of them the same doors—multiple times. And this guy named Barack Obama ends up getting elected to President.

We were nonpartisan but we were encouraging folks who historically didn't vote to vote. And there was a massive turnout not just African-Americans—Latino, Asian, African immigrants. Lots of people came out and voted who hadn't voted before, and Virginia, which had voted, since 1964, since Lyndon Johnson, had voted conservative and Republican basically, voted for much more—the more progressive candidate we'll say in a nonpartisan sense.

And we did that as a nonpartisan organization.

We have different legal statuses, so we were not saying vote for Barack Obama. We were saying vote for somebody who's going to get you healthcare, vote for somebody who's gonna start changing this country. People could figure out who they wanted to vote for on their own...So we did that in 2007—we're still doing it today...[12]

NVM certainly played a major role when Virginia turned decidedly blue in 2013, when the Democrat team of Ralph Northam (Governor) Justin Fairfax (Lieutenant Governor) and Mark Herring (Attorney General) were all elected.

All had been supported by NVM - which wrote on its Facebook page:

The local progressive community has a lot to be thankful for this year.

We delivered a stunning blow to the Tea Party by electing Terry McAuliffe as Governor, Ralph Northam as Lieutenant Governor and Mark Herring as Attorney General.

We're hoping that means big changes in Richmond!

In 2017, the Democrats made very strong gains in both houses of the state legislature, also with NVM support.

The Republicans had held a 66–34 majority in the House of Delegates before the election and were confident of holding a substantial majority. When the dust had cleared, the Republicans had lost15 seats, their majority down to a razor thin 50–49 advantage.

The election sent shockwaves through the GOP. The media crowed about a "blue wave" on the horizon.

Under all the hype, the left community knew who deserved the real credit.

From an Airlift article "Say Hello to the New Virginia Majority":

Virginia Governor-elect Ralph Northam's victory in the Nov. 2017 VA gubernatorial election is being hailed by the press as 'the first forceful rebuke of Trump and his party.' On a night that saw other exciting and improbable wins, the Northam vote was the widest victory in decades for a Democratic candidate for governor of Virginia.

And yet, in the lead-up to the election, the Democrats had no

Get out the Vote (GOTV) effort aimed at communities of color and others who would be needed to push the eventual winner, Dem. Ralph Northam, over the finish line. New Virginia Majority stepped into the breach to:

- *Register 30,666 voters in 2017*
- *Organize a statewide plan with partners NextGen, Planned Parenthood, SEIU, For Our Future, and Equality Virginia that knocked on 689,000 doors*
- *Run $150,000 in ads on African-American radio stations*
- *Fight for 12 candidates—11 of whom won in November.[13]*

In November 2019, after the Virginia Democratic party had consolidated its control even further, Jon Liss's fellow NVM Co-director Tram Nguyen wrote an op-ed for the New York Times.

Entitled "Democrats could learn a lot from what happened in Virginia", Nguyen held up her organization's accomplishments as an example for other Democrats to follow:

On Tuesday night, Virginia Democrats won their most consequential election in decades. After obtaining a majority in both chambers of the General Assembly, Democrats now have a governing trifecta for the first time since 1993. This is no accident. It comes in the midst of a generational political shift that was put in motion years ago. Virginia's Democrats got where they are today as a result of year-round community organizing and voter engagement.

Local organizations like mine understood the political potential of Virginia when we got started 12 years ago. We are winning because we recognize the power of an electorate that includes and reflects the diversity of our state.

We don't talk to voters only when campaign season rolls around. We try to reach voters of all colors, women, low-income workers and young people where they are, which has made it possible for us to develop a robust base of support along Virginia's so-called Urban Crescent, from Northern Virginia to Hampton Roads.

Long before Election Day, we registered more than 300,000 voters, knocked on more than 2.5 million doors, and organized within communities of color to help win significant policy changes…

I don't say this to brag about our organization, but to make the

case that this type of year-round organizing can pave the way for
victory nationally.[14]

Steve Phillips also chimed in. He had no doubt over who deserved
credit for the stunning victory.

He penned an article for The Nation giving much kudos to NVM:

> The evidence is in from the 2017 elections, and the verdict is
> clear—the constituencies that twice voted to put a black man in
> the White House remain the majority in this country. Democrats
> spent a year wailing and navel gazing as they tried to figure out
> how to woo Trump supporters, but it turns out that the way to win
> is to mobilize the New American Majority—people of color and
> progressive whites.
>
> In Virginia... it was the 'Obama coalition' of people of color and
> progressive whites—what I call the New American Majority—
> that propelled Democrats to victory. In both of those states, the
> Democratic candidates for governor lost the white vote but won the
> election because 80 percent of people of color supported them, pro-
> viding the same kind of cornerstone that Obama enjoyed.
>
> What does all of this mean for 2018? It means that by inspiring
> and investing in the core components of the Obama coalition, namely
> people of color and progressive whites, Democrats can capture con-
> trol of the House of Representatives and replace Republican gover-
> nors in key states such as Georgia, Florida, Arizona, Maryland,
> Illinois, Ohio, and Massachusetts...
>
> Lastly, winning elections isn't just about inspirational words
> and impressive candidates. It's also about the basic, expensive,
> and labor-intensive blocking and tackling involved in helping busy
> people overcome the many barriers to participation in the polit-
> ical process. Ample empirical evidence has proven that the best
> way to increase voter turnout is to work with trusted messengers
> to engage their friends and neighbors. That means putting money
> into organizations with credibility in communities of color and a
> track record of conducting effective electoral work.
>
> One of the unsung heroes of the Virginia election is New
> Virginia Majority. Its co-director Tram Nguyen spent years coor-
> dinating a coalition of community-based organizations, and that

work paid off decisively as people of color turned out to vote in record numbers this year.[15]

Considering that Steve Phillips and the late Susan Sandlers directly funded the New Virginia Majority through their Sandler Phillips Center, it is no coincidence that the New Virginia Majority uses the "New Virginia Majority" tactics.[16]

Tram Nguyen, 2017 Democracy Alliance: Building 'Permanent Progressive Power in States'

NVM leader Tram Nguyen has taken part in Sandler-funded Democracy Alliance events,[17] and she also serves on the advisory board of the Sandler Phillips Center. She was also one of the Center's 2020 Fannie Lou Hamer Mentors – a program named in honor of the eponymous far-left "civil rights" activist of the 1950s and 1960s.

Other Fannie Lou Hamer Mentors included Steve Phillips and former PowerPAC stalwarts:

- Anathea Chino, Co-founder, Advance Native Political Leadership
- Andy Wong, President & Co-founder, PowerPAC.org
- Angela Glover Blackwell, Founder, PolicyLink
- Crystal Zermeno, Strategy Director, Texas Organizing Project
- Emi Gusukuma, Executive Vice President & General Counsel, Sandler Phillips Center
- Julie Martinez Ortega, Washington DC Office Director & Chief Data Scientist, Sandler Phillips Center[18]

From the Sandler Phillips website

Also on the list was Laphonza Butler, former President, SEIU Local 2015 and now junior US Senator for California under Kamala Harris.

Butler was appointed by Governor Gavin Newsom to fill out the term of the late Senator Dianne Feinstein.

Kamala Harris, Laphonza Butler, circa 2019

When the far-left Center for Popular Democracy honored Laphonza Butler at their October 2016 fundraising gala, Susan Sandler, Steve Phillips and the San Francisco Foundation sponsored the event.[19]

Imagine that - our favorite old Maoist, Steve Phillips, has strong connections to both California senators and helped elect the President who paved the way for them.

The New Virginia Majority endorsed Kamala Harris and Tim Walz according to a September 5, 2024 Press Release. They write in part:

> *This November, we have an opportunity to elect someone who shares our values and stands with many of our policy priorities - who will fight for Virginians by lowering costs for working families, ensuring our communities are safe and that women have the right to make decisions about their own bodies. Vice President Harris has played a decisive role in some of the most progressive victories of the Biden administration...*[20]

New Virginia Majority Endorses Harris/Walz September 5, 2024

Felons voting

New Virginia Majority also has another secret weapon up the sleeve of its Mao jacket. One that has been now replicated in many states – felon voting.

NVM worked directly with Governor McAuliffe to personally pardon thousands Virginia felons so that they too could vote.[21]

In fact, Governor McAuliffe was even given the "Owen W. Hill Freedom Award" for his work on creating tens of thousands of new Democratic voters with his over 200,000 individually signed pardons.

Freedom Road Socialist Organization, LeftRoots[22] and Asians 4 Black Lives activist Claire Tran[23] worked for New Virginia Majority in the 2008 and 2014 election cycles.[24]

She has no doubt that NVM can take full credit for felon re-enfranchisement in Virginia.

Claire Tran wrote in Freedom Road Socialist Organization/ LeftRoots-linked website Organizing Upgrade (now "Convergence"):

> NVM did not ignore the disenfranchisement of people who were
> formerly incarcerated. Revolutionary thinking is about changing
> the terrain of struggle. Disenfranchisement of formerly incarcer-
> ated people in Virginia, as in many other states, was created with
> an explicitly racist intent.
>
> They worked on an eight-year fight to give people who had been
> formerly incarcerated back their right to vote – and they won.
> NVM showed that they had real power on the ground and advo-
> cated for re-enfranchisement and when it passed, they did the work
> to register people.[25]

NVM almost immediately signed up 25,000 pardoned felons to add to their vote pool and continued working through the list for several years.[26]

Tram Nguyen also wrote in the New York Times:

> The restoration of voting rights provides another example. Virginia's
> state constitution bars anyone with a felony conviction from voting
> until their rights have been restored by the governor. For more than
> nine years, we organized formerly incarcerated women and men to
> help them demand that their full civil rights be restored.
>
> The former governor, Terry McAuliffe, restored the voting
> rights of more than 173,000 Virginians during his term, more than
> any other governor in Virginia's history. In 2016, of the nearly
> 20,000 men and women who registered to vote for the first time
> as a result of the restoration of their rights, a whopping 79 percent
> voted. They were a key voting bloc in Virginia, the only Southern
> state that Hillary Clinton won.[27]

Roughly 2,500,000 Virginia voters cast ballots in the "Old Dominion's" November 2017 elections. Given that NVM helped to get 200,000 felons voting, signed-up at least 160,000 minority voters and was part of a huge Get Out The Vote effort, isn't it reasonable to give Jon Liss' team some credit for the Democrats excellent showing?

Republicans work in election cycles. Maoists work in decades.

Influence on government

NVM also claims credit for other changes which have undoubtedly accelerated Virginia's move to the left.

In the 2020 state legislative session, NVM claims credit for several changes to state election law:

+ Established Election Day as a state holiday
+ Established absentee voting without a needed excuse (e.g. business trip, student attending college, etc.)
+ Created a 45-day early vote and absentee voting period before primary and general elections
+ Repealed strict photo ID requirements for voting[28]

The relationship between the New Virginia Majority and the Virginia Democratic leadership was very close.

Tram Nguyen, Co-Executive Director of NVM, was even named to Governor Ralph Northam's Transition Committee on November 15, 2017.

Pictured is Tram Nguyen left, with several NVM comrades and Governor Ralph Northam and Lieutenant Governor Justin Fairfax:

The Virginia Democrats know full-well who put them in power.

The China connection

NVM also gets help from way further West than the Sandler Philips Center of San Francisco – from Wuhan, China to be specific.

Steve McClure is a US research associate working at Wuhan University's Key Laboratory of Information Engineering in Surveying, Mapping and Remote Sensing.

While earning a "later in life" PhD in Geography from George Mason University, Steve McClure met many Chinese students and visiting professors.

In 2010, he "was invited to work at an international geospatial laboratory based at a university in central China."[29]

Steve McClure is also a lifelong radical, associated for decades with the US Maoist movement and the FRSO/Liberation Road – which to this day upholds China as the leader of world socialism.

In an August 2020 article entitled "Covid19, Wuhan, and the US Left", the FRSO/Liberation Road website described Steve McClure this way:

> *Steve from Wuhan is an American pinko commie who had the good fortune to live and work in Wuhan for the better part of the last decade...*[30]

In January 2020, Steve McClue told the China Daily:

Stephen C McClure, 64, is a US research associate working at Wuhan University's Key Laboratory of Information Engineering in Surveying, Mapping and Remote Sensing (LIESMARS). [Photo provided to chinadaily.com.cn]

> *I have been working at Wuhan University for nine years, helping students, faculty, and staff polish academic papers on subjects ranging from computer science to electrical engineering, helping authors through the publication process.*

But that's not all Steve McClure was doing.

McClure has also been supplying, on contract, sophisticated geopolitical data to NVM.

Geo-demographic data is an extremely valuable tool in modern electioneering, especially to groups like NVM, whose model is based on identifying and targeting specific minority households and neighborhoods.

In other words, it is very helpful to know where the Iranians or South Asians, or Puerto Ricans live so that "culturally appropriate" campaigners may be deployed to maximum efficiency in voter registration and GET OUT THE VOTE drives.

"Wuhan Steve" has proven very valuable in this regard.

From a Steve McClure blog post: "Action research, mapping and civic engagement in Virginia" published on August 25, 2011:

> *I have been recently working with Virginia New Majority to make a series of maps to inform planning for precinct walks in Virginia State house districts. It is collaborative, involving emails, exchanges of data back and forth, and skype calls.*
>
> *The core data are lists of individual households by pan-ethnic census categories, geocode them. and use a point density method to aggregate those households visually, and also aggregate the counts of households by precinct and display those numbers atop the cluster map.*[31]

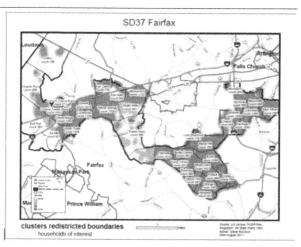

A Steve McClure map for New Virginia Majority

Steve McClure also wrote a blog post, circa 2012, entitled "Actionable Intelligence and Prince William County":

> *In the general elections of 2008 Virginia voted democratic for the first time since 1964 with Obama carrying the state. Demographic shifts and increased voter participation rather than a shift in political allegiances account for this outcome.*

> *This demographic shift was an artifact of the dynamics of capital accumulation, uneven development and class struggle in a period of neoliberalization, prefiguring zoning and land use patterns.*
>
> *Focusing on Prince William County, Virginia, I applied spatial interpolation techniques in a GIS to translate the 2008 election returns from the geography of precincts to year 2000 zoning classification areas for further quantitative analysis. The goal was to produce actionable intelligence for working class organizations building popular power at the base.[32]*

Is this legal? If Steve McClure is using any Chinese Communist Party-owned facilities or equipment to produce these maps, could this be considered an illegal "in kind" foreign donation?

Is Beijing in any way sanctioning or even assisting Steve McClure's operation to influence US elections in favor of the Democrats?

WINNING THE SOUTH

FRSO/Liberation Road has long targeted Southern States using their own interpretation of the "Rainbow Coalition" strategy.

FRSO/Liberation Road explicitly labels the Southern states the "New Confederacy" because in their eyes, the South is a stronghold of conservative Christians and Republicans, racists and worst of all – Trump supporters.

FRSO/Liberation Road wants to 'Crush Trump'

FRSO/Liberation Road goal is to destroy the conservative culture and politics of the South by employing their version of Steve Phillps's New American Majority strategy.

Besides New Virginia Majority, FRSO/Liberation Road has a whole network of controlled and allied organizations operating in nearly every Southern State.

The include:

+ Florida – Florida Rising (formerly New Florida Majority)
+ Georgia – New Georgia Project
+ Kentucky – Kentuckians for the Commonwealth
+ North Carolina – Durham for All, Guildford for All, Forsyth Freedom Federation, New Hanover for All, Down Home North Carolina, The Carolina Federation

+ Tennessee - Memphis for All, Nashville Justice League and the City Council Movement in Knoxville

+ Texas – Texas Organizing Project

FRSO/Liberation Road also has significant influence in Jackson, Mississippi through their strong relationship with the city's ultra radical mayor Chokwe Antar Lumumba – who owes his job partially to Maoist "on the ground" support.

FRSO/Liberation Road Celebrates Chokwe Antar Lumumba

FRSO/Liberation Road theorizes that if can turn Georgia, North Carolina, Arizona and one or two other Southern states blue, the electoral college map dictates that it will be virtually impossible for the Republicans to ever win the White House again.

Flip Texas or Florida – just once – and the GOP will be finished as a national force.

Then if a President Harris grants amnesty for up to 30 million illegal immigrants, turning most of them into reliable Democratic Party voters, the Republicans will be annihilated nationwide.

America will then become a one-party state dominated by China.

That is the communist plan for the American socialist revolution.

FRSO/Liberation Road considers themselves as part of the "Multi-racial, pro-Democracy United Front"; another way of saying "Rainbow Coalition" or "New American Majority". Remember the phrase "United Front" during the Tim Walz chapter.

Their goal is to defeat what they view as a reactionary and racist "New Confederacy" to usher in a socialist America.

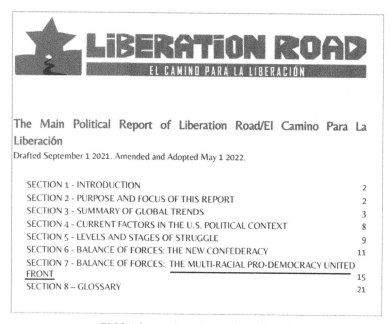

The Main Political Report of Liberation Road/El Camino Para La Liberación

Drafted September 1 2021. Amended and Adopted May 1 2022.

FRSO/Liberation Road: 'Main Political Report"

An article emphasizing the urgency of flipping the Southern states entitled "The Importance of the Fight for the South–and Why It Can and Must be Won" appeared in the FRSO/Liberation Road-linked website Organizing Upgrade (now "Convergence"), on September 4, 2017.

The authors, former Line of March Maoist Bob Wing[33] and "Wuhan Steve" McClure, argue in part that winning the South is imperative for building a leftist majority due to the South's significant number of electoral votes (38%).

Further, the South is not a monolith, Wing and McClure explain. To win, the left must have a detailed, state-by-state and county-by-county strategy. The strategy aims to leverage the South's substantial congressional representation, emphasizing "diversity", particularly in regions where black Americans are the majority, hijacking these delegations for political advantage:

CONVERGENCE

STRATEGY

The Importance of the Fight for the South– and Why It Can and Must be Won, By Bob Wing and Stephen C. McClure

 by Bob Wing · September 4, 2017

Electoral action to win political power in the South is a strategic, not an optional, component of any strategy to defeat the right. As regards to elections and political power, we argue:

(1) A critical mass of Southern states can and must be won if we are to block or defeat the right in presidential elections. Three of the five or so critical battleground states are in the South: Florida, Virginia and North Carolina. Southern blue and battleground states plus Washington D.C. hold 38 percent of the electoral votes needed to win.

(2) Winning an anti-rightwing congressional majority depends on winning in the South, as the South has a bigger congressional delegation than any other region and Southern congresspersons also hold key leadership posts within the Republican Party's congressional hierarchies.

(3) There are tremendous opportunities to build progressive political power and governance at the local level in the South as 105 counties have a Black majority.

While some might dismiss the South, focusing strategically on the Northeast and Pacific Coast as central to a progressive program and the Midwest as the main political battleground, the South's dynamic growth, historical legacy of Black struggle and powerful political weight make it a critical battlefield.

The nuance is that the South cannot be won as a bloc, but only state by state and county by county. In fact, winning the South in large part means understanding that it is not a monolithic entity and winning it piece by piece: i.e. politically deconstructing the South.[34]

Do Republicans or "moderate" Democrats think in such long-term strategic terms?

In Maoist terms, "politically deconstructing the South" means ending the "White Republic".

Bob Wing and his former Line of March comrade Gerald Lenoir said just that in a September 2021 podcast.[35]

In July 2024, FRSO/Liberation Road posted a policy piece on their website focusing on the left's tasks for the 2024 election.

While not mentioning the Harris/Walz ticket, the National Executive Committee, FRSO/Liberation Road was explicitly anti-Trump.

BLOCK, BROADEN, BUILD

The 2024 Elections and the Threefold Tasks of the Left

Preface

This document is written as a contribution to struggle over the position of US socialists in the difficult circumstances of the 2024 elections. A formal position paper of Liberation Road, it aims to challenge us to appreciate the seriousness of the political moment, to unite around an inside/outside orientation with strategic and tactical clarity about the need to defeat the right, while being clear about our profound contradictions with other forces within a united front in which backward elements largely lead.

This document's priorities and preoccupations are thus shaped and limited by that task. While we have attempted to be broad and speak to the many dimensions of the dynamic challenges we face, we have not and could not be total in scope or depth. As Marxists we understand the need for materialist analysis to understand the underlying dynamics that shape our politics and society. For a more detailed elaboration of our positions, see our <u>Strategic Orientation</u>, <u>Main Political Report</u>, and <u>Unity Documents</u>.

We wrote this paper prior to the apparent attempt on Donald Trump's life on July 13. We talk in it paper about the increasingly violent rhetoric of the MAGA right. Trump's violent rhetoric incites political violence of all kinds, including against himself. We know that when political violence is authorized, the people most commonly targeted are immigrants, people of color, women, queer and trans folks, and the left. This only makes it more clear that we must mobilize and organize to reject MAGA and all it stands for in November.

In Solidarity,
The National Executive Committee
Liberation Road

Interestingly, the anti-Trump screed blames the former president for the Butler, Pennsylvania assassination attempt: "Trump's violent rhetoric incites political violence of all kinds, including against himself." It is noteworthy that this narrative has been adopted by many figures in the legacy media.[36,37,38,39]

This verbiage should be expected from a pro-Chinese Communist Party organization, but unfortunately Americans now have to hear it from the legacy media, as well.

STATE POWER CAUCUS

Of all the Phillips/Sandler funded organizations, the State Power Caucus (SPC) is easily the most ambitious, and probably least well-known.

In October 2020, the terminally ailing Susan Sandler wrote a post on Medium announcing the launch of a $200 million fund in "support of organizations working to advance racial justice."

Susan Sandler launches $200 million fund for racial justice

September 15, 2020

Philanthropist Susan Sandler, the daughter of Giving Pledgers Herb and Marion Sandler, former co-CEOs of Golden West Financial Corporation and World Savings Bank, has announced the launch of a $200 million fund in support of organizations working to advance racial justice.

In a blog post published Monday, Sandler wrote that the Susan Sandler Fund will be housed at the Sandler Foundation, a private foundation established in 1991 by her parents. The fund will be led by Vivian Chang, who co-founded Oakland Rising and held senior executive positions at the Asian Pacific Environmental Network, Green for All, and the East Bay Community Foundation before joining the Sandler Foundation in 2018 as grants director.

Screenshot from Philanthropy News Digest

In her post, Sandler explained that the "Susan Sandler Fund" would be housed at the Sandler Foundation, a private foundation established in 1991 by her parents.[40]

The fund would be led by Vivian Chang, who co-founded Oakland Rising and held senior executive positions at the Asian Pacific Environmental Network. Chang also worked for Green For All before joining the Sandler Foundation in 2018 as grants director.[41]

Susan Sandler forgot to mention that Oakland Rising and the Asian Pacific Environmental Network are both FRSO/Liberation Road-aligned organizations. Green for All was founded[42] by the former STORM Maoist-turned-Obama Green Jobs Czar, turned CNN pundit Van Jones.

In 2004, Vivian Chang and Van Jones attended a year-long course together at the Steve Phillips/ FRSO/Liberation Road-linked radical training school, the Rockwood Leadership Institute in Oakland, California.[43]

In her post, Susan Sandler also wrote that the fund would be guided by a "theory of change she developed over her years as a philanthropist that is focused on supporting people of color-led organizations working to boost the power and influence of historically marginalized communities."[44]

According to the left-wing website Inside Philanthropy, Susan Sandler had very firm views about the role of her new fund:

> *Although it's housed at the Sandler Foundation and draws on the family's charitable coffers, it differs from the parent organization in its theory of change. Sandler describes the approach as focused on 'power, not persuasion.' She continues: 'A lot of foundation funding is geared towards persuading people in power to change their minds, and that objective is usually pursued by supporting the development of well-researched reports, studies, and analyses... I do not subscribe to this view as the best way to bring about change.'*[45]

An initial round of awards announced by the Susan Sandler Fund included grants to the Asian American & Pacific Islander Civic Engagement Fund, Advance Native Political Leadership, the Arizona Center for Empowerment, the New Georgia Project, the New Florida Majority Education Fund, the New Virginia Majority Education Fund, PICO California, the Texas Organizing Project and the State Power Caucus.[46]

The grantees chosen by Sandler and Chang "all operate in the realm of civic participation and voter engagement." In the case of some, like New Florida Majority and New Virginia Majority, Sandler has given to the 501(c)(3) education funds associated with 501(c)(4)s specifically dedicated to building the "New American Majority" state by state.[47]

All these organizations are to some degree in the far-left FRSO/ Liberation Road "orbit".

Unsurprisingly, New Virginia Majority's Jon Liss serves on the State Power Caucus leadership team.

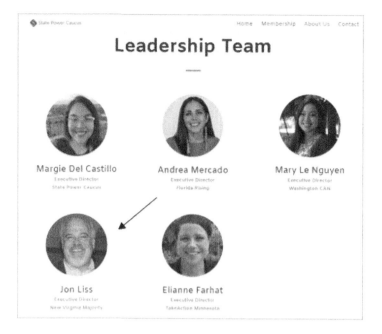

Several other well-known Maoists have served in leadership positions with the network since its founding in July 2017, including former Line of March comrade Bob Wing[48] and Claire Tran[49] of FRSO/Liberation Road and LeftRoots.

Initially known as the State-based Power Caucus, the SPC was founded in 2017, partially as a reaction to the election of President Trump:

According to SPC member organization California Calls:

> *Our goal is to develop a clear and collective understanding of what statewide governing power might look like and how it can be built, articulate an alternative vision to the Trump agenda and the dominant narrative of our time and strategize about how to influence the national landscape towards a strategic long-term state-based power building approach.*[50]

To this end, the SPC initially sought to unite twenty state-based organizations from thirteen states into a cohesive alliance.[51]

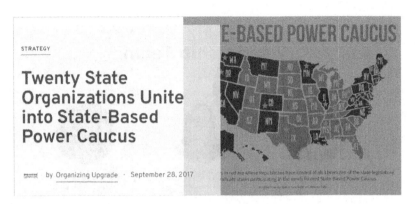

More than that, it was also a way to increase FRSO/Liberation Road control and coordination of some very significant mass organizations.

Wrote Jon Liss in June 2019 article entitled "Seize the Moment: Paving the Road for a Mass Left":

> *These organizations come from a variety of traditions: there are former ACORN groups, and groups that grew out of the workers center movement or the Right to the City Alliance. They are generally left: pro-Black, pro-immigrant, pro-women and pro-worker. Most work on voter mobilization and deep community organizing.*
>
> *Most would welcome dozens of members of left organizations supporting their work. Most are creating a constituency that often votes for Democrats but is also committed to radical democracy and deep transformational change…*
>
> *Bringing together left organizations has value and begins to move the needle.*
>
> *Moving cadre into a positive role of building state power organizations brings together a left that is often isolated and aloof from popular organizations into relationship with organizations that have real capacity, but suffer from the absence of the conscious left.*[52]

While SPC has members all over the country, the focus is still the Southern states.

The goal is to destroy the Republican strongholds in the South to move the entire country to the far-left.

In October 2021, Jon Liss and the SPC were profiled by Blue Tent, "which conducts research and analysis to identify the best giving opportunities for donors looking to advance progressive change:"[53]

> ...the caucus is a peer-to-peer space focused on building a progressive movement that dethrones decades of right-wing rule across the country. The group's map of member organizations helpfully highlights those states where all three branches of the state legislature are under Republican control. The caucus has a presence in seven such states: Texas, Missouri, Mississippi, Florida, South Carolina, Ohio and Kentucky.

STATE-BASED POWER CAUCUS

Note: The states in grey are where Republicans have control of all 3 branches of the state legislature. Stars indicate states participating in the State-based Power Caucus.

The group was founded in 2017 by New Virginia Majority leader Jon Liss, who told Blue Tent he sees a lot of potential for a sea change in Southern politics.

   'I think most of us who do work in the South have an analysis that while the South is seen as a bastion of conservatism, it could actually be a bastion of a progressive movement,' said Liss. 'The South could be a solid South for racial equity, a solid South for income distribution that's fair and equitable, for healthcare, etc.'[54]

The SPC is no small enterprise.

In June 2019, Jon Liss wrote an Organizing Upgrade/Convergence article outlining the tasks ahead for the 2020 election.

Jon Liss doesn't think small. The article was entitled "Toward a Movement 40 Million Strong."

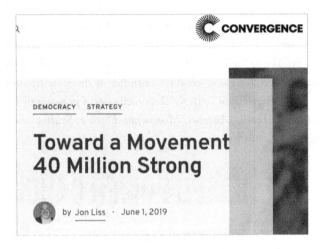

Here are some excerpts:

> *Inspired by the disaster of Trump and Trumpism two years out most organizers are engaged in barroom or coffee shop speculation about the 2020 election.*
>
> *Among the two dozen announced Democratic candidates, many debate: will it be Sanders or Warren, with their attacks on corporate Democrats? Will it be one of Hilary's heirs, with their cozy relationship with Wall Street? Will Harris be the first Black woman nominated by a major party?*
>
> *All of it is idle speculation unless 'we' collectively organize tens of millions of the 108 million eligible voters who didn't vote in 2016. That's right, one hundred and eight million eligible voters chose not to register or to vote in 2016. The non-voting block is disproportionately young, poor and people of color.*
>
> *This is by design.*
>
> *For the formerly incarcerated, people of color, and Black Southerners, rules and administrative practices are designed to prevent millions of potential voters from registering or voting…*
>
> *However, despite, or perhaps because of this, dozens of state-based power building organizations have banded together to lead efforts to build a bottom up long term front against Trump and Trumpism. Over the last twenty-five years, state power*

organizations have grown to fill the political space created by the decline of Democratic Party local organization, the breakup and collapse of ACORN, and low levels of voter turnout. This reflects a shift from narrow Alinskyism and its very limited political engagement…

These organizations have deep strategic knowledge and practice in their particular states. Starting in the summer of 2017 many leading state-power organizations have come together as a caucus to support peer-to-peer learning and incubate innovate organizing practices. Included among the organizations that have been leading the State Power Caucus are New Virginia Majority, The New Florida Majority, California Calls, Washington Community Action Network, and Kentuckians for the Commonwealth.

All told, there are 22 organizations from 15 states involved in the Caucus. Importantly, these organizations recognized the need to develop a systematic and long-term alternative to Trumpism.[55]

Jon Liss reveals the New American Majority-style strategy to mobilize the "unorganized social base", who is "more Black, more immigrant, more working class and poor". He also clarifies the basis for his 40 million voter mobilization target:

We've also begun to assess the collective impact of state-based organizations. Looking at 2016, our rough estimate is that at most 4 million people were contacted and encouraged to vote. This is our high-water estimate. The actual number who actually voted is probably much lower still.

Now, recall the 108 million people who were eligible but not voting? They are largely our 'core' constituency, or in other terms, they are our unorganized social base. This 108 million when compared to the voting electorate is more Black, more immigrant, more working class and poor.

If we initially target just half of the 108 million, and we acknowledge that some in that half are going to disagree with our values and politics, some aren't going to vote no matter what, and some are in geographies that we just can't reach, we believe our real voter mobilization target number is 40 million, and we've agreed as a caucus to that number as our target. That's our natural consistency.[56]

The race-obsessed voter registration strategy would make Steve Phillips proud! Liss continues to explain that the SPC tactics will ultimately bring about the "defeat [of] white nationalism and move past neoliberal corporatism [the free market] ...by building a bottom up movement of 40 million people..."

> *These are the voters or potential voters who put AOC and Ilhan Omar into Congress. They are our friends and family, and they are the everyday members and supporters of our organizations that fight for racial justice at the state and local level.*
>
> *The State Power Caucus is committed to working more effectively, efficiently and collaboratively with national social justice networks. Together, we look to take a big leap forward and move from mobilizing 4 million and organizing many less to mobilizing and organizing many times more.*
>
> *The long game to defeat white nationalism and move past neoliberal corporatism is by building a bottom up movement of 40 million people.*
>
> *At a minimum that is a movement where people vote consistently and consciously. Where people share our values for racial, gender and social justice and where people believe they have the capacity to rule.*[57]

Ironically, this plan by CCP-aligned activists to massively impact the 2020 election was partially foiled by the "China virus" – Covid-19, but the SPC is still very active and gearing up for Harris/Walz 2024 and beyond.

Current SPC membership consists of:

+ Arizona - Arizona Center for Empowerment (ACE)
+ California - Alliance of Californians for Community Empowerment (ACCE) Institute, Asian Americans and Pacific Islanders Empowerment Education Fund (AAPI Force – EF), California Calls Education Fund, PICO California Action Fund.
+ Florida - Florida Immigrant Coalition Incorporated, Florida Rising Together
+ Georgia - New Georgia Project Incorporated

* Illinois - Grassroots Collaborative
* Kentucky - Kentucky Coalition
* Michigan - We The People Michigan
* Minnesota TakeAction Minnesota Education Fund
* Mississippi - One Voice
* Missouri - Missouri Organizing and Voter Engagement Collaborative aka MOVE (MOVE)
* New York - Public Policy and Education Fund of New York, New York Communities Organizing Fund, Inc.
* North Carolina - Carolina Federation Fund
* Ohio - Ohio Organizing Collaborative
* Oregon - Pineros y Campesinos Unidos del Noroeste (PCUN)
* Pennsylvania - Pennsylvania Stands Up Institute
* Texas - Texas Organizing Project (TOP) Education Fund
* Virginia - New Virginia Majority Education Fund
* Washington - Washington Community Action Network (WACAN) Education & Research Fund[58]

Most of these organizations are very well funded and can mobilize hundreds of staffers and volunteers in any given election.

Collectively, these organizations, mostly led by pro-China communists, could mobilize several million, perhaps 10s of millions of voters in November 2024 and beyond.

How different would US elections be without this significant communist influence?

Do you think a Kamala Harris Justice Department would ever investigate this network?

SEED THE VOTE

The SPC is not the only Maoist-led electoral alliance working for Democratic Party victories.

The Bay Area-based Seed the Vote network has also played a major role in the last two election cycles.

In December 2019, the Seed The Vote Education Committee (which included former Line of March Maoist Max Elbaum and ex-STORM communist Jason Negron-Gonzales) released details of "a new political project led by organizers in the Bay Area...mobilizing to defeat Trump in 2020."[59]

According to the Education Committee, STV's goals went well beyond ending the Trump presidency but were part of a program to drive America much further into socialism:

> The Trump era has been all about the naked aggression of the far right, but cracks are appearing. Trump is battling impeachment, a result not only of his criminality but of the changes that the blue wave brought to Congress. Last month we saw further losses for the right in Virginia, Kentucky and Pennsylvania – the result of sustained organizing by hundreds if not thousands. That work didn't start this year; it's the culmination of many years of work. None of this was spontaneous. When we organize, we can win. When we step up to fight, we can win.
>
> Those are the lessons of last year, and this week – lessons that we have to apply to 2020. Seed the Vote is a project in the Bay Area attempting to create a vehicle to do just that. We want to leverage the experience, capacity, and expertise of organizers and activists in California in support of long-term organizing in our neighboring states.
>
> Our goal is not just to push Trump out of office, but to help shift the balance of power in the states where we are working in favor of communities of color, social justice organizations, and labor. We want to be tactically and politically smart, and move our politics and organizations forward.[60]

So, the activists launched Seed the Vote:

> *The possibility of Trump's re-election in 2020 is a real one. And it's one we are determined to stop. When we – a group of left activists rooted in community and labor organizing in the San Francisco Bay Area – gathered this spring, it was with the urgency that came from seeing our communities under relentless assault from a white nationalist, authoritarian administration.*
>
> *But we also knew that 2020 – with the size, energy, and leftward shift among the opposition to Trumpism – would give us an opportunity: if we plan carefully and think big, we can make a difference at the ballot box in 2020, the kind of difference the Left failed to make in 2016. And we thought we could do this while building a stronger and more cohesive Left.*
>
> *So we launched Seed the Vote. Our practical focus is centered on bolstering 2020 electoral efforts to defeat Trump and the GOP in two key states, Nevada and Arizona. We are already building infrastructure and recruiting to (1) deploy several hundred Bay area activists to work with partnering unions and community-based organizations in Nevada and Arizona for two-week periods in October 2020; and (2) connect volunteers with remote call-in and text efforts from the Bay Area to register voters, protect voting rights and increase turnout in key constituencies in November 2020.*
>
> *We are also considering partnerships in more states and expanding our field work depending on capacity—this may include connecting some Bay Area folks back to their home states and/or work with college students. We launched Seed the Vote as a project of a federal PAC.*[61]

The "federal PAC" referred to here is the Everyday People PAC, which is closely affiliated with the Chinese Progressive Association – San Francisco.

> *This effort is not only designed to impact the 2020 election outcome. We are including a training component to provide our volunteers with the skills and experience to lead electoral engagement work, ranging from advanced canvassers to team leaders who can train and supervise others, to campaign managers. And our program is crafted to increase the capacity and reach of partner*

organizations in Nevada and Arizona, as well as participating organizations in the Bay.

Seed the Vote is an active investment in the long-haul work of building the independent electoral strength of social justice organizations rooted in communities of color and the working class.[62]

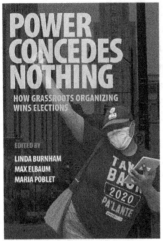

Power Concedes Nothing: How Grassroots Organizing Wins Elections

As one studies these connections, the same names and racial voting registration strategies appear time and again. Seed the Vote is using the "New American Majority" strategy in order to create a one party state.

So it should not surprise readers that the FRSO/Liberation Road-aligned Convergence Magazine reported that the Democracy Alliance sponsored a launch event for the 2022 book "Power Concedes Nothing: How Grassroots Organizing Wins Elections". The book was edited in part by Seed the Vote Maoists Max Elbaum and Maria Poblet.[63] Other contributors included Ai-jen Poo, Jon Liss, Alicia Garza, Andrea Cristina Mercado, Maurice Mitchell, Nse Ufot[64] and others in the Steve Phillips/Kamala Harris orbit.

The Democracy Alliance was not the only organization hosting a book launch for "Power Concedes Nothing". On April 14, 2022, The People's Forum also hosted an event featuring co-editors ex Line of March Maoist Linda Burnham and Deepak Pateriya, a long time activist who not-so-coincidentally participated in a year-long training at the Rockwood Leadership Institute in 2013.[65]

The People's Forum operates openly from a posh building on 37th Street in Manhattan. They are known for being deeply involved in "much of the pro-Hamas violence and chaos in NYC", and The People's Forum receives funding directly from the Chinese and Cuban communist parties.[66]

Communist to the core

There is zero doubt that STV is a communist-led operation – with "Chinese characteristics".

Note that the graphic below lists several STV "branches." They include the Chinese Progressive Association Action Fund, FRSO/Liberation Road and LeftRoots.

Seed the Vote is a project of Everyday People PAC and Center for Empowered Politics.[67]

The Treasurer of the Everyday People PAC is FRSO/Liberation Road comrade Michelle Foy,[68] who as previously noted doubles as the Finance and Administration Director of the Chinese Progressive Association – San Francisco (CPA-SF).[69]

The Center for Empowered Politics is led by Alex Tom, a LeftRoots comrade and the former Executive Director of the CPA-SF.[70]

Alex Tom certainly knew why he was involved in the 2020 elections.

He told a May 22, 2020, webinar on "US and China Relations" hosted by the San Francisco-based Center for Political Education:

...we just got to stay eyes on the prize now from anti-Asian vio-
lence being documented to attacks on China and defending China
to me the main thing is we got to get rid of Trump...[71]

Emily Lee, a LeftRoots comrade,[72] was a co-founder and currently
serves as the STV Executive Director.[73] Lee previously served as
political director of the CPA-SF.[74]

Fellow STV Coordinating Committee member[75] and Everyday
People PAC Director Le Tim Ly[76] was CPA-SF Deputy Director,
but now serves as Chief Financial Officer.[77]

Le Tim Ly

Long-time FRSO/Liberation Road comrade Sarah Jarmon[78] is also another very prominent STV activist.

Sarah Jarmon

Alicia Garza of LeftRoots, Black Lives Matter and the CPA-SF also played a strong support role in the 2020 election.

STV is the same old gang - with many of the same old funders.

In 2019/20 Steve Phillips's brother and sister-in-law James and Gretchen Sandler gave the Everyday People PAC $75,000 each, while Le Tim Le donated well over $60,000 on behalf of the CPA-SF.[79]

In 2022, the Sandler Foundation chipped in a cool $75,000.[80]

Victory, 2020

In the lead up to the 2020 election, Seed the Vote partnered with organizations all over the country, but especially in several key "swing states."

The key core organizations were;

+ Arizona – Living United for Change in Arizona (LUCHA)
+ Florida – New Florida Majority
+ Georgia – New Georgia Project
+ Michigan – Detroit Action
+ Pennsylvania – Pennsylvania Stands Up
+ Wisconsin – Black Leaders Organizing Communities (BLOC)

Other groups pitched in including several labor unions, especially in Nevada, the Black Lives Matter spinoff Dream Defenders in Florida, The Carolina Federation in North Carolina, the Texas Organizing Project and several state affiliates of the Working Families Party.

Many of these groups were led by activists connected in some way to the Maoist movement.

Detroit Action Managing Director Laura Misumi, an activist in her own right, is the daughter of former San Francisco League of Revolutionary Struggle member-turned-LeftRoots-comrade Don Misumi.[81]

Laura Misumi is also closely tied to the Chinese Progressive Association – San Francisco/Alex Tom's Center for Empowered Politics.[82]

Jennifer Disla, Detroit Action's Organizing Director was formerly with the Maoist-led Organization for Black Struggle in Missouri.[83]

New Florida Majority's leader Andrea Mercado was formerly with the LeftRoots FRSO/Liberation Road-led National Domestic Workers Alliance.[84]

New Georgia Project was founded by Stacey Abrams, a longtime Steve Phillips protégé and former PowerPAC+ board member.

The closely-allied Carolina Federation is led by FRSO/Liberation Road comrade Sendolo Diaminah,[85] while the Texas Organizing Project is led by former Staford University activist and PowerPAC+ board member Michelle Tremillo.[86]

Seed the Vote activists were able to mobilize nearly over 4,500 and phone bankers mainly focused on the "communities of color" in the main cities of a handful of key swing states.

Pennsylvania Stands Up alone made more than four million "voter contacts" through the course of the campaign.

It all paid off.

STV quite rightly claims credit for defeating President Trump in 2020.

On November 4, the day after the election, Becca Guerra of the Democracy Alliance's "New American Majority Fund" convened a meeting with several Seed the Vote affiliate leaders.

Becca Guerra stated that the New American Majority Fund was a "proud sponsor, funder and co-conspirator with these leaders…" The election was a "step in our path to our liberation".[87]

The gathered leaders, while not all as successful as they'd hoped, were jubilant at defeating Trump and happy with multiple victories and advances at state level.

Several of the participants quoted numbers, to emphasize the incredible amount of work their organizations had done to flip their respective states.

Alex Gomez of LUCHA explained the 10 years of work leading up to the big night and being able to "drive over 8 million calls and knock on over a million doors".

Nse Ufot of New Georgia Project claimed the organization had "knocked on a million doors."

Brandon Snyder of Detroit Action boasted of targeting "192,000 black and brown working-class Detroiters who were low propensity...made 858,000 calls, 90,000 text messages". They were able to "register and engage 12K same day voters and 20,000 first time voters."

BLOC leader Angela Lang claimed full credit for reversing Trump's 2016 20,000+ margin to an almost identical figure for Biden/Harris.[88]

Those figures are telling as they clearly indicate that several key, very close races in the handful of "battle ground states" that decided the election were heavily influenced by this Maoist-led network.

Indeed, in a similar post election webinar organized by Convergence Magazine, LeftRoots comrade Adam Gold claimed the network members "were focusing on seven states and six of those went to Biden..."[89]

And there was no rest for the wicked.

Within a few weeks, STV had moved hundreds of people into Georgia to win two vital Senate races for the far-left Jon Ossoff and the even further left Reverand Raphael Warnock. This, all on the back of 600,000 new voter registrations by the New Georgia Project.[90]

From a Seed the Vote election review:

> We sent 450 volunteers to Georgia to support in-person canvass programs with our local partners. Partners included New Georgia Project Action Fund (NGPAF), Asian American Advocacy Fund PAC (AAAF), Showing up for Racial Justice (SURJ), UNITE HERE, Care in Action, and Georgia Latino Alliance for Human Rights Action Network (GLAHR Action) and Mijente PAC. Volunteers made calls and participated in door-to-door canvassing to get out the vote ahead of the Senate run-off elections. The leadership of these organizations was integral to the victories of Raphael Warnock and Jon Ossoff for US Senate, not only their efforts in this election, but their long-term work registering and turning out voters over many years.[91]

Seed the Vote
January 4, 2021 · 🌐

"I'm here in Georgia through Seed the Vote to help reach Asian American voters with in-language lit to encourage them to make our voices heard and turn out to vote for the Georgia Senate runoff election! Seed the Vote partner Asian American Advocacy Fund has knocked on the doors of 72,000 Asian American voters. Today, I got to practice speaking some of my limited Lao with a Laotian voter! They didn't know about the election, but said they will be voting for Ossoff/Warnock on Tuesday!" Wayne Yeh, Seed the Vote volunteer w/ Asian American Advocacy Fund

In 2022, STV focused on the mid-term elections in the battle-ground states of Arizona, Pennsylvania, Georgia, Nevada, Wisconsin, and North Carolina.

From STV's 2022 election evaluation report:

> For the 2022 midterms, Seed the Vote ran or supported door knocking programs in Philadelphia, Pennsylvania; Atlanta, Georgia; Phoenix, Arizona; Reno, Nevada; and Durham, North Carolina. We supported our partners' phone bank programs in Pennsylvania, Georgia, and Wisconsin, and ran a phone bank program in Arizona in partnership with LUCHA.
>
> The nature of each partnership differed, depending on the needs and capacity of each partner. In Philadelphia, Reno and Phoenix we partnered with UNITE HERE, and hired field leads to run volunteer programs that operated alongside UNITE HERE's paid member door knocking program.
>
> This meant that UNITE HERE staff could focus their efforts on their paid member door knocking program, and STV held all of the training, canvass support and logistics for volunteers. In Durham we connected volunteers to Durham for All's existing door knocking program, and in Atlanta we did the same with SURJ. We set up a late partnership with PA United, in Western Pennsylvania, and sent a few volunteers out to join their door knocking program.
>
> Our partnership with AAAF (Asian American Advocacy Fund PAC, also in Atlanta, was a hybrid: we plugged out of state volunteers into their existing program but had a STV volunteer leader play a role in leading our volunteers.
>
> We also partnered with UNITE HERE for the December runoff in Georgia, leading two volunteer teams working with different union locals in neighboring Atlanta counties.[92]

Seed the Vote for Warnock

STV boasted:

> In Nevada we knocked on over 37,000 doors, in a senate race won by fewer than 9,000 votes.
> We knocked on over 40,000 doors for the Georgia runoff, in a race won by under 100k votes.[93]

In 2024, STV is out there doing it all over again in Nevada, Arizona, Pennsylvania, Wisconsin and Michigan.

The pattern is clear; Steve Phillips's rich friends provide the money. The Chinese Progressive Association – San Francisco, Seed the Vote, LeftRoots and FRSO/Liberation Road organise the manpower.

MAOIST MASS MOVEMENT

Kamala Harris is being pushed into the White House by an alliance of mega-wealthy donors, many with ties to China and a "grassroots" Maoist mass movement.

Seed the Vote's Max Elbaum explained the depth and breadth of this movement in an August 8, 2024, Convergence article:

> *Squad members—Cori Bush, Ilhan Omar, AOC and Ayanna Presley —have all endorsed Kamala, as have the AFL-CIO and numerous national unions (Service Employees International Union, American Federation of Teachers, National Education Association) and grassroots progressive organizations (Community Change Action, March for Our Lives, Black Voters Matter).*
>
> *Of particular note is the increased cooperation among progressive national and local groups reflected in common messaging and coordination of practical efforts. On July 25, the Working Families Party, Center for Popular Democracy Action, and People's Action jointly announced their endorsement of Harris and 'pledged to mobilize their national member bases to knock on over 5 million doors in key battleground states, including Michigan, Wisconsin, Pennsylvania, Nevada, and Arizona.'*
>
> *The Working Families Party also has been joined by SURJ, Seed the Vote and the Movement for Black Lives (M4BL) in a common 2024 effort of political education and action situated within a long-term strategy to gain governing power. In explaining WFP's plan to 'make 2024 a win for working people' and forge a new center of gravity within the progressive movement, WfP director Maurice Mitchell wrote:*
>
> *'We must block MAGA extremists from seizing governing power, and we must build the most viable, durable political vehicle that is beholden and accountable to the people and not the wealthy and corporations.'[94]*

It's hopefully clear by now that race-based Maoism is the guiding philosophy of the Kamala Harris presidential campaign, many senior Democratic Party politicians, much of the leftist donor class, many influential legal activists and pretty much all the pro-China US left – especially FRSO/Liberation Road, LeftRoots and the Chinese Progressive Association – San Francisco.

It should also be clear that the Kamala Harris's career has been supported at every stage by rich donors influenced by that same philosophy who are happy to fund leftist electoral groups who share similar views.

This "Maoist Mafia" may soon completely dominate US politics.

The New Virginia Majority and its allied organizations, the State Power Caucus, and Seed the Vote are all part of this network.

Also closely connected are Black Lives Matter and the nationally organized Working Families Party led by Maurice Mitchell – also of Movement for Black Lives.

Maurice Mitchell is pictured in the next image with socialist Congressmember Jamaal Bowman (D-NY) and Ash-Lee Henderson of FRSO/Liberation Road, LeftRoots and also the Movement for Black Lives.

The June 2024 webinar was sponsored by the Working Families Party, Movement for Black Lives and Seed the Vote:

As previously noted, LeftRoots came out the 2013 "Ear to the Ground Project" funded by among others Steve Phillips, Susan Sandler and Quinn Delaney.

The project was also aided by Black Lives Matter founder Alicia Garza who made sure "our i's were dotted, and our t's were crossed".[95]

In late 2023, LeftRoots dissolved in preparation for the launch of a new "cadre party" – in cooperation with FRSO/Liberation Road.

The "call" for this new Maoist party, the "North Star Socialist Organization" (NSSO) was "finished in the days after [the] Joe Biden announced that he would not run for reelection and before the 2024 Democratic National Convention."

This call was finished in the days after the Joe Biden announced that he would not run for re-election and before the 2024 Democratic National Convention. Vice President Kamala Harris seems to have a lock on the Democratic Party nomination. She has begun campaigning and is currently vetting possible vice-presidential running mates.

MOVEMENT MISSION 2024 by the North Star Socialist Organization's National Leadership

NSSO also noted that "Vice President Kamala Harris seems to have a lock on the Democratic Party nomination. She has begun campaigning and is currently vetting possible vice-presidential running mates."[96]

Incidentally, Ash-Lee Henderson of FRSO/Liberation Road is part of the NNSO leadership team.[97]

In the statement, NSSO issued a call to all comrades to commit themselves to the upcoming election.

Sign up with your friends and family to canvas with an independent political organization in a swing state (Arizona, Georgia, Michigan, Nevada, North Carolina, Pennsylvania and Wisconsin)

to encourage voters to vote against Trump and for Harris. While on the doors, you can talk about not just what the Right hopes to do to our communities, but what our organizations can win, if we defeat the Right's campaign.

Trump's path to victory relies on low voter turnout. The problem is that millions of voters are likely to stay at home unless someone makes a strong case for why it is in their interest to defeat Trump...

We have to mobilize and support independent political organizations which are so important because they combine electoral and ongoing campaign-based organizing. For a list of independent political organizations, you can contact Working Families Party or Seed the Vote.[98]

Lastly, NSSO called on its comrades to support Kamala Harris, invoking the name of the famed French Afro-Caribbean Marxist Frantz Fanon:

The Black revolutionary Frantz Fanon once wrote that 'each generation must out of relative obscurity discover its mission; fulfill it or betray it.' We believe our mission for the rest of this year is to block the MAGA Right by electing Kamala Harris and to build the Left. Now, it's up to us to fulfill it.[99]

Now it's up to us to stop them.

CHAPTER 6

KAMALA HARRIS AND THE MAOIST MAFIA

KAMALA HARRIS'S "INNER circle" is highly incestuous, nepotistic and deeply Marxist/Maoist. The Kamala Harris presidential campaign is guided by a philosophy that could be described as 'race-based Maoism,' where policies and campaign strategies are tailored through the lens of racial identity, drawing parallels to Maoist ideologies of class struggle but applied within a racial context.

Kamala's little acolytes

Few photographs distill the essence of the movement to elect Kamala Harris to the US presidency than the two featured below.

Taken in 2015, at a gathering of the "progressive" Young Elected Officials Network, the top photo shows left to right Hawaiian official Kaniela Ing, Kamala Harris's protégé Lateefah Simon, San Francisco activist/politicians Jane Kim and Matt Haney, and South Dakota politician and tribal leader Kevin Killer.

The adjoined following image omits Kaniela Ing and Kevin Killer, but includes Meena Harris (second from right), Kamala Harris's niece, the daughter of her sister Maya Harris.

Jane Kim ✓ is with **Kevin Killer** and 2 others.
July 25, 2015 · 🌐

Bay Area representing with other young electeds. Matt Haney, Lateefah Simon, Meena Harris w/youngest Native American State Reps Kaniela Ing (HI) + Kevin Killer (SD)

Those featured in the previous image are all part of the movement to promote Kamala Harris to high public office.

The group is a microcosm of the Rainbow Coalition/New American Majority movement - Native Hawaiian (Kaniela Ing), Korean American (Kim), Black (Lateefah Simon), White "progressive" (Matt Haney), Native American (Kevin Killer) and Asian American/ Black (Meena Harris). For the Rainbow Coalition strategy, which has since evolved into the New American Majority, different groups could unite in a spectrum of colors, much like a rainbow. The goal is to bring together the races, along with progressive whites, to shut out conservative voices and ultimately create a one-party state.

Kaniela Ing would later become a member of the Honolulu branch of Democratic Socialists of America. He stood unsuccessfully for Congress in 2018 with full socialist support and endorsement.

In recent years, Kaniela Ing has led the Green New Deal Network, a 50-state campaign with a national table of 14 organizations, mostly connected to FRSO/Liberation Road and Democratic Socialists of America: Center for Popular Democracy, Climate Justice Alliance, Grassroots Global Justice Alliance, Greenpeace, Indigenous Environmental Network, Indivisible, Movement for Black Lives, MoveOn, People's Action, Right to the City Alliance, Service Employees International Union, Sunrise Movement, US Climate Action Network, and the Working Families Party.[1]

From the Green New Deal Network:

> Today, the Green New Deal Network, hub of the Green New Deal movement, announced their endorsement of Vice President Kamala Harris for President…
>
> While GNDN had not endorsed President Biden, the coalition has been consistent in opposing former President Trump. Vice President Harris' unifying energy, strong track record on climate, and focus on new solutions inspired the decision to jump in the race. The Network specifically cited Harris' record on championing environmental justice, electrifying school buses, and taking on Big Oil.
>
> 'Our coalition represents the communities that Democrats need to win, but so many of our friends and family have felt too defeated or silenced to fight. In just 10 days, Kamala Harris has reinspired millions of our people to get off our asses and take back our freedom from billionaires and corporate clowns like Donald

Trump,' said Kaniela Ing, National Director of the Green New Deal Network…

This election will come down to groups like ours turning our people out, and we're all in.[2]

Kevin Killer is now the South Dakota-based President of the Oglala Sioux Tribe (OST).

Readers will not be surprised to learn that Kevin Killer served for several years on the Advisory Board of Steve Phillips's political staff "of color" talent bank Inclusv.[3]

Killer is fully on board with Steve Phillips's race-obsessed "voters of color" agenda.

In August 2021, Oglala Sioux Tribe President Kevin Killer attended a meeting in Washington DC chaired by Vice President Kamala Harris and Secretary of the Interior Deb Haaland.

Killer "addressed the concerns of OST" about the "marginalization of the Native American vote, drawing on his experience as a South Dakota State legislator to deliver a well written speech in a statesman like manner."[4]

Kevin Killer left, Deb Haaland second from right, Kamala Harris right

According to Native Sun News Today:

> *Killer next spoke about the impact the Native vote can have on election outcomes: 'Over half of the States have a sizeable Native population. When barriers to our participation are removed, we make a difference in local, state, and federal elections.'*
>
> *Nineteen years ago, John Thune went to bed way ahead in his senate race against incumbent Tim Johnson. Thune was the GOP Golden Boy who had never tasted defeat. The only county left to tally was Shannon County on the Pine Ridge Reservation, and when Thune woke up next day, that county had gone overwhelmingly for Johnson, and Johnson held onto his senate seat by a 528-vote whisker. So, Killer's assertion was far from hyperbole.*
>
> *Killer then implored of his hosts: 'We need your Administration to carry out the trust responsibility it owes to Native people and increase pressure on Congress to pass comprehensive voting rights legislation.*[5]

Killer demanded the following: 1.) Pass the "Native American Voting Rights Act" to ensure on-reservation polling and registration, 2.) the DOJ be engaged in redistricting cases to give Native Americans "voting power", 3.) mandate voter registration services in federal agencies serving tribes and 4.) establish a USPS contact to facilitate voter registration and mail-in voting.

In his words:

- ✦ *Pass the Native American Voting Rights Act (attach it to any voting bill that moves – the civil rights community is supportive the federal government has authority under the federal trust responsibility to enact it; and it remedies issues unique to Native communities by mandating on reservation polling and registration).*
- ✦ *Involve DOJ in upcoming redistricting cases. There are still 'at large' elections being used in Indian Country at the county level that are diluting Native American power.*
- ✦ *Every federal agency that interacts with tribes should be required to offer registration (IHS, BIA, Department of Agriculture when distributing SNAP benefits).*

> ✦ *A point of contact at the USPS to start addressing the
> lack of residential addressing and lack of residential mail
> delivery which makes it very difficult to register to vote
> and vote by mail[6].*

True revolutionaries are meticulous. These people will exploit
every possible opportunity to tilt the political odds in their favor.

This kind of leftist election lobbying and maneuvering is being
done almost every day in almost every state capitol.

By August 2024, Kevin Killer was boasting of his work with Vice
President Harris on "voting rights for Native communities" and promoting the upcoming "Native Men for Kamala" call.

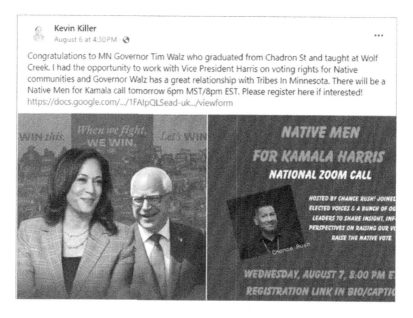

Lateefah Simon, as previously noted, is a longtime Kamala Harris
protégé, friend and supporter.

Meena Harris is also an activist in her own right and a strong
political supporter of her aunt. During Kamala Harris's successful
2016 campaign for the US Senate, Meena Harris served as a senior
advisor on policy and communications.[7]

She also works very closely with her friends Lateefah Simon and
Black Lives Matter founder Alicia Garza.

Alicia Garza, Meena Harris, Lateefah Simon

Meena Harris even interviewed Alicia Garza on her activism for the popular young women's magazine "Glamour".[8]

Just like her famous aunt, Meena Harris supports all the "Maoist" campaigns – fighting against imaginary[9] "anti-Asian hate", supporting Black Lives Matter, working to defund the police and so on.

The following passage is from a July 2020 San Francisco Chronicle article on Meena Harris's campaign to rename a San Francisco school named after George Washington in favor of far-left San Francisco poet Maya Angelou:

> *At the time of writing, the founder of the Phenomenal Woman Action Campaign— had been ramping up a grassroots effort to rename S.F.'s George Washington High School after one of its esteemed Black alums, the late poet-activist Maya Angelou.*
>
> *Meena Harris and her collaborators — among them BART Board of Directors President Lateefah Simon and Alicia Garza, co-founder of Black Lives Matter — had blown right past their 10,000-signature petition goal to remove the name of the slave-owning Founding Father that's been on the building for 84 years, and were inching their way to 20,000.*
>
> *'I wasn't planning for the emotional roller coaster of this time in our history,' says Harris, who in recent months had masterminded the Phenomenally Asian campaign to help reverse the racist rhetoric around the coronavirus, as well as the Phenomenally Black crusade to support the momentous surge of the Black Lives Matter movement in*

the wake of senseless Black deaths, past and present. Looking toward the future, she is forthrightly pro defunding the police — that is, reinvesting some of local law enforcement's big budgets into communities and programs that help Black citizens thrive.[10]

The Phenomenally Asian Campaign, "masterminded" by Meena Harris, sold tee shirts. It was promoted under the umbrella of her "Phenomenal" organization, described as a "consumer and media company that elevates the stories of women and underrepresented communities…"[11]

The proceeds went to the National Asian Pacific American Women's Forum (NAPAWF),[12] which was founded by "100 founding sisters" after attending the "Beijing World Conference on Women" in 1996.[13]

The organization, which approaches their work with a "reproductive lens"[14] was very active in promoting the false narrative that hate "incidents" against Asian Americans escalated in the wake of Covid-19. Their findings were based on a 2022 "survey".[15]

The NAPAWF's lies were regurgitated by the official newspaper of the Central Committee of the Chinese Communist Party, the People's Daily.[16]

San Francisco Democratic Party rising star Matt Haney knows Meena Harris very well.

They have collaborated on several political and cultural projects.

Meena Harris ⊘ is with Lateefah Simon and Matt Haney.
June 18, 2020 · ⊗

What if, on Juneteenth, the San Francisco School Board announced that it would rename George Washington High School after Maya Angelou? Matt Haney tried to do this four years ago and received death threats. Our time is now. Sign the petition!
https://www.change.org/mayaangelouhighschool

Matt Haney calls Meena Harris his "sister".

Matt Haney is also very close to Kamala Harris.

He has worked with her since 2008 when they campaigned together for former President Barack Obama in Iowa.

Matt Haney, Kamala Harris, Meena Harris, 2008

Harris even made a point to personally swear in Matt Haney when he won a seat on the San Francisco School Board.

Matt Haney
@MattHaneySF

I first met @KamalaHarris in Iowa where we were both campaigning for Barack Obama. I worked for her campaign in 2010 when she ran for AG, she swore me into School Board, & she's inspired me with her leadership as Senator. Let's get this daughter of the Bay into the White House.

4:54 PM · Aug 11, 2020

On July 25, 2024, Jane Kim, by now the leader of the California Working Families Party, trumpeted the national party's commitment to "keeping Donald Trump a one term President" and their "overwhelming" endorsement of Kamala Harris.

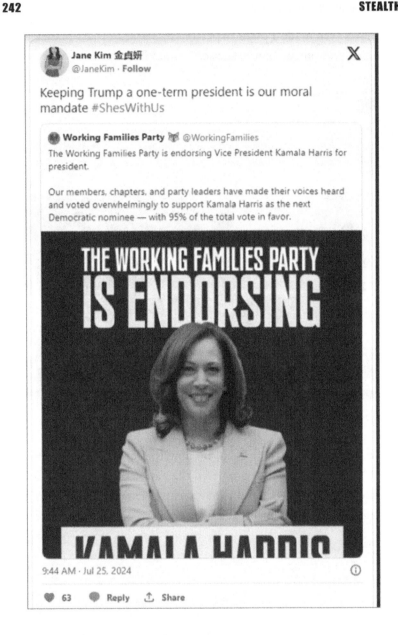

A 95% endorsement, no less.

WHO IS JANE KIM?

Jane Kim is one of the most well-known younger activists in the Bay Area. She is involved in virtually every main current of the San

Francisco area and is tied in to almost every component of Kamala Harris's local support base.

As a political science student at Stanford University in the late 1990s, Jane Kim chaired the Asian American Students Association[17] which had been previously run for years by comrades from the former League of Revolutionary Struggle.

Also, a leader of Concerned Students for Asian American Studies, Jane Kim pushed for Asian Studies at Stanford University[18] and condemned "racism" in the pages of the Stanford Daily.[19]

Stanford Daily, February 4, 1998, page 4

In 2012 and 2017, Jane Kim served alongside Alicia Garza and several old Maoists, on the Host Committees for the Chinese Progressive Association–San Francisco's 40th[20] and 45th[21] Anniversary celebrations respectively.

Kim regularly attends CPA–SF events and has enjoyed the organization's support on the campaign trail.

Jane Kim, CPA-SF, November 2016

Jane Kim was also mentored by notoriously pro-China San Francisco power broker, the late Rose Pak.

In October 2016, after Rose Pak underwent kidney transplant surgery in China, San Francisco "dignitaries" including Charlotte Shultz (wife of former US Secretary of State George Schultz) organized the largest welcome ceremony in the history of SF Airport for their beloved Godmother.

From the San Francisco Chronicle:

> *From the greeting by San Francisco Mayor Ed Lee and two former mayors to the Rolls-Royce ride — complete with police escort — it would be hard to imagine anyone from President Obama on down topping the welcome for Chinatown majordomo Rose Pak on her return to the city.*
>
> *The 300 greeters who took the drive out to the airport Monday for Pak's welcome–home from China, where she underwent months of kidney treatment, included former Mayors Gavin Newsom and Willie Brown, Supervisors Aaron Peskin, Jane Kim, Norman Yee and David Campos, Public Defender Jeff Adachi and City Attorney Dennis Herrera.[22]*

L-R Norman Yee, Willie Brown, Rose Pak, (podium), 2nd from right Charlotte Schultz, Jane Kim

Incidentally, the Norman Yee pictured in the previous image is a long time San Francisco Supervisor, a Chinese Progressive Association – San Francisco supporter[23] and a former PowerPAC+ board member.[24]

The far-left Rose Pak Democratic Club endorsed Jane Kim's San Francisco Supervisor run in 2016.

They also gave a nod to Norman Yee and Kamala Harris's long-time protege Lateefah Simon.

Jane Kim also endorsed her friend and comrade Lateefah Simon.

Jane Kim ✔
November 2, 2016 · 🌐

Vote down the ballot! Support two incredible, smart public service candidates (and friends!!) running for BART Board Lateefah Simon + Bevan Dufty!

Though Rose Pak died in September 2016, Jane Kim continues to benefit from her legacy.

In 2018, The Rose Pak Democratic Club announced their sole endorsement of Jane Kim for the San Francisco mayoralty race.

According to the club's press release Jane Kim stated:

> I am proud to receive the sole endorsement for San Francisco Mayor from the Rose Pak Democratic Club. As mayor, I will continue to support the causes Rose Pak championed—preserving the cultural institutions of Chinatown, ensuring our immigrant families can stay in their homes, and uplifting the voice of the Chinese

community in San Francisco. Rose Pak was my mentor, and I will honor her legacy by fighting for the people she dedicated her life to protect…[25]

Jane Kim is also very close to Steve Phillips and his operations.

When Steve Phillips launched his book "Brown is the New White" on February 4, 2016, at the Impact Club in Oakland, Jane Kim was a featured speaker.[26]

When Steve Phillips launched Democracy in Color on July 25, 2016, at the Democratic National Convention in Philadelphia, Jane Kim was there with Stacey Abrams, Alida Garcia and Aimee Allison.

In 2016, Steve Phillips's PowerPAC+ endorsed both Kamala Harris for US Senate and Jane Kim for California State Senate.

Kamala Harris - U.S. Senate, California

Since her election as state Attorney General in 2010, Kamala Harris has been a fierce advocate for the people of California. She actively defended marriage equality during the battle over Proposition 8, successfully brought charges against major corporate polluters, and orchestrated the largest foreclosure reform package in the nation on behalf of California homeowners. Kamala recognizes that California leaders must be "smart on crime," and she has combated transnational gang activity and dismantled several major human trafficking operations. Born in Oakland to an Indian American mother and Jamaican American father, Kamala is the first female, first African American and first Asian American to serve as Attorney General for the state of California. On January 13, 2015, Kamala announced her candidacy for the U.S. Senate. You can read more about Kamala HERE.

Jane Kim - California State Legislature

Jane Kim is current San Francisco Supervisor and candidate for State Senate, District 11. Jane is a proven progressive leader who has fought to expand access to affordable housing, protect renters, close the income gap and improve public schools. Jane understands that the major challenges we face are not just local issues - they are statewide and even national issues and require support at the broadest levels. She is running for Senate to ensure we have a representative in Sacramento who will work to address those challenges – housing the homeless, creating more affordable housing, family-sustaining jobs, relieving transit gridlock and strengthening public education. You can read more about Jane HERE.

Jane Kim was also supported by the California Donor Table (originally the Progressive Era Project) – founded by Steve Phillips, Susan Sandler, Quinn Delaney, her husband Wayne Jordan, and Democracy Alliance Chairman Rob McKay.[27]

On November 17, 2016, the leftist "gay rights" group, the Courage Campaign hosted the Sixth Annual Spirit of Courage Awards in Hollywood, to honor two "courageous champions and inspiring leaders" State Senator Holly Mitchell and Steve Phillips.

Jane Kim introduced Steve Phillips to the crowd, describing him as a "leader in the New American Majority".

Jane Kim 金貞妍
@JaneKim · Follow

Honored @CourageCampaign invited me to introduce Steve Phillips, leader in the new American majority. #cantstopwontstop #brownisthenewwhite

1:06 AM · Nov 18, 2016

In 2023, Jane Kim, California Director of the Working Families Party, spent most of the year studying at the Steve Phillips/ FRSO/ Liberation Road-linked radical training school the Rockwood Leadership Institute in Oakland, CA.[28]

Goodwin Liu and Kamala Harris

Jane Kim's partner, Associate Justice of the California Supreme Court, Goodwin Liu is also very much part of the "movement".

Goodwin Liu went to Stanford University and earned a bachelor's degree in biology in 1991.[29]

At Stanford, Goodwin Liu was a contemporary of Steve Phillips and was politically active in the same radical circles.

Liu was elected to the student government on the "People's Platform", the electoral wing of the League of Revolutionary Struggle. He served on the Council of Presidents (student government) with fellow Peoples Platform activist Ingrid Nava, a reported LRS comrade and future PowerPAC+ board member.

Left to right, Jay Tucker, Jamie Green, Goodwin Liu and Ingrid Nava are trying to become the third People's Platform slate in three years to win the COP election.

The people behind the platform

The Standford Daily, April 6, 1990

After Yale Law School, Goodwin Liu clerked for the late leftist Justice Ruth Bader Ginsburg.[30]

In the early 2000s, Goodwin Liu was also part of the leadership of Chinese for Affirmative Action (CAA), a Maoist-oriented group, founded in 1969 to use alleged "anti-Asian racism" to push for affirmative action, hate speech laws and other attacks on Constitutional liberties.

CAA Chinese for Affirmative Action (CAA) · Follow
      June 18, 2012 · San Francisco, CA · 🌐   ...

Judge Lillian Sing, Judge Goodwin Liu, Commissioner Norman Yee and Judge Julie Tang— with
Goodwin Liu and Norman Yee at Empress of China.

CAA campaigned heavily for the appointment of Goodwin Liu to the US Court of Appeals.[31]

CHINESE SPY RUSSELL LOWE

Around the time, of Goodwin Liu's involvement, longtime San Francisco activist Russell Lowe was a prominent CAA staff member.[32]

In 2018, it was revealed that Russell Lowe was also a Chinese Communist Party spy.

For nearly 20 years, Lowe worked for Senator Dianne Feinstein - including while she served as Chair of the Senate Intelligence Committee. When the news broke that Lowe was a CCP spy, Senator Feinstein minimized his importance, referring to him as a mere driver.[33] In fact, Russell Lowe "served officially as 'office director' and importantly, as Feinstein's California liaison to the Asian-American community."[34] Lowe was important enough to have been listed as a contact for Dianne Feinstein, as in the case of this Department of the Navy Environmental Impact document (archived) from 1997:[35]

10. DISTRIBUTION LIST

Title	First	Last	Organization	Branch	City	State
			Elected Officials			
Mr.	John	Hass	Senator Boxer's Office		San Francisco	CA
Mr.	Russell	Lowe	Senator Feinstein's Office		San Francisco	CA
The Honorable	Mazzoni	Kerry	State Assembly Representative		Sacramento	CA
The Honorable	Patricia	Ecklund	City of Novato		Novato	CA
Mayor Pro Tem	Carole	Dillon-Knutsen	City of Novato		Novato	CA
Councilmember	Michael	DiGiogio	City of Novato		Novato	CA
Councilmember	Ernest	Gray	City of Novato		Novato	CA
Councilmember	Cynthia	Murray	City of Novato		Novato	CA
Supervisor	John	Kress	Marin County		San Rafael	CA
Supervisor	Annette	Rose	Marin County		San Rafael	CA
			Marin County Board of Supervisors		SanRafael	CA
Supervisor	Harry	Moore	Marin County		San Rafael	CA
Supervisor	Harold	Brown	Marin County		San Rafael	CA
The Honorable	Lynn	Woolsey	US Representative		Washington	DC

Environmental Impact Statement prepared by the Dept of the Navy, November 1997 (Screenshot)

Russell Lowe was also in contact with the Chinese Consulate in San Francisco.

The following Facebook post from the Chinese Student Association of California State University, East Bay shows Russell Lowe left, Consul Chen right and center Christine Fang, (aka Fang Fang) another alleged Chinese spy.

CSUEB Chinese Student Association is at CSUEB.
September 22, 2011 · 🌐   ···

Office Director of U.S. Senator Dianne Feinstein California Russell Lowe & Consul CHEN

Reportedly Eric Swalwell also addressed this event.[36]

Congressman Eric Swalwell was later thrown off the House Intelligence Committee for his close relationship with Christine Fang.[37]

Russell Lowe is also a very close friend and longtime political collaborator with Bay Area activist Eric Mar.

One of three Maoist brothers (Warren and Gordon), Eric Mar is an Asians 4 Black Lives activist, longtime Chinese Progressive Association – San Francisco leader, past Vice Chair of the San Francisco Democratic Party's Central Committee, former San Francisco Supervisor[38] an ex-Rainbow Coalition activist[39] and a one-time League of Revolutionary Struggle supporter.[40]

Russell Lowe left, Eric Mar, right

Eric Mar also knows Steve Phillips.

Steve Phillips with Eric Mar, September 2013

Eric Mar also travels in the same circles as Alicia Garza and Pam Tau Lee of Chinese Progressive Association-San Francisco, LeftRoots and the League of Revolutionary Struggle fame.

L-R: Eric Mar, Alicia Garza and Pam Tau Lee

And Eric Mar made a revealing comment on a "Threads" post on July 22, 2024. "Despite my criticisms of her, VPOTUS Kamala Harris gives us a chance to defeat the rise of MAGA/Trumpism," Mar said. "We need to 'Block and Build' as suggested by Convergence [Magazine]."[41] Convergence Magazine, which was founded as Organizing Upgrade, is aligned with FRSO/Liberation Road.

On their website, Convergence states in part that they aim to "dismantle racial capitalism, and win the change we need by **building a new governing majority** that is driven by a convergence of grassroots social movements, labor movements, socialists, and progressives [emphasis added]."[42]

The "Block and Build" strategy referenced by Eric Mar in his Threads post seeks to "Block" the "MAGA" movement and to "Build" the progressive alliance.

From the Convergence website:

The main dynamic shaping this moment is the drive by a powerful right-wing bloc to impose authoritarian rule and a white Christian Nationalist agenda on the country. This bloc, gathered under the banner of 'Make America Great Again' (MAGA), has already captured the Republican Party and the Supreme Court, and holds trifectas (governorships and legislative majorities) in 22 states. The drama being played out today centers on whether MAGA will succeed in gaining full federal power in 2024 or soon after; and, if they are beaten back, what will be the character of the anti-MAGA governing coalition.

The strategy elaborated in this syllabus is aims to block MAGA's bid for power and while doing so build enough independent progressive clout to start the country down the road to a robust multiracial, gender-inclusive democracy and an economy that works for all on an environmentally sustainable planet.[43]

Screenshot from the FRSO/Liberation Road-aligned Covergience Website

An important acknowledgement must be made here of Eric Mar's reference to his "criticisms" of Kamala Harris. This exemplifies a strategy commonly used within leftist political circles to maintain accountability among progressive figures. This tactic was notably evident during the Obama era, where far-left groups, including communists, regularly critiqued the President. These criticisms served to push Obama towards adopting more radical socialist policies.

Similarly, the critique serves a dual purpose: it pressures Kamala Harris in this instance to lean further left while also providing a veneer of moderation. Critics might argue, "How could Kamala Harris be a communist if communists criticize her?" This rhetorical question is designed to reassure Americans, suggesting that Harris isn't as far-left as her detractors claim.

This approach mirrors the Chinese Communist Party's (CCP) strategy known as "Big help with a little bad mouth," where mild criticism is used to mask deeper cooperation or alignment. This strategy will be further explored in the context of Tim Walz's interactions with China in the final chapter, illustrating how criticism can be a tool for strategic manipulation rather than genuine opposition.

All criticism is tactical.

 ericmar415 07/22/2024   · · ·

Despite my criticisms of her, VPOTUS Kamala Harris gives us a chance to defeat the rise of MAGA/Trumpism. We need to "Block and Build" as suggested by ⊙ _convergencemag

Eric Mar Threads Post Dated July 22, 2024

But, back to Goodwin Liu.

On February 24, 2010, President Barack Obama nominated Goodwin Liu to fill a vacancy on the US Court of Appeals for the Ninth Circuit (California, Oregon, Washington).

On May 26, 2010, this country's most influential pro-China organization, the Committee of 100 (C-100), issued a statement in support of Goodwin Liu's nomination.

Goodwin H. Liu Statement; Committee of 100 (C-100) Screenshot

Committee of 100 Chair John Chen wrote, "C-100 urges the Senate to confirm Professor Goodwin Liu. His ascension to the bench would signal that talented people of all backgrounds are integral to our justice system." [44]

To put it very gently, the C-100 has deep and long-term ties to Chinese Government officials and has been "noted to avoid criticism of the Chinese Communist Party and its policies." [45]

A 2020 Newsweek article reported that committee members have been "targets" of [the Chinese Communist Party's] "United Front Work Department pressure and influence operations." [46] The section on Tim Walz will delve into the CCP's "United Front" strategy.

While most C-100 members are businesspeople, professionals and academics, few are former Maoist radicals – the most notable being former Stanford University academic Gordon H. Chang. [47]

Chang, a lifelong Maoist, was one of the main leaders of the League of Revolutionary Struggle[48] at Stanford in the 1980s, when Steve Phillips and his comrades were active within the organization.

But why would the Chinese Communist Party-friendly C-100 possibly want a Maoist-affiliated leftist serving on the 9th Circuit?

Maybe they hoped that Goodwin Liu would affirm Maoist-inspired racial legislation?

Or possibly they hoped that Liu would strike down policies coming from a future Republican President, seeking to curtail the endless waves of legal and illegal immigration entering this country – as happened several times during the Trump presidency.

Despite intensive leftist lobbying, Senate Republicans, alarmed about Liu's well-deserved extremist reputation, refused to confirm him. On May 19, 2011, the Senate rejected cloture on Liu's nomination in a 52–43 vote and on May 25, Liu informed President Obama that he was withdrawing his name from consideration.[49]

However, a consolation prize was soon forthcoming.

On September 1, 2011, UC Berkeley School of Law professor Goodwin Liu won confirmation as the newest Associate Justice of the Supreme Court of California. The unanimous vote by the three-member Commission on Judicial Appointments came after Liu's supporters spoke on his behalf at a public hearing in San Francisco—there was no opposing testimony.[50]

One of those testifying in Liu's favor was former Obama mentor and fellow Harvard Law Review editor Chris Edley, Jr., then a Boalt Hall, UC Berkeley Dean and Professor of Law.[51]

Chris Edley, Jr. is married to former Stanford University radical,[52] one time President Clinton Deputy Chief of Staff, Obama nominee for Ambassador to Mexico,[53] and PowerPAC+ board member Maria Echaveste.[54]

Here's an October 2014 photo of Steve Phillips, center, then California Lieutenant Governor Gavin Newsom left, Susan Sandler second from left, Nevada Lieutenant Governor candidate Lucy Flores second from right and Maria Echaveste right:

From the Steve Phillips Facebook page

Here's another photo from 2015, also from Steve Phillips's Facebook page: left to right, Steve Phillips, Susan Sandler, Chris Edley, Jr. and Maria Echaveste at a Berkeley eatery:

From the Steve Phillips Facebook page

The three-member judicial commission which approved Goodwin Liu consisted of Chief Justice Tani Cantil-Sakauye, California's senior appeals court justice Joan Dempsey Klein, and California Attorney General Kamala Harris – who quickly offered her congratulations:[55]

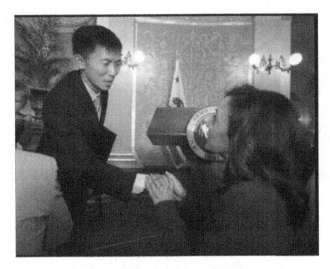

From Kamala Harris Facebook page

But more disappointment for Goodwin Liu was to come.

Kamala Harris and Rob Bonta

On March 24, 2021, Governor Gavin Newsom nominated Assemblyman Rob Bonta to be California's next Attorney General, filling the vacancy created when Xavier Becerra was confirmed as President Biden's Secretary of Health and Human Services.

Justice Goodwin Liu had been "prominently mentioned as a possible nominee" and he had gathered many "significant endorsements".[56]

Justice Liu and Rob Bonta had been classmates at Yale Law School.[57]

John Liu issued this statement in response to Governor Newsom's announcement:

> I am delighted and proud to see my friend and law school classmate Rob Bonta nominated for Attorney General. California is fortunate to have such talented and diverse leaders in public service, and this nomination is especially meaningful for Asian Americans, especially particularly at a time when our community is experiencing great vulnerability and many are fearing for their safety.
>
> Our Chief Justice last week underscored the continuing need to tackle 'the disease of racism,' and I've always known Rob to be a strong leader in combatting discrimination and protecting the rights of all persons, including groups that for too long have been marginalized or ignored.[58]

When Rob Bonta stood for a full four-year term in 2022, he earned a very powerful endorsement – from no less than former California Attorney General and serving US Vice President Kamala Harris.

Rob Bonta
@RobBonta   ...

BIG ENDORSEMENT NEWS! I'm proud to have been endorsed by VP @KamalaHarris. As our former AG, VP Harris knows firsthand the importance of protecting our fundamental rights. I'm grateful to have a partner in the White House to advance those rights for all Californians.

3:44 PM · Oct 21, 2022

Van Jones chimed in as well – praising Bonta for his radical-left "soft on crime" policies:

Van Jones ✔
@VanJones68   ...

.@GavinNewsom has a chance to make a huge statement by appointing @RobBonta, a lifelong champion of criminal justice reform, as CA's next AG. Rob has led fights to end cash bail, rollback mandatory minimums & outlaw private prisons. It would be a big moment for our movement.

9:46 PM · Feb 22, 2021

If Goodwin Liu leaned a little Maoist, Rob Bonta was, if anything, even worse.

In 2012, Alameda County Supervisor and former Assemblymember Wilma Chan announced she has endorsed Alameda Vice Mayor Rob Bonta for the State Assembly in the 18th District.

Bonta was "humbled and energized" by Chan's endorsement.[59]

"Supervisor Chan is a legend in the East Bay in her commitment to children and families, and trailblazing accomplishments for Asian Americans and I deeply appreciate her endorsement," Bonta said. "I am honored and motivated to advocate on behalf of the people and issues for which we share a passion."[60]

As previously noted, Wilma Chan had formerly been a Maoist, a leader of both the League of Revolutionary Struggle and the Chinese Progressive Association – San Francisco.

In August 2013, Assemblyman Bonta keynoted the Asian Pacific American Labor Alliance (APALA) 12th Biennial Convention in Las Vegas.

APALA is largely led by Maoist-leaning activists from Line of March, League of Revolutionary Struggle etc., and was founded by former Communist Workers Party comrade Kent Wong.[61]

Until recently, APALA was led for many years by Greg Cendana, a former board member of Steve Phillips's PowerPAC+,[62] and a co-founder with Phillips of the Inclusv organization.[63]

Steve Phillips
June 18, 2014

Look who I ran into at the US Capitol!— with **Gregory Allan Datu Cendana.**

Rob Bonta is also an official "APALA Lifetime Warrior" for his "continued leadership and support to APALA's efforts to fight for social and economic justice."[64]

There is an even closer Bonta/Maoism connection.

Rob Bonta is the son of lifelong Bay Area Filipina American activist Cynthia Bonta.

During the 1970s and 1980s, many young Filipino Americans supported the Maoists of the Communist Party of the Philippines/New People's Army in their guerilla war against the pro-American Ferdinand Marcos government.

Cynthia Bonta was a member of the pro-communist Union of Democratic Filipinos (KDP),[65] which later merged into the openly Maoist organization Line of March.

Cynthia Bonta was also active in the Coalition Against the Marcos Dictatorship, a KDP front group which was later renamed the Anti-Martial Law Coalition.

Coalition Against the Marcos Dictatorship (CAMD) Protest

When Rob Bonta was in the running for the Attorney General position, Filipino Americans and other "AAPI" leaders called on California Governor Gavin Newsom to appoint him.

"Today we uplift Rob Bonta for our choice for CA Attorney General," said Robert Chua, Northern California Chair of the Fil Am Democratic Caucus.[66]

State Treasurer Fiona Ma, a former Kamala Harris 2020 Presidential campaign co-chair[67] also threw her support behind Bonta.

"This is what it takes to get people from our community to get appointed grassroots support," said Ma. "We saw this happen with Kamala Harris."[68]

"Rob Bonta's march from his early days in the labor movement sitting on his parents lap across from Cesar Chavez…to this day-it is a special moment," said Joselyn Geaga-Rosenthal of the Asian Pacific American Labor Alliance.[69]

Joselyn Geaga, a former radical activist, is the sister and comrade[70] of long time former Southern California KDP/Line of March leader Jaime Geaga – who served for 10 years as a Los Angeles Central Area Planning Commissioner.[71]

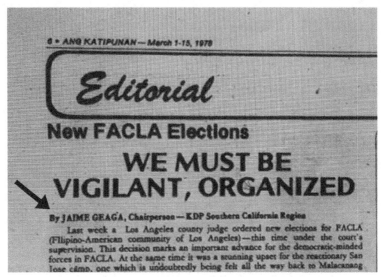

Newspaper of the Union of Democratic Filipinos

Rob Bonta is also very close to his mother's lifelong friend and fellow Maoist comrade Lillian Galedo.

Lillian Galedo left, Rob Bonta, 2020

Like Cynthia Bonta, Lillian Galedo was active in the KDP/Line of March.[72]

When Jesse Jackson declared his candidacy for the 1984 presidential election, the KDP organized Filipinos to join in the Rainbow Coalition and helped to form "Filipinos for Jackson".

Lillian Galedo was one of the key Jackson/Rainbow Coalition supporters.[73]

Until her retirement in 2017, Lillian Galedo ran the "social and economic justice" organization Filipino Advocates for Justice (previously Filipinos for Affirmative Action) for several decades.

Rob Bonta
Like This Page · April 27 · ☻

So proud to honor Filipino Advocates for Justice on the well-earned retirement of their incredible executive director Lillian Galedo after 37 years. You are my friend and all of our inspiration!

Rob Bonta served on the board of Filipino Advocates for Justice for several years under Lillian Galedo.[74]

In October 2020, California Assemblymember Rob Bonta "partnered" with Filipino Advocates for Justice for an activist event named in honor of 1940s Filipino American labor activist and Communist Party USA comrade Larry Itliong.[75]

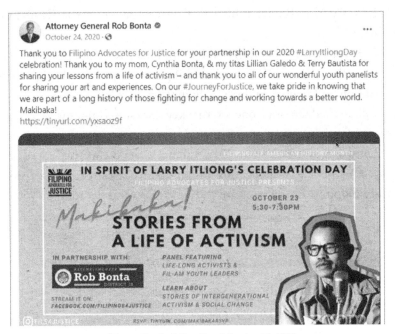

Attorney General Rob Bonta ✓
October 24, 2020 · 🌐   •••

Thank you to Filipino Advocates for Justice for your partnership in our 2020 #LarryItliongDay
celebration! Thank you to my mom, Cynthia Bonta, & my titas Lillian Galedo & Terry Bautista for
sharing your lessons from a life of activism – and thank you to all of our wonderful youth panelists
for sharing your art and experiences. On our #JourneyForJustice, we take pride in knowing that
we are part of a long history of those fighting for change and working towards a better world.
Makibaka!
https://tinyurl.com/yxsaoz9f

Rob Bonta Facebook Post Dated October 24, 2020

In one of his first acts as California Attorney General, Rob Bonta drafted legislation that would prevent California state employees from being fired for being a member of the CPUSA.[76]

The proposal was symbolic, as the law hadn't been enforced for decades. If it had been, and applied to Maoists as well, it would likely have collapsed the entire California education system.

Rob Bonta backed down after he got strong pushback from some Republican legislators and many anti-communist Vietnamese Americans.[77]

Bonta also enjoyed a very close working relationship and friendship with Kamala Harris.

As far back as 2014, the duo worked together on anti-truancy legislation - Assembly Bill 2141.

Rob Bonta was personally active in all of Kamala Harris's latter electoral campaigns and is honored to have her "friendship and support."

In May 2020, at the beginning of the Covid-19 pandemic, Senator Harris and Assemblymember Bonta penned a joint article for Asian Journal News "Standing up for the AAPI community amid America's leadership crisis."

The article promoted the perennial Maoist themes – "hating Trump" and countering "anti-Asian hate".

According to Harris and Bonta:

> We are in a crisis — one that requires unifying leadership. But that's not what we are getting from the president of the United States. The staggering death toll and human suffering haven't changed Donald Trump's lack of empathy and tendency to strike out at those who speak truth. Rather than show moral leadership and take real action to help people, Trump has resorted to race-baiting and spreading misinformation. This has helped perpetuate hate against the Asian American & Pacific Islander (AAPI) community.[78]

Harris and Bonta trotted out the usual baseless, undocumented and usually completely bogus "incidents" to prove their propaganda points.

No police reports. No convictions. No evidence beyond Facebook memes and rumors.

But Maoist propaganda always works best when there are few verifiable facts to get in the way of the narrative. They continued:

> The number of hate-fueled incidents – ranging from verbal harassment to physical assault – against the AAPI community remains dangerous. These incidents include cases like people being spit on, having bottles thrown at them, and being physically assaulted in the subway and other public places. The racist fearmongering has also hurt AAPI-owned small businesses.
>
> The increase in instances of profiling, intolerance, intimidation, and hate is disturbing and inexcusable. Any witness to these acts has the responsibility to speak up, report, and condemn them. And the Commander in Chief must show real leadership that unifies our country instead of sowing hate, especially during a national crisis…
>
> Given the lack of leadership in the White House, the two of us

have worked hard to address these issues head-on by demanding an end to discrimination against the AAPI community; calling for the administration to address bias; and requesting funding to combat discrimination.

Funding, that would, of course, go straight to Bonta and Harris's friends and their Maoist-oriented "anti-racist" organizations, which is precisely what happened as will be revealed.

As Vice President, Kamala Harris pushed the narrative even further. But this time, she was able to promote the so-called "COVID-19 Hate Crimes Act".

Vice President Kamala Harris ✔
@VP

Hate crimes and violence against Asian Americans and Asian immigrants have skyrocketed during the pandemic. That's why our Administration has taken actions to address these xenophobic attacks. We must continue to commit ourselves to combating racism and discrimination.

2:34 PM · Feb 12, 2021

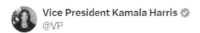

Vice President Kamala Harris ✔
@VP

In the past year alone, there have been more than 3,800 anti-Asian hate crimes. We urge the Senate to pass Senator @MazieHirono's bill, the COVID-19 Hate Crimes Act – which expedites review of hate crimes. We must do everything we can to #StopAsianHate.

7:46 PM · Apr 14, 2021

A year after Bonta and Harris's joint article, Kamala Harris used her platform as Vice President to falsely claim that Asian Americans are victims of voter suppression and hate crimes brought on by alleged anti-Asian sentiment in the wake of Covid-19.

On May 20, 2021, Harris said:

So early on in the pandemic, 1,100 anti-Asian hate incidents had been reported. Over a year later, just about a year later, we are now up to more than 6,600 and nearly two in three were reported by women.

Kamala Harris's figures were based on data from "Stop AAPI Hate," whose founders are Russell Jeung, Asian American Studies professor at San Francisco State University, Manjusha Kulkarni, Executive Director at AAPI Equity Alliance, and Cynthia Choi, co-executive director of the Chinese for Affirmative Action (CAA) - Goodwin Liu's former organization.

The group compiles their information by collecting "anonymous anecdotes about so-called 'microaggressions' and 'hate incidents'".[79] This is added to a report and regurgitated as fact by the media and politicians promoting a narrative.[80] There is no way to confirm that the "hate crimes" took place. There is certainly no due process for the accused.

Some examples of these vicious crimes according to the report:

> A white man catcalled me, then aggressively followed me down the block, and got inches from my face and yelled "Ch*nk!" and "C*nt!" after realizing I was Asian. Lots of neighbors were standing outside their homes and no one intervened. (Brooklyn, NY)
>
> As I was shopping, a white woman and what I am assuming was her husband came into the aisle I was in. They gave me dirty looks and just looked me up and down like they were disgusted with me. I tried to ignore it the best I could so I just walked away. To add to the story, I am a part of the LGBTQ+ community so I was wearing a mask that showed love and support for the community. As I walked away, the woman proceeded to walk up to me and stop me. She looked me up and down and said these exact words: "Oh so you're one of them?" And I was of course confused but then I remembered I had on the LGBTQ+ mask. I politely responded "Excuse me?" She proceeded to say slurs that were both directed towards Asians and the LGBTQ+ community. (Jefferson, KY)
>
> Two white, middle-aged men, who have been my neighbors for over fifteen years, approached me threateningly on the street, pulled down the corners of their eyes and said, "Go back to Wuhan, b*tch and take the virus with you!" When I called them vile, they then called me a "Thai wh*re" and threatened to beat up my husband. (West Vancouver, Canada)
>
> During an Asian American protest, a white man driving a silver Mercedes drove past the first wave of Asian protesters yelling out of

his window at them, "Stupid f*cking Asians!" Afterwards, he drove to where the remaining Asian protesters stood and was witnessed by multiple protesters aggressively driving onto the walkway where several protesters were gathered. Several elderly Hmong women jumped out of the way. An 8-year-old boy, who stood in the path of the oncoming vehicle, was startled into action and quickly moved out of the way towards safety. (Elk Grove, CA)

I came into the coffee shop at Mercato and people started leaving the area where I sat one by one. People started coming in and they sat on the other side of the coffee shop away from me. I became isolated on one side of the coffee shop. (Naples, FL) [81]

A month before the Harris/Bonta article in April 2020, the Stop AAPI Hate founders wrote a joint op-ed published at the Los Angeles Times titled "Op-Ed: Trump's racist comments are fueling hate crimes against Asian Americans. Time for state leaders to step in".[82]

Stop AAPI Hate has a very strong interest in proving their narrative. After all, they received $10 million from California taxpayers.[83] Additionally, Kamala Harris's friend Phil Ting "secured $1.4 million in state funds" for the Stop AAPI Hate website.[84]

Kamala Harris with Phil Ting

Harris's May 20, 2021, comments were made in her official capacity as Vice President at the "AAPI Unity Summit" hosted by the AAPI Victory Fund. The founder of the AAPI Victory Fund, Shekar Narasimhan, introduced Kamala Harris.

The LA Times reported[85] in 2016 that the AAPI Victory Fund is "focused on voter registration and turnout in battleground states" for the Asian American and Pacific Islander population. Currently, the group boasts that they are "the only national political action committee" dedicated to "increasing AAPI representation in elected offices and winning elections for candidates that share our progressive values."[86]

This vision is perfectly aligned with the "New American Majority" strategy of racial voter registration designed to ultimately give the Democratic Party a one-party state. So, it makes sense that AAPI Victory Fund founder Shekar Narasimhan also sits on the board of the Democracy Alliance.[87]

Last word from the Committee of 100

The Committee of 100 was interested in a judge like Goodwin Liu, so might they also be interested in a prominent leftist Senator or Presidential candidate with lots of Maoist connections?

On November 9, 2020, Zhengyu Huang, President of C-100 issued a statement congratulating Joe Biden and Kamala Harris on their recent election victory:

> *Committee of 100 congratulates President-elect Joseph Biden and Vice President-elect Kamala Harris on their 2020 election victory...*
>
> *With geopolitical tensions rising and nationalistic and anti-immigration sentiments inflamed over recent years, this is a critical moment in US history to showcase how various racial and ethnic groups have contributed to US prosperity. C100 supports the full inclusion and advancement of the more than five million Chinese Americans in the US and we believe that America is stronger because of our immigrant heritage and diverse citizenry. We encourage the new US administration to openly address issues of systemic bias against all Americans across our great democracy.*
>
> *C100 looks forward to the opportunity to engage the Biden/Harris administration and the newly elected US Congress in promoting the full participation of Chinese Americans in all aspects of American life and to engage in fair and constructive relations between the leaders and people of the United States and Greater China.*[88]

That's the Chinese propaganda line right there. America needs to deal with its "systemic racism" and its "anti-Asian bias" and Biden/Harris are just the people to do it.

It is also clear that Vice President Harris has gone out of her way to push these Chinese propaganda points during her term of office.

In February 2023, representatives of the Committee of 100, plus the previously mentioned AAPI Victory Fund, as well as the Council of Korean Americans and the Japanese American Citizens League were invited celebrate the Lunar New Year at the private home of Vice-President Harris.

Committee of 100

Press Releases

AAPI Victory Fund, Committee of 100, Council of Korean Americans, and Japanese American Citizens League Celebrate Lunar New Year with Vice President Kamala Harris

17th February 2023

The four groups issued a press release on February 17, commenting on their visit with Vice-President Harris, though from its tone and content, it may as well have been issued by the Chinese Consulate:

> *In the midst of growing hatred and violence against the AAPI community, it's been a blessing to be able to come together and celebrate traditions and holidays of such deep meaning, particularly with friends at Committee of 100, Council of Korean Americans, and the Japanese American Citizens League – with whom we look forward to growing in partnership,' said Brad Jenkins, CEO and President of the AAPI Victory Fund. 'We also thank Vice President Kamala Harris for opening her home to our community to celebrate the Lunar New Year.'*
>
> *'On behalf of Committee of 100… We are grateful for the opportunity to work with the Korean American and Japanese*

American communities towards shared goals and visions,' said Zhengyu Huang, President of Committee of 100. 'We look forward to working together to combat xenophobia, racism, and violence directed at the AAPI community and to celebrate the vibrant AAPI cultures as part of American culture.'

'We are especially thankful to Vice President Kamala Harris for honoring Asian Americans and graciously opening her residence to us,' said Abraham Kim, Executive Director of the Council of Korean Americans (CKA). 'The event was an inspiring first step towards our shared vision of strengthening AANHPI collaboration across boundaries...'

...added David Inoue, Executive Director of the Japanese American Citizens League. 'We look forward to further building on both our shared and unique experiences to collaborate across the spectrum of Asian and other communities that make up the rich fabric of our country. Just as the Lunar New Year brings a sense of hope, we look forward to a bright future working together in solidarity.'[89]

With Kamala Harris, all roads lead back to the Chinese Communist Party.

CHAPTER 7

TIM WALZ'S MIDWESTERN COMMUNIST ROOTS

TIM WALZ, HAILING from the Midwest, was chosen by Kamala Harris as her running mate, which reveals more about Harris's alignment with Marxist/Maoist ideologies than it does about representing traditional heartland American values.

EARLY LIFE

The son of a public-school administrator and "community activist", Tim Walz was born in West Point, Nebraska on April 6, 1964. Raised in a rural community, Walz graduated from Butte High School.[1]

Walz enlisted in the Army National Guard, and started teaching at an Indian Reservation, where he became inspired to become a teacher. In 1989, he graduated from Chadron State College with a bachelor's degree.

From Tim Walz's Congressional biography:

> *During his adolescence, Tim's parents instilled in him the Catholic values that propelled him into a life of service. When Walz enlisted in the Army National Guard at the young age of 17, he had no way of knowing he would spend more than two decades serving America as a member of the Guard. After high school, Walz worked a number of odd jobs before accepting a temporary teaching position at the Native American Reservation in Pine Ridge, South Dakota. It was his experience*

Meet Tim

at the Pine Ridge reservation that convinced Tim to follow his father's lead and become an educator.

Prior to his retirement, Tim Walz was the highest ranking enlisted National Guard soldier in southern Minnesota. In 1989, Walz earned a B.S. in social science education from Chadron State College in Nebraska. That year he earned the title of Nebraska Citizen-Soldier of the Year.[2]

Walz's biography mentions that he "earned the title of Nebraska Citizen-Soldier of the Year", a claim that follows a longtime pattern of padding his resume. In fact, Eliana Johnson of the Washington Free Beacon found that the assertion "is a significant exaggeration that makes it sound like Walz was the sole recipient of an award."

Johnson writes:

Walz was one of 52 reservists in 1989 who were invited to a brunch in Omaha for the '31st Annual Citizen Soldiers Awards,' put on by the Aksarben Foundation, a local non-profit that, at the time, owned a race track and funded community events through horse betting.[3]

This deception is one of many one finds when studying Tim Walz's life.

Tim Walz goes to China

In China in January 1987, Hu Yaobang was accused of "bourgeois liberalization"[4] (oriented toward free market and individualism over the collective). While he was forced to resign from his position as General Secretary of the Chinese Communist Party, he was still attending Politburo meetings. It was at one of these meetings on April 8, 1989, that he suffered a heart attack and ultimately died April 15, 1989, at age 73.

Hu Yaobang's death sparked the movement which culminated in a military crackdown on June 4, 1989, known as the Tiananmen Square massacre. The death toll for the massacre varies widely and is obscured by the Chinese Communist Party. On the first anniversary of the massacre, Time Magazine reported that "Chinese Red Cross sources told reporters that 2,600 people died and 10,000 were injured, although the organization later denied it."[5]

Shortly after the massacre, Tim Walz went to China to teach English to young Chinese students. The experience profoundly shaped Walz's perspective and life trajectory.

"No matter how long I live I'll never be treated that well again," Walz said as reported at a local Nebraska paper in 1990. "They gave me more gifts than I could bring home. It was an excellent experience," he continued. Walz did reference the Chinese Communist Party's response to the Tiananmen Square uprising, saying that the massacre will "always" invoke "bitter memories" in China.[6] These jabs to the Chinese Communist Party are reminiscent of what author Peter Schweizer warns is a Chinese tactic referred to as "Big Help With A Little Bad-Mouth".[7]

As explained by author Seamus Bruner, Director of Research for the Government Accountability Institute:

> *The Chinese Communist Party has an expression for this [tactic]. It is called 'Big Help With A Little Bad-Mouth'. So, you are allowed to say a few bad things every once in a while about the CCP as long as you're friendly towards them, as long as you don't call for say - sanctions; as long as you bash Donald Trump for his so-called trade war with China...*[8]

While Walz praises the Chinese Communist Party, he also pays lip service to the crimes of the CCP for Western consumption.

As time moved forward, Walz's dedication to China only grew deeper. Tim and his wife's 1995 honeymoon was a "trip to China with 60 kids in tow."[9] According to an article titled "Honeymoon in China" dated January 09, 1994, Walz *chose* the five year anniversary of the Tiananmen Square massacre, June 4, 1994, for his wedding date because - according to his bride-to-be Gwen Whipple - "[He] wanted to have a date he'll always remember."

Not only did Walz deliberately choose the day of the Tiananmen Square massacre for his wedding date, he and his bride decided to "make two trips with groups of 25 to 30 high-school students for two weeks in China."

From the 1994 profile:

> *Tim Walz should have no problem remembering his wedding anniversary date. Or his upcoming honeymoon overseas. The 29-year-old Alliance teacher and lifelong student of the Far East will marry fellow teacher Gwen Whipple on June 4, 1994 - the fifth anniversary of the uprising in China's Tiananmen Square. 'He wanted to have a date he'll always remember,' Whipple said. For their honeymoon, Walz and Whipple will make two trips with groups of 25 to 30 high-school students for two weeks in China.*[10]

The author of the 1994 article also revealed that the young teacher "visited Vietnam, Japan, Taiwan, and Korea in the summer of 1992." Walz additionally claimed that "a friend in China's foreign affairs department" arranged a 1993 trip "[W]ith eight other adult sponsors [who] took 26 teenagers to China in 1993."

Tim Walz and and American student in China

Walz "always has been fascinated by Communist China," the article continued. "He remembers from his childhood pictures of Mao Tse-tung, hung in public places and carried in parades," the author explained.[11]

Walz reportedly conceived of having his honeymoon in China while he was first teaching there. A "friend helped contact the authorities and funding came through from the government." The students on Walz's trips enjoyed a "special status" that "let them go places other people can't." The students would also be taken to a university to teach them about Chinese governance. Tim Walz also reportedly urged students to "downplay their America-ness."[12]

Back to Tim Walz's Congressional biography:

> *With his teaching degree complete, Harvard University offered Walz an opportunity to gain a new perspective on global education by teaching in the People's Republic of China. Working in China during 1989-1990, Walz was a member of one of the first*

government sanctioned groups of American educators to teach in Chinese high schools.[13]

Tim Walz's implication that he was approached by Harvard for the China opportunity appears to be a part of the previously discussed pattern of resume inflation.

The Washington Free Beacon called out Walz's deception:

> …*In the same 2006 campaign biography he used to launch his congressional campaign, Walz cites a yearlong stint teaching in China. It's another credential he has inflated over the years, telling voters that Harvard hand picked him to travel to Asia.*
>
> *'Harvard University offered Walz an opportunity to gain a new perspective on global education by teaching in the People's Republic of China,' the biography claims. His congressional biography, published after Walz had won his seat, said the same thing. Indeed, a 2018 version indicated that Walz taught in China 'through a program at Harvard University.'*
>
> *The program in question is the WorldTeach program, a nonprofit founded by Harvard undergraduates, including the Nobel Prize-winning economist Michael Kremer, in 1986. For a time, the program was funded by Harvard's Phillips Brooks House Association, which the Harvard Crimson has characterized as 'a student-run community service group' that disburses resources to an array of nonprofit organizations and facilitates volunteerism for Harvard students. WorldTeach, which is currently dormant, does not appear to have ever been an official program of Harvard.*
>
> *Walz, who is casting himself as a homespun midwesterner and mocks Republican vice presidential nominee J.D. Vance for attending Yale Law School, now omits any mention of Harvard from his biography.*[14]

Nevertheless, Walz's teaching stint at Foshan No 1 High School, Guandong Province China greatly defined his young career.

The future vice-presidential candidate "seized the opportunity to develop a program of cooperation between American and Chinese students"[15] after his return to the United States.

Through his "Educational Travel Adventures, Inc.", Walz "conducted annual educational trips to China for high school students".

Walz's new organization even included a "scholarship program that allows students to travel and study in China regardless of their financial situation."[16] The Chinese Communist Party (CCP) government contributed "a large part of the cost"[17] to Tim Walz's enterprise.

Tim Walz, front row, center

The Daily Dot quotes Michael Lucci of the anti-CCP organization State Armor Action on how Chinese authorities would likely have manipulated Tim Walz:

> *The CCP cultivating Tim Walz is textbook 'sub-national influence,' Lucci explained, laying out a five-step program of alleged infiltration and cultivation that he says the Chinese Communist Party has run on Walz, including establishing a relationship early in his life, 'softening' his views on the country by frequent visits, maintaining a relationship with him, having Walz 'parrot' Chinese Communist Party propaganda, and 'capitaliz[ing] on the relationship at an opportune time' after playing the long game.*

Given his military connections and the obvious propaganda value of bringing impressionable young Americans to China, it's inevitable that Chinese intelligence services would have targeted young Tim Walz.

Tim Walz taught for a time at a Chinese university. He served at one point as a visiting Fellow of International Relations at the Macau Polytechnic University, a position that "helped develop his knowledge of China's unique international status".[18]

Almost certainly Tim Walz would have earned the close attention of the Chinese spy services by this point.

Tim Walz in Congress

After being elected to Congress in 2006, Tim Walz continued advocating for and traveling to China.

On June 4, 2009, then Congressional-Executive Commission on China member Tim Walz spoke at a hearing of the commission marking the 20th anniversary of the Tiananmen Square Massacre. During his speech, Walz compared the 1863 execution of 38 Dakota men[19] (not women and children, as stated by Walz) for their role in the massacre of civilians as ordered by President Abraham Lincoln to the Tiananmen Square massacre:

To watch what happened at the end of the day on June 4 was something that many of us will never forget, we pledge to never forget, and bearing witness and accurate telling of history is absolutely crucial for any nation to move forward. I thank the Chairman for this very insightful and timely hearing, and the nature of it in terms of where we go from here, how our relationships are shaped and what happens.

Every nation has its dark periods that it must come to grips with. This Nation is no exception, and we still struggle with that. I took the first teaching job that I had at a place called Wounded Knee in South Dakota that many of us in this room know well, and I hail from the city of Mankato, Minnesota that has the distinction of being the site of the largest mass execution of Native Americans in American history, 38 men, women, and children hung the day after Christmas in 1863. Those are issues that all must be addressed, and every nation, as it matures and it deals with its human rights issues, moves to become a better nation.[20]

In 2013, Tim Walz became the Vice Ranking and then Ranking Member on the Congressional-Executive Commission on China. He would remain on the Commission until he ran for governor.

In 2014, Walz greeted a Chinese delegation and claimed that "When we work together and when we collaborate together, there's nothing we can't solve."[21]

In November 2015, Tim Walz travelled to China, Hong Kong and Tibet as part of a Congressional delegation led by then-Speaker of the House Nancy Pelosi. The delegation included several other far-left Congressmembers including Jim McGovern (D-MA), Joyce Beatty (D-OH), Alan Lowenthal (D-CA), Ted Lieu (D-CA), and Betty McCollum (D-MN).

From a Pelosi press release:

In Beijing, the delegation met with the Premier of the People's Republic of China, Li Keqiang; National People's Congress Chairman, Zhang Dejiang; and National People's Congress Vice Chairman, Zhang Ping:

The delegation and Chinese officials discussed the importance of building upon President Obama and President Xi's agreements on

*climate change, protection of cyber space and countering the prolif-
eration of nuclear weapons.*

*At Peking University, the delegation participated in a climate
change forum with students who shared their determination to
address the climate crisis...* [22]

On his return to the US, Tim Walz told the Star-Tribune that the
Chinese should be commended for its "spectacular" infrastructure. "I
think China rightfully feels a sense of pride on that ... but I think
it's safe to say the human rights aspects are lagging a little behind," he
said.[23] The bland rebuke is a clear example of the afore-mentioned "Big
Help With A Little Bad-Mouth".

In a 2016 interview with Agri-Pulse, Governor Walz stated:

*I've lived in China and as I've said I've been there about 30
times...I don't fall into the category that China necessarily needs
to be an adversarial relationship; I totally disagree...* [24]

So, Walz was a great advocate for the Chinese Communist Party
while he was in Congress. His lifelong advocacy for China continued
after being elected in 2018 as Governor of Minnesota.

Tim Walz as Governor

In October 2019, the US-China Peoples Friendship Association
(USCPFA) held its national convention in Minneapolis, Minnesota, a
state deeply affected by trade disputes due to its significant soybean
exports to China. This backdrop set the stage for the event where Tim
Walz was not only a participant but a featured speaker.[25]

Shillman Journalism Fellow at the David Horowitz Freedom Center,
Daniel Greenfield, analyzes the significance of Tim Walz's role in the
event, giving context to so-called "Friendship Associations" and Walz's
appearance as a battering ram against President Donald Trump:

*With the United States and China engaged in a heated trade war,
the US-China Peoples Friendship Association (USCPFA) sched-
uled its national convention in Minneapolis.*

*Minnesota's soybean trade made it China's best leverage against
President Trump's tariffs and the regime was fortunate to have one
of its own in the governor's residency.*

> Gov. Tim Walz was the highest ranking elected official with
> the broadest ties to China. And so it surprised no one when the
> US-China Peoples Friendship Association listed him as one of its
> speakers at the convention alongside notable Communist influence
> operation figures.

Greenfield explained that Walz went on an overseas trip with his Lieutenant Governor Peggy Flanagan, a once "Senior Trainer" at Wellstone Action, which will be discussed in the next section. As described by Greenfield, the trip was "actually a propaganda move to stir up opposition to Trump's trade war":

> Earlier that year, Walz had gone on a foreign trip to Asia along
> with his Lt. Gov: leaving no one in charge of Minnesota. While the
> trip was ostensibly undertaken to find alternative trading partners
> to China, it was actually a propaganda move to stir up opposition
> to Trump's trade war.
> In September 2019, Gov. Walz returned claiming that the state's
> farmers 'remain in desperate need of a US trade deal with China.'
> 'There's just no substitute for 1.6 billion consumers who are
> hungry to get our China trade negotiations normalized,' he claimed.

The US-China Peoples Friendship Association convention may sound innocuous but is a part of the Chinese Communist Party's "United Front" influence operations as discussed later in this chapter. From Greenfield:

> And next month in October, it was time for the USCPFA conven-
> tion. While the USCPFA represents itself as an alliance of ordinary
> citizens seeking better relations, it had started out as a Communist
> front group. Revolution magazine wrote that 'Communists, mem-
> bers of the Revolutionary Union (and later the Revolutionary
> Communist Party) were instrumental in the formation of the ear-
> liest local Friendship Associations in 1971 and played a significant
> role in the creation of the national association and in the building
> of locals across the country.'
> In his book 'Red Destinies', historian Colin B. Burke wrote that
> the USCPFA 'like the Party's front organizations of the 1930s and
> 1940s it was advertised as a liberal, non-political organization

supporting peace and cultural understanding. But in 1971, the founders had other missions: Advance the interests of Communist China and world communism.'

Governor Tim Walz had to be very naïve - or very complicit – to take part in the USCPFA convention considering his fellow speaker Li Xiaolin. Greenfield continues:

> *When Gov. Tim Walz showed up at the USCPFA convention, the most obvious sign of the organization's close ties to China's influence operation came from Walz's fellow speaker. ...Li Xiaolin, the president of the Chinese People's Association for Friendship with Foreign Countries (CPAFFC), which leads a billion-dollar Chinese influence operation flagged by the US State Department for 'directly and malignly influencing' American politicians.*
>
> *Another politician might have pleaded ignorance, but Gov. Tim Walz had been promoted as 'one of a select few members of the Legislative Branch with extensive, on-the-ground experience in the Middle Kingdom.' He had probably spent more time in China than any major American elected official.[26]*

*"Forty Years and Beyond:
Friendship, Successes, and Challenges"*

USCPFA 27th
National Convention
October 18 –20, 2019
Minneapolis, Minnesota

PRESENTATIONS (subject to confirmation)

University of Minnesota Asian Studies Prof. Emeritus **Edward (Ted) Farmer**, and early founder of USCPFA Minnesota Chapter: Ted Farmer has been a teacher and deep thinker about modern China since the 1960's, and brings deep insight into US-China relations during the 20th and 21st centuries.

Mr. **Wing Young Huie**, winner of 2019 Minnesota Book Award in Memoir and Creative Nonfiction for his book *Chinese-ness*: Mr. Huie is a professional photographer, mentor, and lecturer whose perspective on growing up Chinese-American in mid-20th century Minnesota is beautifully captured in this award winning book.

Ms. **Sarah Lande**: who provided Midwestern hospitality to Xi Jinping in Iowa in 1985 and again in 2012, will share her reflections on those experiences with President Xi and Iowa's then-Governor (now US Ambassador to China) Terry Branstad.

Minnesota Governor **Tim Walz**: Gov. Walz is an educator and former Congressman who taught in China (Taiwan) in the 1980s; he has been invited to speak about his experiences and Minnesota's connections with China.

Mme. **Li Xiaolin**, President, Chinese People's Association for Friendship with Foreign Countries (You Xie) has been invited.

Representatives of the Harbin Foreign Affairs Office have indicated they will attend to share their experiences with the USCPFA-MN. Harbin has been Minneapolis' Sister City in China for over 25 years.

SCHEDULE

- Friday morning and afternoon, October 18: National Board meeting at hotel.
- Friday afternoon: Arrival and registration; free time at Minnesota Valley National Wildlife Refuge (adjacent to Hotel)
- Ongoing: "40 Videos for 40 Years"
- Friday evening, October 18: Welcome reception and dinner. Greetings from USCPFA leaders; MC and comedy by Jack Tsai and/or Harkness and Shapiro (pioneering student visitors to the PRC)
- Saturday morning, October 19: Breakfast, Opening Plenary Session; presentations; discussion groups for resolutions or amendments
- Lunch at hotel [speaker TBD]
- Saturday afternoon, October 19: Field trip via bus to St. Paul – Changsha China Friendship Garden and Minneapolis Institute of Art Asian Art Collection.
- Saturday evening, October 19: Gala Convention banquet at hotel with awards and performances
- Sunday morning, October 20: Breakfast regional meetings; presentations, closing Plenary Session
- Convention ends at noon Sunday

Members who wish to submit resolutions, bylaw amendments and / or statements of candidacy for President or Treasurer should mail or email documents by August 1, 2019, to Paul Morris, Agenda Committee, 2234 NE 25th Ave., Portland, OR 97212, pemorris07@gmail.com.	The Membership Committee will send each chapter a notice with the September 1, 2019, cut-off date for membership valuation to determine members eligible for voting at the Convention. One copy of the Plenary Guide will be sent to each chapter leader to duplicate and share as necessary.

Tim Walz's USCPFA convention co-speaker Li Xiaolin is Chinese Communist Party "royalty".

She is the daughter of Li Xiannian, president of China from 1983 to 1988 under paramount leader Deng Xiaoping[27] and then chairman of the Chinese People's Political Consultative Conference from 1988 until his death. He was a full member of the CCP Politburo from 1956 to 1987, and of its Standing Committee from 1977 to 1987.

Li Xiannian was regarded as the *most left wing* of the so-called "Eight Elders" of the CCP,[28] who were notorious for ordering the military crackdown on protesters in Beijing, the previously mentioned "Tiananmen Square Massacre" of June 1989.[29]

Li Xiaolin served as First Secretary of the Chinese Embassy the USA. From 1992 to 2007, Li alternatively served as deputy director and director of the Department of the Americas at the Chinese People 's Association for Friendship with Foreign Countries, as well as vice-chairperson and deputy CCP secretary of the CPAFFC.[30]

Tim Walz shared the podium with a bona fide CCP "princess". How does Li Xiaolin feel about her father ordering the murder of thousands during the Tiananmen Square Massacre?

CCP 'UNITED FRONT' INFLUENCE OPERATIONS

Tim Walz has been deeply linked to events hosted by the Chinese American Association of Minnesota (CAAM) and the St. Paul branch of the Overseas Chinese Service Center (OCSC). Both organizations have ties to the Chinese Communist Party's United Front Work Department, which is a part of a larger CCP "United Front" influence operation strategy, as revealed by a Daily Caller investigation.[31]

These Overseas Chinese Service Centers are more commonly known as "secret Chinese police stations" and have been used by the Chinese Communist Party to intimidate and even kidnap overseas Chinese who may be critical of the Beijing regime.[32] The Overseas Chinese Service Centers challenge the very principles that maintain national boundaries and sovereignty.

Since 2016, CAAM and another local nonprofit have been hosting the St. Paul branch of the OCSC program.[33]

According to a 2022 report published by the House Select Committee on the Chinese Communist Party, the "United Front" strategy is used for nefarious means:

> United Front work is a unique blend of engagement, influence activities, and intelligence operations that the Chinese Communist Party (CCP) uses to shape its political environment, including to influence other countries' policy toward the PRC and to gain access to advanced foreign technology.[34]

The Central United Front Work Department (UFWD) "reports directly to the CCP's Central Committee", according to a House Select Committee on the CCP in a 2023 memo "United Front 101".[35] The United Front web consists of "an extensive network of organizations and individuals... [who] look to influence universities, think tanks, civic groups, other prominent individuals and institutions, and public opinion broadly."[36]

Walz's participation in these CCP-linked events include a 2022 fundraiser for his own gubernatorial campaign, which "was organized by CAAM's former president" KaiMay Yuen Terry.

June 2, 2022, Walz Fundraiser found at Archived 'Minnesota Chinese World' article

June 2, 2022, Walz Fundraiser found at Archived 'Minnesota Chinese World' article

Interestingly, an August 2024 article from "Minnesota Chinese World" detailing some of the events featuring Tim Walz was deleted after Philip Lenczycki, the author of the Daily Caller piece, "reached out for comment." The archived version[37] details some of these events, gushing that Walz [translated by Google] "has forged an indissoluble bond with the Chinese community in our Twin Cities of Minnesota, and is often invited as a VIP guest to participate in relevant charity activities in our Chinese community."

According to Lenczycki, Yan Bingwen, the Overseas Chinese Service Centers "co-head", was at the CAAM Fundraiser, along with OCSC "propaganda chief," Deng Qing:[38]

Image posted on X by Philip Lenczycki on August 27, 2024

Philip Lenczycki pointed out that several Republican Senators have reached out to the Justice Department about the CCP-linked Overseas Chinese Service Centers based in part on his reporting.[39] "We write to express our grave concerns regarding reports of 'Overseas Chinese Service Centers' (OCSCs) operated by an intelligence service of the People's Republic of China (PRC) in conjunction with the PRC's national police force," the letter began. "US- based OCSC representatives met with officials of the PRC's national police force, the Ministry of Public Security (MPS), on a trip to China to discuss the use of technology to conduct 'cross-border remote justice services' overseas."

Further, Chairman on the House Committee on Oversight and Accountability, Representative James Comer has launched a probe into Tim Walz's CCP connections. In a letter to FBI Director Christopher Wray dated August 16, 2024, Comer requested "[A]ll documents and communications in the FBI's possession, including that of the Foreign Influence Task Force's, regarding any Chinese entity or individual with whom Mr. Walz may have engaged or partnered."[40]

Comer's letter cited research from investigative journalist Natalie Winters, who exposed Walz's address at the US China Peoples Friendship Association 2019 convention. Lenczycki quoted Winters as saying that the United Front Work Department "weaponizes American leaders against their own people by pushing them to advocate for policies favored by the CCP".[41]

Tim Walz's extensive engagements with entities linked to the Chinese Communist Party raise serious questions about his judgment and loyalty. Whether he's turning a blind eye to these connections for personal gain, such as political or financial benefits; or if he actively supports the CCP's agenda, the national security implications are deeply concerning.

As observed by Gordon G. Chang, noted CCP critic and author of "Plan Red: China's Project to Destroy America": "Speak like a communist, act like a communist, cavort with communists, and people might actually think you're a communist."[42]

Wellstone socialism

Tim Walz is very much part of the Wellstone movement, a near cult-like political current running through Minnesota politics that began after Senator Paul Wellstone died in a plane crash during his 2002 reelection campaign.

Senator Paul Wellstone

Tim Walz, in common with many in Minnesota, was a huge admirer of the late Senator. A 2022 article at the MinnPost quoted Tim Walz as stating: "...walking by the Wellstone for Senate office my senior year of college changed the entire trajectory of my life. I would not be where I am today if not for Senator Paul Wellstone and his vision for Minnesota." Walz continued to say it was "Wellstone's passion that inspired me to run for Congress in Southern Minnesota. Senator Wellstone never wavered from his convictions or his commitment to improving the lives of working people."[43]

Governor Tim Walz ✓
October 25, 2022 · 🌐   ...

Paul Wellstone's passion inspired me to run for Congress in Southern Minnesota. Senator Wellstone never wavered from his convictions or commitment to improving the lives of working people. 20 years after his death, Minnesotans continue to feel his legacy and loss.

Few Minnesotans seem to understand, or want to admit, that Paul Wellstone was a committed socialist.

Paul Wellstone was basically "Bernie Sanders before Bernie Sanders". Like the Senator from Vermont, Paul Wellstone was active in Jesse Jackson's Rainbow Coalition[44] and was deeply connected to the US's largest Marxist organization, Democratic Socialists of America (DSA).

In the late 1970s, Wellstone was involved with the New American Movement (NAM), a pro-China coalition of former Students for a Democratic Society radicals and Communist Party USA dissidents which merged into DSA in 1982.[45]

In the 1980s, Wellstone was the faculty adviser for the Young Democratic Socialists chapter at Carleton College, where he was teaching at the time.[46]

In 1990, DSA's Democratic Left, November/December issue stated:

> *Twin cities DSA in Minnesota continues its resurgence with ongoing support of Paul Wellstone's campaign for the Senate seat currently held by Republican Rudy Boschwitz.*
>
> *Local activists are doing literature drops and helping to raise money for this watershed campaign...Contributions, made out to Wellstone for US Senate, can be sent to the DSA national Office and will be forwarded to the campaign.[47]*

In 1996, DSA played a major role in re-electing Wellstone to the US Senate – says DSA leader Christine Riddiough:

> *Before I got to Minnesota the race was neck and neck, but in that last week before the election-coinciding with DSA's active involvement-Wellstone pulled out to a strong lead, finally winning by nine percent.*
>
> *I worked with the campaign's superbly organized grassroots efforts. I concentrated on organizing DSA members and members of the gay and lesbian community to round up volunteers for Wellstone. Then I rolled up my sleeves for endless rounds of calls to Wellstone supporters to make sure they got out to vote.*[48]

That year, national DSA formally endorsed Bernie Sanders for Congress in Vermont, and Paul Wellstone for US Senate in Minnesota.

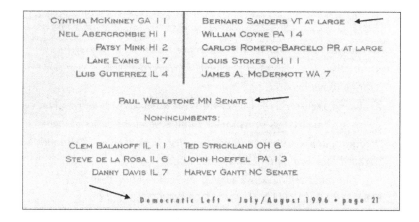

From 2000, Minnesota DSA decided to "focus all of its efforts as a group the next two years on reelecting Senator Paul Wellstone, who is closest to DSA's ideology. Although divided on Gore vs. Nader, they are 100% united behind Wellstone."[49]

DSA almost certainly believed that Wellstone was preparing to run for US President someday.

Tim Walz and the Wellstone 'Mafia'

Tim Walz began his political career training with Wellstone Action, a far-left training school established by Paul Wellstone's sons Paul and Mark, to fulfill their father's socialist legacy.

From the Jerusalem Post:

> In 2005, a high school geography teacher in rural Mankato, Minnesota, arrived at a politics boot camp named for a progressive Jewish senator, where he honed his skills in grassroots organizing and voter outreach.
>
> Nearly two decades later, Tim Walz is the Democratic vice presidential candidate.
>
> 'I'm excited because he's a winner,' David Wellstone said about Walz on Tuesday, following his selection. 'And he operates with integrity.'
>
> Wellstone, alongside his brother Mark, is the co-founder and former co-chair of Wellstone Action, the progressive training organization named in memory of their father, Minnesota Sen. Paul Wellstone. The brothers saw the organization as a way of inculcating their father's brand of populist progressivism in a new generation of politicians.
>
> Camp Wellstone, the boot camp Walz attended, was designed to teach aspiring leaders in Minnesota and beyond the basics of door-knocking and coalition-building in a few days. David Wellstone recalled that Walz immediately stood out.
>
> 'You could tell he was a leader,' he said, adding that the camp worked to mold the teacher into a candidate who could win.
>
> 'I would like to think, and I do think, that when Governor Walz went through Camp Wellstone, it helped shape the way that he politicked,' Wellstone said. Wellstone believes the camp formed 'the way that he connected to people, the way that he listened to people, which is what my dad did.'[50]

Since 2003, Wellstone Action (now known as "re:power"), is "proud to have supported over 100,000 candidates, elected officials, campaign managers, and community organizers from across the country through training, coaching, facilitation, campaigning, and capacity building."[51]

Like Steve Phillips's "New American Majority" strategy, it appears that re:power has embraced Maoist-style, race-based politics. Re:power is "dedicated to building a liberated multi-racial democracy", the group posted on August 24, 2024.[52]

re:power
@repowerorg

VP Kamala Harris is the first woman of color to become a major-party presidential nominee.

re:power is dedicated to building a liberated multi-racial democracy where such moments are possible. We hope her nomination inspires women of color to become leaders in their communities!

3:00 PM · Aug 21, 2024

X Post from re:power dated August 21, 2024

Many thousands have gone through "Camp Wellstone" in rotating sessions held all over the country. Thousands of alumni have gone on to play prominent roles in Minnesota and US politics.[53]

By 2010, forty of the 112 Democratic-Farmer-Labor (DFL) party lawmakers elected to the state legislature that year were Camp Wellstone alums.[54] DFL can be described as the Minnesota branch of the Democratic Party.

Other key Minnesota Wellstone alumni included Tim Walz and his future chief of staff Josh Syrjamaki, DFL chairman Ken Martin and State Auditor Rebecca Otto.[55]

Tim Walz and future Secretary of State Mark Ritchie graduated from the same Camp Wellstone three-day "bootcamp" in 2005. They were both trained by Peggy Flanagan, who today serves as Tim Walz's Lieutenant Governor.[56] As an aside, Tim Walz referred to Peggy Flanagan as his "mentor at Camp Wellstone" in 2017.[57]

Re:power Facebook Post dated August 14, 2024

Current St. Paul Mayor Melvin Carter was also among the trainers at the 2005 gathering.

Keith Ellison, currently Minnesota's Attorney General was also a Wellstone Action trainer, his onetime Chief of Staff Kari Moe is also a Wellstone alumnus.[58] "Paul Wellstone inspired me to run for office," Keith Ellison wrote on Facebook on October 25, 2020. "He was a hero to me and so many others. His spirit lives on in the struggle for justice. Stand up, keep fighting," he continued.[59]

Keith Ellison ✓
October 25, 2020 · 🌐   ...

Paul Wellstone inspired me to run for office. He was a hero to me and so many others. His spirit lives on in the struggle for justice. Stand up, keep fighting.

Remembering Paul, Sheila, Marcia, Mary, Tom, and Will today.

The current US Attorney for Minnesota Andy Luger is yet another Camp Wellstone graduate,[60] as is Minnesota Secretary of State Steve Simon.[61]

Just about every leader of the Minnesota Democratic Farmer-Labor-Party still worships at the Wellstone altar.

Is it fair to say that Minnesota today is run by the Wellstone "mafia"?

How red was Wellstone Action?

Several left leaning media outlets have run articles on Wellstone Action/Camp Wellstone since Tim Walz shot to international fame as Kamala Harris's vice presidential pick.

Most have portrayed the Wellstone operation as a mildly "progressive" training school for "community organizers" and aspiring political candidates.

That's a very misleading and superficial portrayal of the movement.

Many Wellstone people were from the hard left, including founder and longtime Director of Education and Training Pam Costain.

In 1976, Pam Costain, a member of the Twin Cities Women's Union, participated in the "Hard Times Conference" held from January 30 to February 1 at the University of Chicago. This event was organized by the notorious Weather Underground, a terrorist left-wing group known for its bombings in the late '60s and '70s, and their above-ground affiliate, the Prairie Fire Organizing Committee.[62]

The infamous Bernardine Dohrn,[63] a well-known leader of Weather Underground and the wife of the equally infamous Bill Ayres, was actively involved in the Hard Times Conference.

Several Wellstone Action officials were closely connected to the Minnesota Communist Party, included currently-serving Minnesota Attorney General Keith Ellison.[64] Speaking of Keith Ellison, he also addressed a fundraiser held on February 12, 2000, for Weather Underground terrorist Sara Jane Olson keynoted by Bernardine Dohrn.[65,66] That event was hosted by the far-left legal activist group founded by the Communist Party USA, the National Lawyers Guild.[67,68]

For several years, the Wellstone Action Advisory Board included several hard-core leftists and a few Democratic Socialists of America comrades including the infamous Frances Fox Piven[69] - a close friend and ally of Paul Wellstone.[70]

Frances Fox Piven and her equally Marxist husband Richard Cloward[71] were behind President Bill Clinton's 1993 "Motor Voter" law – which was designed primarily to bring more low propensity young and minority voters into the New American Majority.

Frances Fox Piven, second from left, Richard Cloward center

Before Wellstone transitioned to become re:power: more Maoist-leaning influences were starting to become apparent.

Jennifer Pae, for instance, was a Wellstone Action trainer, running Camp Wellstone courses around the country. She was also the former director of FairVote California, where her Deputy Director was Pedro Hernandez[72] of FRSO/Liberation Road.

Elections 2020: Covid-19, the Left
and the uprising against racist violence

Online webinar June 22 at 9pm (eastern time)
Cosponsored by Liberation Road and CCDS socialist education project

Speakers: Pedro Hernandez, Liberation Road; Carl Davidson CCDS, & 3rd speaker TBA

Pedro Hernandez--Pedro is an elections expert, voting rights advocate, and member of Liberation Road

Carl Davidson--Carl is on CCDS National Committee, LeftRoots Compa, Steel Valley DSA, USW Local 3657.

Committees of Correspondence for Democracy and Socialism, 'The Mobilizer', June 2020, pg. 1

Jennifer Pae has also and served as Project Director for PowerPAC[73] and as a PowerPAC+ board member.[74]

Wellstone Action's successor organization re:power has become top-heavy with Steve Phillips and FRSO/Liberation Road-aligned activists.

+ Executive Director Karundi Williams is a 2020 alum of the FRSO/Liberation Road-linked Rockwood Leadership Institute in Oakland California.[75]
+ Board chair Carmen Berkley has served on the Advisory Board of Steve Phillips's staff recruitment organization Inclusv.[76]
+ Board member Sarah Audelo was a 2018 Rockwood Leadership Institute National Alum[77] and served on the Advisory Board of the Movement Voter Project with Van Jones, Marvin Randolph, Andy Wong and several other Steve Phillips collaborators.[78]
+ Board member Aaron Dorfman was a 2010 Rockwood Leadership Institute National Alum.[79]

- Board member Jennifer Epps-Addison was a 2017 Rockwood Leadership Institute National Alum.[80] She was also serves on the Advisory Board of Aimee Allison's She the People organization.[81]
- Board member Katrina Gamble served on the Advisory Board of the PowerPAC.org "partner" organization Movement Voter Project.[82]
- Board member Jessica Morales Rocketto has served on the Advisory Board of Steve Phillips's Inclusv[83] and was a leader of the National Domestic Workers Alliance.[84]
- Board member Justin Myers was a 2021 Rockwood Leadership Institute National Alum.[85]
- Board member Art Reyes III is a leader of the Seed the Vote "partner" group We The People Michigan.[86]
- Board member Luna Yasui was a 2013 Rockwood Leadership Institute National Alum[87] and a former Policy Director of Chinese for Affirmative Action.[88]

Clearly, re:power/Wellstone Action has moved firmly into the "New American Majority" camp.

Minnesota communists secret meeting

On December 5, 1999, a national Communist Party USA (CPUSA) meeting was held at the May Day Bookstore in Minneapolis, Minnesota, for the purpose of re-establishing the party's "Farm Commission".

Party members present were Erwin Marquit, Helvi Savola, Jack Brown, Peter Molenaar, Morgan Soderberg, Bill Gudex, Mark Froemke, Scott Marshall, Gary Severson, Mike Madden, Becky Pera, Charlie Smith and Tim Wheeler.

Mark Ritchie, of the far-left Institute for Agriculture and Trade Policy, also attended and addressed the meeting. In a written report on the meeting by Tim Wheeler, Ritchie is referred to as a "non-party friend". The report was marked "not for publication":[89]

Report on the CPUSA farm meeting, Minneapolis, Dec. 5, 1999
(Not for publication)
The Communist Party USA convened a day-long meeting at the May
Day Bookstore in Minneapolis Dec. 5. to discuss the crisis of family and
independent farmers.
Those present: Erwin Marquit, Helvi Savola, Jack Brown, Peter
Molenaar, Morgan Soderberg, Bill Gudex, Mark Froemke, Scott Marshall,
Gary Severson, Mike Madden, Becky Pera, Charlie Smith, Tim Wheeler.
The meeting took place in an atmosphere of great enthusiasm because
four of those present had just returned from Seattle where farmers were
strongly represented in the fightback against the WTO and globalized
monopoly capitalism. All four gave reports on the "Battle in Seattle."
Mark Ritchie, a non-party friend, executive director of the
Minneapolis-based Institute on Trade and Agricultural Policy, had chaired
the farm-agricultural rally of over 5,000 people in Seattle. He opened our
meeting with a report on Seattle and gave us an in-depth analysis of the
current farm crisis. He spent the entire morning session with us.
His main points: The powerful new coalition in Seattle based on
farmers-labor-environmental-religious and other human rights
organizations "stopped the WTO. It is a tremendous victory." Ritchie, who
is also a member of the U.S. delegation to the WTO, said the key to the
collapse of the WTO Ministerial meeting was a "revolt by Third World
delegates who looked out their hotel windows and saw what was happening
in the streets and said to themselves, 'We are not alone. Millions of
Americans agree with us! We don't have to just go along with the dictates
of the big capitalist powers.'" They rejected the U.S. diktat and the whole
meeting ended in failure.

The fact that Mark Ritchie was able to address and attend a secret
high level CPUSA meeting meant that he had to be extremely-well
trusted by the assembled party leaders.

Mark Ritchie also went on to mention Senator Paul Wellstone
twice, in the context that he and far-left Senator Tom Harkin (D-IA)
were already moving in line with Communist Party agricultural
policies.[90]

Several of the Minnesota attendees listed above would go on to
play a prominent role in Minnesota (and national politics).

The Mark Ritchie connection

Governor Walz has worked closely with Communist Party USA
"non-party friend" Mark Ritchie since they first met in a 2005 Camp
Wellstone training course.

Mark Ritchie

As an organizer with the Minneapolis-based Institute for Agriculture and Trade Policy and as founder of the League of Rural Voters, Mark Ritchie worked with Paul Wellstone to "improve conditions for farmers and other rural Americans."[91]

Veteran Democratic Socialists of America comrade Peter Dreier wrote about Mark Ritchie and Paul Wellstone for the Chicago-based socialist journal In The Times:

> 'Paul was one of the first people that I knew who moved from issue activism and direct action organizing to electoral politics,' Ritchie recalled. 'He had incredible integrity. He was an inspiration. Not just the legislation he worked on. But also the way he connected with people. After Paul died, I was one of a number of people— activists who had worked with Paul—who decided that we ought to run for public office and help keep Paul's legacy alive.' He called Wellstone Action's three-day 'boot camp' for candidates 'the perfect training for coming to terms with what it actually meant to run for office.'[92]

Mark Ritchie was already moving from mainly organizing farm and rural issues to more electorally focused work.

In 2003, Ritchie led National Voice, a "national coalition of over two thousand community-based organizations from across the country working together to increase non-partisan civic engagement and voter participation."

National Voice, through their "November 2" media campaign,

registered over 5 million new voters nationwide, making the effort one of the largest non-partisan voter mobilizations in our nation's history. Over "four hundred Minnesota churches, businesses, unions, schools, and community groups participated in the campaign."[93]

In 2006, Mark Ritchie, running on the Democratic-Farmer-Labor Party ticket defeated incumbent Republican Secretary of State Mary Kiffmeyer, to take the position.

In a July 8, 2006, article at the CPUSA's People's World titled "This Battle Can Be Won!", the author underlined the importance of the elections for Secretary of State, "whose job is mandated as protecting voting rights and election practices".

The unnamed author also wrote "[I]n Minnesota the DFL candidate for Secretary of State Mark Ritchie, of the League of Rural Voters could play a valuable national role."[94]

How did comrade author know?

AL FRANKEN GETS 'ELECTED'

In 2008, Minnesota Secretary of State Mark Ritchie oversaw one of the most contentious Senate races in US history.

After a super close November 4th election, well within the margin for a compulsory recount, and after a legal battle lasting over eight months, the DFL candidate, Al Franken, defeated Republican incumbent Norm Coleman to claim a seat in the US Senate.

Mark Ritchie supervised the recount, during which the lead fluctuated several times, ultimately resulting in Al Franken's victory by a mere 312 votes out of approximately 2.9 million cast. This was a critical victory for the Democrats, giving them a filibuster proof 60 seat majority – which enabled the passing of Obamacare and other "progressive" legislation.

Former Republican Secretary of State Mary Kiffmeyer made it clear that changes in election procedures under Ritchie's administration directly affected the integrity and outcome of the Senate race:

According to Fox News:

> *According to Kiffmeyer, as soon as Ritchie took office he began dismantling much of the framework that had been assembled to ensure honest voting in the state. It was that loosening of election controls,*

she argues, that lead to the eight month standoff between incumbent Senator Norm Coleman and challenger Al Franken in what was one of the closest Senate race ever.

Kiffmeyer is 'absolutely sure' that Ritchie's efforts to eliminate voting regulations ensured Franken's victory.

'The first thing he did when he got into office was to dismantle the ballot reconciliation program we started. Under that program districts are required to check that the number of ballots issued by matching them with the number of ballots cast,' she said, 'that way we know immediately that the vote count is accurate.'

But that isn't what happened, she said. We now have 17,000 more ballots cast than there are voters who voted and no way to determine what went wrong. Why anyone would eliminate that basic check, I don't know,' she said.[95]

Might the fact that Mark Ritchie was a secret CPUSA "non-party friend" offer some sort of explanation?

In a People's Weekly World article, "Minnesota euphoria over Obama win tempered by Senate recount November" published November 22, 2008, comrade Barb Kucera highlighted the vital importance to the left of the controversial election:

Whether Minnesota labor's massive effort to mobilize members in the 2008 elections was a success will ultimately turn on the results of a recount in the US Senate race, Labor 2008 coordinators say.

While most AFL-CIO and Change to Win unions backed Democratic-Farmer-Labor (DFL) challenger Franken, a few labor organizations—notably the Carpenters and Pipe Trades--endorsed Coleman. After all the results were turned in, Coleman led Franken by only 215 votes out of just under 3 million cast. An official recount began Nov. 18 and could take a month, Secretary of State Mark Ritchie said.

Franken's race against GOP incumbent Norman Coleman is important nationally. To get pro-worker bills through the Senate, workers and their allies need 60 votes, out of 100 senators, to cut off GOP filibusters. That includes a presumed GOP talkathon against the Employee Free Choice Act, which is designed to help level the playing field between workers and bosses in union organizing and bargaining first contracts... [96]

Months after the election was finally settled, two activist/computer experts pieced together the consequences of what they say was the loosening of the rules.

Dan McGrath and Jeff Davis, who had formed a small research-watchdog group called the Minnesota Majority, said that their computer assisted-examination of the voting records from the 2008 election showed that Al Franken's 312 vote margin of victory could be attributed to Mark Ritchie's dismantling of election rules, to allow more than 1400 convicted felons to illegally vote.[97]

MARK RITCHIE, INFLUENCE OPERATOR

Mark Ritchie was re-elected in 2010, but did not stand in 2014.

That same year, Mark Ritchie joined The World's Fair Bid Committee Educational Fund, a 501(c)(3) non-profit organization promoting US participation in World Expos.

Mark Ritchie wrote on LinkedIn:

> As co-founder of our bid to host the 2027 Expo in Minnesota I am [excited] by the momentum we have, thanks to our theme 'Healthy People, Healthy Planet' and our alignment with the UN's Global Goals for Sustainable Development.[98]

In 2016, Mark Ritchie became Secretary of the National Advisory Board of the Washington DC-based US Election Assistance Commission – where he still serves, "protecting" our elections nationwide.[99]

When Tim Walz ran for Governor of Minnesota in 2018, Mark Ritchie was right there with him.

From the Albert Lea Tribune:

> The wife of a leading DFL gubernatorial candidate urged participation in Tuesday's primary election Monday morning during a brief meeting at The Interchange Wine & Coffee Bistro. Gwen Walz, wife of Tim Walz, 1st District congressman and candidate for governor, made the comments at the meeting of DFLers including former District 27A Rep. Robin Brown, candidate for District 27A Rep. Terry Gjersvik and former Minnesota Secretary of State Mark Ritchie…

Ritchie said he met Tim Walz in 2005 at Camp Wellstone.
He said during the Great Recession, the congressman 'was always
a voice for those people I knew were having the most difficulty and
were also working the hardest.' [100]

Former secretary of state, wife of Walz encourage people to vote in primary

Published 11:10 pm Tuesday, August 7, 2018

By Sam Wilmes

By January 2019, Mark Ritchie was serving as President of Global
Minnesota, a "nonprofit international education organization" with
more than 2,000 members, 52 corporate members and a $1.5 million
budget.

Global Minnesota
January 18, 2019 ·

This week, we proudly welcomed Mark Ritchie as Global Minnesota's new president. Mark spent
the past few days connecting with the Minnesota Consular Corps and at the Minnesota Council
on Foundations Conference. "It's a true honor to lead the dedicated Global Minnesota team and
serve members who live out our important mission every day." Welcome aboard, Mark!

Global Minnesota worked closely with the Chinese American Association of Minnesota and the St. Paul branch of the "Overseas Chinese Service Center" or secret Chinese police stations.

Governor Walz is indeed very close to Global Minnesota and happily cooperated with his old friend Mark Ritchie on several of the organization's projects.[101]

Mark Ritchie • 2nd   **+ Follow**   ⋯
Minnesota USA Expo 2031 Steering Committee| Expo USA Co-f...
4yr • 🌐

The Governor gave a great speech this morning at the Manova Summit > Manova Summit Office of Governor Tim Walz & Lt. Governor Peggy Flanagan Global Minnesota Expo USA #Manova2019 #healthcare #wellness #innovation #global #usa

On February 1, 2024, the "band" got back together again for a FairVote Minnesota "Symposium on Voting Rights" at the at the University of St. Thomas Anderson Student Center in St. Paul. From the St. Thomas website:

> *The Racial Justice Initiative at the University of St. Thomas, in collaboration with FairVote Minnesota and other nonprofits and universities, is co-hosting an in-person Symposium on Voting Rights: Our Past, Our Present, Our Future on Feb. 1 to kick off Black History Month.*
>
> *The symposium, which recognizes the 60th anniversary of the Civil Rights Act, will convene a diverse and influential gathering*

of thought leaders, students, community members and political figures. Speakers and panelists include Minnesota Gov. Tim Walz, Lt. Gov. Peggy Flanagan, Secretary of State Steve Simon and Attorney General Keith Ellison.

[...]

In this symposium, we will revisit our history of voting rights, think concretely about how we can protect access to the ballot box, and examine changes to our political system that would make it easier for all of us – especially those who have been historically oppressed – to participate and be fully represented," said Racial Justice Initiative Founding Director Dr. Yohuru Williams, a Distinguished University Chair and Professor of History at St. Thomas.

St. Thomas President Rob Vischer will welcome participants and Gov. Tim Walz and Williams will give opening remarks..."[102]

Panels covered the "evolution of voting rights and democratic participation, threats to our democracy, and the future of democracy reform in Minnesota and the country."[103]

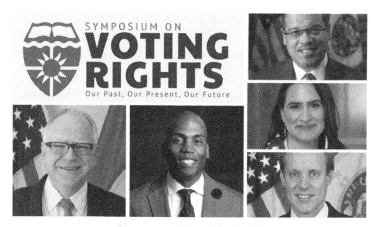

Symposium on Voting Rights Graphic

Confirmed speakers and panelists included "Wellstoners" Governor Tim Walz, Leiutenant Governor Peggy Flanagan, Secretary of State Steve Simon, Attorney General Keith Ellison, and former Secretary of State Mark Ritchie,[104] plus Minnesota House Majority Whip Athena Hollins, a Democratic Socialists of America comrade – one of many in the Minnesota legislature.

Incredibly, since 2016, Mark Ritchie has also served as serves as the Civilian Aide to the Secretary of the Army for Minnesota.

According to the US Army website, Civilian Aides to the Secretary of the Army (CASAs) are:

> ...business and community leaders appointed by the Secretary to advise and support Army leaders across the country...Each is proactively involved in the community and brings to the position an interest in the Army, a high degree of business and civic leadership and an ability to influence the public. CASAs are Special Government Employees who agree to serve as representatives of the Secretary of the Army without salary, wages or related benefits, and are afforded a 3-star protocol status.
>
> CASAs bridge the gap between the Army and civilian community by disseminating information about the Army's objectives and major programs to the public through speeches, personal contact and participation in Army and community events. CASAs assist with recruiting by increasing the positive image of the Army and connecting Army recruiters to key influencers in the community.[105]

In August 2019, Harry Sieben, a former US Army CASA representative for Minnesota, was honored with a CASA Emeritus certificate. The award was presented by Roger Rojillio Combs, representing Acting Secretary of the Army Ryan McCarthy, during a ceremony hosted by Minnesota Governor Tim Walz.

Also, in attendance to recognize Harry Sieben were Major General John Jensen, the Adjutant General of the Minnesota National Guard, and Mark Ritchie, the current Minnesota CASA.

Civilian Aides to the Secretary of the Army
August 28, 2019 · 🌐   ...

Former U.S. Army #CASA for Minnesota Harry Sieben was presented with a CASA Emeritus certificate from Roger Rojillio Combs, representing Acting Secretary of the Army Ryan McCarthy, at a ceremony in Harry's honor hosted by Minnesota Governor Tim Walz at the Minnesota State Capitol. Also attending and recognizing Harry were the Minnesota National Guard Adjutant General MG John Jensen and our current Minnesota CASAs Mark Ritchie and Eric Ahlness.

Harry served in the U.S. Army R... **See more**

Mark Ritchie's old CPUSA "friends" and his former Wellstone comrades must be very proud.

Who, if anybody, vets these positions?

Erwin Marquit and 'Maoist' Keith Ellison

Erwin Marquit, a notable figure within the Minnesota/Dakotas Communist Party, alongside his wife Doris, significantly influenced Keith Ellison's path to Congress. Their involvement, stemming from their participation in the May Day Bookshop CPUSA gatherings, was instrumental in propelling Ellison, who previously worked with Wellstone Action, into the political spotlight.

The following extract from Erwin Marquit's memoirs illustrates yet again the very blurred line between America's communists and Democrats – a line that many subjects in this book have crossed over and over again:

Erwin Marquit

In Minnesota, campaigns for nomination as a candidate in a public election starts with winning support at the precinct caucuses…Ellison's initial campaign had to focus on winning the endorsement at the Fifth Congressional District DFL Convention on 6 May…

Doris and I normally attend the DFL caucuses. I already have indicated that although the DFL caucus rules state that a participant in the caucus cannot be a member of another political party, the Communist Party is technically not a political party in Minnesota if does not field candidates in the election.

Doris and I had been chosen as delegates for the DFL Congressional District Convention, and we campaigned for Ellison before and at the convention. Ellison, with his strong antiwar position and positive reaction to his role in the legislature as a representative of his predominately African American north Minneapolis district, came out first in the first ballots at the convention…Ellison won the nomination in the fourth ballot. He still had to face a primary election in September with the four other candidates, all with heavy political credentials that were running against him. To gather support for Ellison, I suggested to [communists] April Knutson and Jim Knutson that they draft a letter addressed to activists in the peace movement urging them to support Ellison.

Doris and I and the Knutsons then solicited signatures to the letter from among well-known peace activists. In July, we circulated the letter as widely as possible. Doris and I volunteered to cosponsor a fundraiser for Ellison in our home on 24 July…On 21 and 22 July, I went into St. Louis Park, a suburb just west of the city line, a block and a half from our home, to do door knocking. When someone appeared at the door, I would begin by introducing myself

*by name. I was not surprised when one of the first responses I got
was, 'Oh, you're the Communist at the University of Minnesota.'
Two or three others recognized me in a similar manner. The fact
that I was campaigning for Ellison did not seem to bother any of
them.[106]*

Erwin Marquit would go on to hold at least two more fundraisers
in his home for Keith Ellison.[107]

Nor is Keith Ellison shy about his ties to the CPUSA, even con-
tributing an August 2014 article to the party's People's World website:

New grassroots movements show: Never count out working people

by: REP. KEITH ELLISON
august 29 2014					*Print |Email*
tags: Low wage workers, minimum wage, Minnesota, collective bargaining

The last sever
have been rou
working peop
the folks who
products, fix t
machines, fry
chicken and k
place clean sh
never be coun

Neither is Keith Ellison embarrassed or apologetic about his long
history with the Maoists of the Freedom Road Socialist Organization.

In June 1989, Geoff Hahn of Freedom Road's "Forward Motion"
magazine interviewed Keith Ellison on recent police "brutality demonstrations" in Minneapolis.

Said Ellison:

*The responsible activist has to show young people out the, that
white supremacy and capitalism are what's putting them in the
position they're in.[108]*

Unsurprisingly Keith Ellison is also a friend of Kamala Harris's buddy Steve Phillips and is a big fan of his book "Brown is the New White".

Keith Ellison ✓
@keithellison

My friend Steve Phillips just wrote Brown is the New White. Great book!

5:17 PM · Nov 20, 2015

Keith Ellison is also a very big is a big fan of the "Rainbow Coalition" concept.

Perhaps Keith Ellison's "Maoist" sympathies and anti-police attitude may help to explain why Governor Tim Walz chose Ellison to lead the prosecution of police officers accused of George Floyd's killing in May 2020.[109]

The Walz/Froemke/Henry/Harris chain

Another attendee of the secret CPUSA meeting at the May Day Bookshop, Mark Froemke, is the long time District Organizer of the Minnesota/North Dakota Communist Party.[110]

Froemke is also very prominent in the DFL and the labor movement in Northwest Minnesota and parts of North Dakota.

Mark Froemke

Mark Froemke, is the longtime President of the North West Area Labor Council and seems to be on close terms with many prominent DFL figures.

Comrade Froemke's favorite DFLers include former US Senator and Governor of Minnesota Mark Dayton.

Mark Froemke, left, Governor Dayton, right

Mark Froemke also seems to be on very close terms with the former US Senator from Minnesota Al Franken:

Senator Franken with Mark Froemke, January 2012

Mark Froemke with Senator Franken, Froemke Facebook page March 26, 2016

Currently serving US Senator from Minnesota and former Democratic presidential candidate, Amy Klobuchar appears to have no qualms associating with one of the state's most prominent communists:

Facebook, July 2009

Governor Tim Walz is in the club, as well.

Here's a photo from 2022, with birthday greetings to Governor Walz, from leftist labor activist Dale Moerke and comrade Mark Froemke:

Dale Moerke is with **Mark Froemke**.
April 6, 2020 · 🌐

Happy Birthday Governor Tim Walz ! Thanks for your leadership during these difficult times.

Here's an August 2022 shot apparently from the campaign trail, with Walz, Moerke and comrade Froemke:

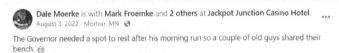

Dale Moerke is with **Mark Froemke** and **2 others** at Jackpot Junction Casino Hotel.
August 3, 2022 · Morton, MN · 🌐

The Governor needed a spot to rest after his morning run so a couple of old guys shared their bench. 😄

#FARMFEST2022 #mnisready

Very shortly after Kamala Harris picked Tim Walz as her running mate, Mark Froemke was interviewed by the Minnesota news station KVRR:

Local AFL-CIO President Mark Froemke told us that labor unions in Minnesota have been able to work with the Governor well, securing what he says has been crucial and important legislation for working class people.

'Legislation that we passed in Minnesota, under the Democratic Party and Governor Tim Walz, who's done an outstanding job.'

Froemke added that he's excited by what Walz will bring to the national stage.

'It would be good for Minnesota, because we'd be giving our best of the best to not only help our country, but to help guide it. So we would be very proud,' Froemke said.

'She couldn't pick a better person.'[111]

From a communist perspective, comrade Froemke is right.

Mark Froemke is also a very close friend and comrade to his counterpart, the leader of the Iowa/Nebraska Communist Party, Joe Henry.

Mark Froemke ▶ Joe Henry
October 4, 2023 · 🌐

Have a great birthday today Joe

Mark Froemke and Joe Henry work very closely together on union campaigns such as the United Autoworkers strike of 2021.

Joe Henry left, Mark Froemke, right

A Communist Party USA member since 1982[112] Joe Henry has been active in Iowa and Washington DC for decades as a union activist, realtor and longtime Polk County (Des Moines) leader[113] and former candidate for Chair of the Iowa Democratic Party.[114]

Henry also served on the Des Moines Civil Service Commission from 2013 to 2020.[115]

Henry has also served simultaneously on the Communist Party's Political Action Committee[116] – which exerts considerable influence on the Democratic Party at every level and on the CPUSA's powerful Labor Commission.[117]

Mark Froemke knows just about every important Democrat in Minnesota and Joe Henry knows them all in Iowa – including former Democratic Congressmember Dave Loebsack, another Camp Wellstone alum.[118]

Joe Henry left, Representative Dave Loebsack right

Joe Henry is also a Midwestern and national official with the League of United Latin American Citizens (LULAC), the "nation's largest and oldest Hispanic civil rights organization."[119]

Comrade Henry was also heavily involved in the groundbreaking 2007-2008 Obama campaign in Iowa.

Joe Henry updated his cover photo.
June 29, 2017 · 🌐

Meeting candidate Barack Obama for the first time in 2007 in Des Moines to discuss issues of importance for the Latino Community.   He was articulate, completely informed on the issues and was very professional and kind.

Campaign leaders. Joe Henry at Barack Obama's left shoulder

It is during this campaign that Joe Henry likely first met Kamala Harris, who had travelled to the Midwest to help her friend Barack Obama defeat Hillary Clinton in the Democratic primaries.

When Kamala Harris began returning to Iowa in 2018 in preparation for her 2020 presidential run, Joe Henry was on apparently her "must visit" list.

Harris and Henry posed for a "photo op" at an October 2018 Iowa State Capitol event hosted by the Asian & Latino Coalition.

From Joe Henry's Facebook page

Joe Henry plays a prominent role in the Asian & Latino Coalition, which is formally led by his brother Mitch Henry.[120]

Kamala Harris was back in Iowa in February 2019 for a "Kamala Harris for President" event at the Iowa State Capitol, hosted again by the Asian & Latino Coalition and Joe Henry's LULAC.

Al Womble added a new photo — with **Kamala Harris** and **Joe Henry** at Iowa State Capitol.
February 24, 2019 · Des Moines, IA · 🌐

In August 2019, Asian & Latino Coalition was one of the few Iowa organizations to formally endorse Kamala Harris for president.[121]

On the heels of that endorsement, the Harris Iowa campaign announced the formation of a "Latinx Steering Committee", which included Mitch Henry.[122]

Kamala Harris was back in Iowa in November and December 2019, staying in the home of a business client of Joe Henry's.

Joe Henry
November 27, 2020 · 🌐

This special moment was held at my clients home in Des Moines last year. Senator Harris needed a place to spend November and December 2019. We won't ever forget that special time at ▆▆▆ Grand Avenue, Des Moines.

M.TIKTOK.COM
VP-ELECT Kamala Harris ♡ on TikTok
Happy thanksgiving!! 🦃🍂 here's a video from *LAST YEAR* of Kamala on thanksgiving. #kamalaharris #GivingThanks #fyp #viral

Through these events, Joe Henry worked closely with Deidre DeJear, a Harris protégé[123] who served as Iowa Campaign Chair for the 2019 Kamala Harris presidential campaign as well as black out-reach director for the 2012 Obama re-election campaign.[124]

DeJear has also worked with Harris and the White House on ini-tiatives, including "reproductive care and voting rights issues".[125]

In 2018, Deidre DeJear ran unsuccessfully for Iowa Secretary of State – with Kamala Harris's enthusiastic endorsement.[126]

Had she won, might Deirdre DeJear have turned out to be an Iowa Mark Ritchie?

In 2022, Deidre DeJear ran unsuccessfully for Governor of Iowa against popular Republican incumbent Kim Reynolds.

Joe Henry, of course, endorsed her.

I am honored to have the support of Joe Henry! Joe has spent his career fighting for workers, voting rights, and to create an Iowa that is welcoming to everyone. Thank you, Joe! #WorthTheWork

So did Aimee Allison, Steve Phillips's longtime comrade and polit-ical collaborator.

Aimee Allison said of Deirdre DeJear:

> Dejear ran Obama's Black outreach in Iowa resulting in victory in that state, and ever since she has organized and built and moti-vated a multiracial base in a state most dismiss as too white for a Black woman to win. She knows that Black + Latino + Asian American + progressive white voters can win statewide and she proved that with Obama.

Aimee Allison with Deirdre DeJear, June 2, 2022

Where have we heard this formula before?

Deidre DeJear is now supporting and endorsing the Kamala Harris for President campaign in Iowa.

In December 2023, Joe Henry and Darryl Morin, both leaders of Wisconsin-based voter mobilization group Forward Latino were invited to meet with Vice President Harris and her husband Doug Emhoff at their official Washington DC home, the Naval Observatory.

Joe Henry کی Vice President's Mansion - Washington, D.C. د ک .
December 23, 2023 · Washington D.C. · 🌐

While in Washington DC last week, my good friend Darryl Morin and I visited Vice President Kamala Harris at her house, the Naval Observatory.

An amazing experience!

Was a possible Harris Presidential run in 2024 a topic of discussion?

Did the presence of Joe Henry, a leading member of the openly pro-China, Communist Party USA inside the official residence of the Vice-President of the United States of America raise any security "red flags"?

In early August 2024, the supposedly non-partisan LULAC broke with nearly a century of tradition to endorse the Harris/Walz ticket.

From NBC News,

> The 95-year-old League of United Latin American Citizens has endorsed Vice President Kamala Harris and Minnesota Gov. Tim Walz, breaking with its past practice of not formally supporting any political candidates.
>
> The historic endorsement of the Democratic presidential ticket

is the first for the civil rights group, which formed in 1929 to pro-
tect the rights of Americans of Mexican descent.

The endorsement was made through its political action com-
mittee, the LULAC Adelante PAC. LULAC is a nonprofit with
a social welfare arm, and under federal tax law it cannot make
political endorsements.

'We are proud to endorse Kamala Harris and Tim Walz
because of the real issues facing Latino communities and all
Americans across the nation; we can trust them to do what is right
for our community and the country,' Domingo Garcia, chairman of
LULAC Adelante PAC and LULAC's immediate past president,
said in a statement...

LULAC had been considering creating a PAC for a few years,
the organization said. But the prospect of another Donald Trump
presidency created an urgency to do it now, said LULAC CEO
Juan Proaño.

'The politics of hate mongering and scapegoating Latinos and
immigrants must be stopped,' Garcia said in the statement.

LULAC said its councils, essentially chapters based at the local
level, will step up support for the Democratic ticket in key battle-
ground states. LULAC has 535 councils and 140,000 members,
86% of whom are registered voters, LULAC said. The organiza-
tion has not previously done national get out the vote work.

In a statement, Julie Chavez Rodriguez, Harris-Walz 2024
campaign manager, said the campaign was honored to earn
LULAC's endorsement.

'They've never backed away from the fight for the communi-
ties they represent, and Vice President Harris has never stopped
fighting to create opportunities for Latino families,' she said.[127]

Did long time LULAC board member Joe Henry[128] have anything
to do with this decision? Did his realtor sales skills come in useful?

Possibly. Joe Henry currently serves as a non-voting LULAC board
member – and as an Advisor to the LULAC President for Civic
Engagement and Elections.

He is effectively LULAC's political guru.

**Advisor to the President for Civic
Engagement and Elections
Joe Henry**
Des Moines, IA

From the LULAC webiste

It's all about winning the "New American Majority".

The vetting team that chose Tim Walz was led by Harris campaign chair Jen O'Malley Dillon, former Attorney General Eric Holder (who was mentored as a young man, by the late Percy Sutton,[129] the same old communist sympathizer who helped Obama get into Harvard, all those years ago) and Kamala Harris's brother-in-law Tony West. [130]

That's why Tim Walz was chosen. Kamala Harris needed an older white man on the ticket. Perhaps an older "Maoist" white man?

INDEX

ENDNOTES

FOREWORD

1 Connors, Ben, Communist Workers Party, "The Expert Red", February 1985, page 4

2 Ibid.

3 Brookhiser, Richard, City Journal, "The Resistible Rise of Margaret Chin", Spring 1991, Link: https://www.city-journal.org/article/the-resistible-rise-of-margaret-chin

4 Viser, Matt, Washington Post "The story behind Kamala Harris's 'When we fight, we win' slogan", August 22, 2024, Link: https://www.washingtonpost.com/politics/2024/08/22/kamala-harris-slogan-when-we-fight-we-win/

5 Lindsay, James, New Discourses", "The New Discourses Podcast with James Lindsay, Episode 147", September 3, 2024, Link: https://newdiscourses.com/2024/09/the-unhappy-rebellion-of-radical-joy/

6 Link: Poster Crazed, "Mao's Words Bring Joy by Chinese Government", Link: https://www.postercrazed.com/Maos-Words-Bring-Joy-by-Chinese-Government_p_13576.html

7 Communist Party USA, "We're not going back . . . forward together!", March 5, 2021, Link: https://cpusa.org/article/were-not-going-back-forward-together/

CHAPTER 1

1 Romano. Andrew Yahoo News. How Kamala Harris, Joe Biden's new running mate, was shaped by 'the People's Republic of Berkeley' August 16, 2019, Link: https://news.yahoo.com/how-kamala-harris-was-shaped-by-the-peoples-republic-of-berkeley-182310899.html.

2 Haines, Erin Washington Post Kamala Harris wants America to turn protest into policy. Is she the one to make it happen? June 19, 2020, Link: https://www.washingtonpost.com/politics/2020/06/19/there-was-this-tool-that-they-had-figured-out-was-powerful-kamala-harris-working-system-justice/

3 Laney College, Ethnic Studies News & Updates. "Loss of Dr. Mary Lewis". Link: https://laney.edu/ethnicstudies/about/ethnic-studies-news-accomplishments-and-photos/

4 Sedensky, Matt, Associated Press. "For Harris, memories of mother guide bid for vice president", August 14, 2020. Link: https://web.archive.org/web/20210114031827/https://www.sentinelandenterprise.com/2020/08/14/for-harris-memories-of-mother-guide-bid-for-vice-president/

5 Murch, Donna, Haymarket Books. "Assata Taught Me: State Violence, Racial Capitalism, and the Movement for Black Lives", March, 2022. Link: https://www.haymarketbooks.org/books/1650-assata-taught-me

6 iii Romano. Andrew Yahoo News. How Kamala Harris, Joe Biden's new running mate, was shaped by 'the People's Republic of Berkeley' August 16, 2019, Link: https://news.yahoo.com/how-kamala-harris-was-shaped-by-the-peoples-republic-of-berkeley-182310899.html

7 Alexander, Robert Jackson, "Maoism in the developed world", page 33, Bloomsbury Publishing, 2001, ISBN 9780275961480

8 Romano. Andrew Yahoo News. How Kamala Harris, Joe Biden's new

running mate, was shaped by 'the People's Republic of Berkeley' August 16, 2019, Link: https://news.yahoo.com/how-kamala-harris-was-shaped-by-the-peoples-republic-of-berkeley-182310899.html

9   Robinson, Cedric J. Black Marxism: The Making of the Black Radical Tradition. University of North Carolina Press, 1983, Preface.

10   Ibid.

11   Bloom, Joshua; Martin, Waldo E. Jr. (2013). Black against Empire: The History and Politics of the Black Panther Party. University of California Press. p. 315. ISBN 9780520953543.

12   History Matters "The Only Good Pig Is a Dead Pig": A Black Panther Paper Editor Explains a Political Cartoon Link:
   http://historymatters.gmu.edu/d/6460/

13   Investor's Business Daily editorial, Barack Obama—The Radical Mansourian Candidate, 09/24/2012 Link https://www.investors.com/politics/editorials/khalid-al-mansour-helped-barack-obama/

14   Peoples World, James and Esther Jackson: shapers of history December 15, 2006, Link: https://www.peoplesworld.org/article/james-and-esther-jackson-shapers-of-history/

15   Investor's Business Daily editorial, Barack Obama—The Radical Mansourian Candidate, 09/24/2012 Link https://www.investors.com/politics/editorials/khalid-al-mansour-helped-barack-obama/

16   Ibid.

17   Judicial Watch FBI Files Document Communism in Valerie Jarrett's Family JUNE 22, 2015, Link: https://www.judicialwatch.org/corruption-chronicles/communism-in-jarretts-family/

18   Myles, Dee People's World Vernon Jarrett: a partisan journalistic giant June 4, 2004, Link: https://www.peoplesworld.org/article/vernon-jarrett-a-partisan-journalistic-giant/

19   The Berkeley Revolution, UC Berkeley. "A Digital Archive of the East Bay's Transformation in the late 1960s & 1970s. Link: https://revolution.berkeley.edu/projects/rainbow-sign/

20   MSNBC Transcript Into America Kamala Harris and the Rainbow Sign, November 2020, Link: https://www.msnbc.com/podcast/transcript-kamala-harris-rainbow-sign-n1248462

21   Ibid.

22   Gale, "Maya Angelou (1928-2014)", Link: https://www.gale.com/intl/databases-explored/literature/maya-angelou

23   Dilawar, Arvin, Jacobin, "The Socialism of James Baldwin", Link: https://jacobin.com/2021/01/james-baldwin-socialism-blank-panthers

24   Morgan. Kelli, Against the Current The Life and Memory of Elizabeth Catlett Link: https://againstthecurrent.org/atc160/p3685/

25   Zak, Ian Literary Hub, Odetta, the Shy Folk Singer Who Defied McCarthyism's Fear Tactics, April 20, 2020, Link: https://lithub.com/odetta-the-shy-folk-singer-who-defied-mccarthyisms-fear-tactics/

26   Judis, John, In These Times, "Democratic Socialism Will Prevail": An Interview with Ron Dellums in 1976 "July 30, 2018, Link: https://inthesetimes.com/article/ron-dellums-death-democratic-socialist-dsa-antiwar-1976-interview

27   Thompson, Chris East Bay Express, Lenore Anderson Out as Ron Dellums' Crime Aide, June 2, 2008
     Link: https://eastbayexpress.com/lenore-anderson-out-as-ron-dellums-crime-aide-1/

28   St. John, Paige, Los Angeles Times. "'Campaign Manager' for criminal justice", October 31, 2014. Link: https://documents.latimes.com/campaign-manager-criminal-justice/

29   Californians for Safety and Justice, "What We Do". Link: https://safe-andjust.org/about-us/

30   Luthi, Susannah, Washington Free Beacon. "As Crime Worsens in California, Soros-Backed Group Mobilizes Against Referendum To Restore Tougher Criminal Penalties", April 23, 2024. Link: https://freebeacon.com/california/as-crime-worsens-in-california-soros-backed-group-mobilizes-against-referendum-to-restore-tougher-criminal-penalties/

31   Ibid.

32   MSNBC Transcript Kamala Harris and the Rainbow Sign, November 2020. Link: https://www.msnbc.com/podcast/transcript-kamala-harris-rainbow-sign-n1248462

33   Ibid.

34   Ibid.

35   Alan, Adrian, The Professional Gunfighter. "Meet the Police Officers Murdered by the Black Panthers", February 10, 2016. Archive: https://web.archive.org/web/20200718075651/https://progunfighter.com/murdered-by-the-black-panthers/

36   Foote, Patrick, Peoples World, Remembering Shirley Chisholm November 30, 2016, Link: https://www.peoplesworld.org/article/remembering-shirley-chisholm/

37   Ibid.

38   Ibid.

39   McLaughlin, Ken, Stanford Daily, The Stanford Daily Archives. "Marxist Offered Economics Post", Page 1, May 13, 1975. Link: https://archives.stanforddaily.com/1975/05/13?page=1

40   Stanford Daily, "Faculty column misstates record", page 2, November 12, 1976. Link: https://archives.stanforddaily.com/1976/11/12?page=2&section=MODSMD_ARTICLE7

41   Ibid.

42   Kahan, Hazel, PM Press, "Professor emeritus Michael Zweig on why he wrote "Class, Race and Gender"", Link: https://blog.pmpress.org/2023/10/23/professor-emeritus-michael-zweig-on-why-he-wrote-class-race-and-gender/

43   Schneider, Markus, University of Denver, College of Arts, Humanities & Social Sciences. "In Memoriam: Tracy Mott", November 8, 2021. Link: https://liberalarts.du.edu/news-events/all-articles/memoriam-tracy-mott

44   Alt, Theresa, Democratic Left, "DSA House Parties Help Send Sanders to Senate", Winter 2006, 2007, page 4

45   Communists in the Democratic Party, page 68, January 1, 1990 by Inc. Concerned Voters, ISBN-13': ʃ978-0962742705

46   The National Guardian, "Right Wing smears IPS as "KGB front",

December 10, 1980, Link: https://www.cia.gov/readingroom/docs/CIA-RDP90-00806R000100510016-7.pdf

47   Proyect, Louis, "Oil, NATO and Yugoslavia", April 1, 1999, Link: https://wsarch.ucr.edu/wsnmail/99/msg00291.html

48   Fleischman, Harry, Democratic Left, "On the Left", July/August 1992, page 10

49   "Winning America: Ideas and Leadership for the 1990s", edited by Marcus Raskin, Chester Hartman pages 24, 25, ISBN-10: 0896083438

50   Former leaders of the Students for a Democratic Society, The Nation. An Open Letter to the New New Left From the Old New Left, April 16, 2020, Link: https://www.thenation.com/article/activism/letter-new-left-biden/

51   Union for Radical Political Economics, "History of URPE ", Link: https://web.archive.org/web/20110416094209/https://urpe.org/about/history.html

52   Economic Policy Institute, "Barry Bluestone Northeastern University", Link: https://www.epi.org/people/barry-bluestone-2/

53   Democracy Collaborative, Gar Alperovitz, Link: https://democracycollaborative.org/gar-alperovitz

54   Pattberg, Mike, The Yankee Radical, "Short Takes", March 2006, page 2, Link: https://web.archive.org/web/20060716214127/http://www.dsaboston.org/yradical/yr2006-03.pdf

55   Democratic Left, "Cablegram to Portuguese Socialists and M.F.A." September 1975, page 2

56   Institute for Policy Studies 30th Anniversary brochure, 1993

57   SDS Home, "NATIONAL VIETNAM EXAMINATION", Link: https://web.archive.org/web/20090623062157/https://www.sds-1960s.org/exam.htm

58   Democratic Left, "New Directions", March-April 1996, page 16

59   Scholars Strategy Network, "Jeff Faux", Link: https://scholars.org/scholar/jeff-faux

60   Fleischman, Harry, Democratic Left, "On the Left", May-June 1990, page 8

61   Haimerl, Amy, Crain's Detroit Business, "Duggan appoints Carol O'Cleireacain deputy mayor for economic policy", October 16, 2014, Link: https://www.crainsdetroit.com/article/20141016/BLOG017/141019893/duggan-appoints-carol-ocleireacain-deputy-mayor-for-economic-policy

62   Wachtel, Howard, Democratic Left, "Structural Causes Lead to Multifaceted Assault", February 1980, page 10

63   Institute for Policy Studies 30th Anniversary brochure, 1993

64   Union for Radical Political Economics, "History of URPE ", Link: https://web.archive.org/web/20110416094209/https://urpe.org/about/history.html

65   Ibid.

66   The Yankee Radical, "21st Century Socialism", May-June 2010, page 1, Link: https://web.archive.org/web/20130528164436/http://www.dsaboston.org/yradical/yr2010-05.pdf

67   "Winning America: Ideas and Leadership for the 1990s", edited by Marcus Raskin, Chester Hartman pages 24, 25, ISBN-10 : 0896083438

68   Radosh, Ron, National Review, "The Obama Vision: Book review of 'Radical-in-Chief'", November 15, 2010, Link: https://www.hudson.org/domestic-policy/the-obama-vision-book-review-of-radical-in-chief-

69   Holmes, Tamara, Howard University, "Raising Up Kamala", Link: https://magazine.howard.edu/stories/raising-up-kamala

70   Kaminsky, Gabe, Washington Examiner, "How Kamala Harris's former boss 'destroyed' his Senate career", August 2, 2024, Link: https://www.washingtonexaminer.com/news/investigations/3107560/kamala-former-boss-destroyed-senate-career/

71   The Stanford Daily, "Stanford Men join Mexican political move", Volume 87a, Issue 9, July 23, 1935, page 1, Link: https://archives.stanforddaily.com/1935/07/23?page=1&section=MODSMD_ARTICLE4

72   Diament, Sean M., University of California, Berkeley, "The Pragmatic Idealist: An Exposition and Review of Alan Cranston – Senator from California: Making a "Dent in the World" by Judith Robinson, Telegraph Hill Press, 2012", Calif. J. Politics Policy 2013; 5(4): 755–767. Archive Link: https://web.archive.org/web/20240711113554/https://escholarship.org/content/qt5t51g60p/qt5t51g60p_noSplash_917fddc1d32b02481d79bc058b34c4a9.pdf?t=nhwwat

73   Communists in the Democratic Party, page 37 January 1, 1990 by Inc. Concerned Voters, , ISBN-978-0962742705

74   Albats, Yevgenia (1999). The State Within a State: The KGB and Its Hold on Russia--Past, Present, and Future. New York: Macmillan. page 250. ISBN 0-374-52738-5. Retrieved 27 November 2010.

75   Yevgenia Albats, Senator Edward Kennedy Requested KGB Assistance With a Profitable Contract for his Businessman-Friend, Izvestia 24 June 1992, page 5.

76   Useful Stooges, "David Karr KGB Creep" Link: https://usefulstooges.com/2019/08/27/12338/

77   Communists in the Democratic Party, page 37 January 1, 1990 by Inc. Concerned Voters, ISBN-13 : 978-0962742705

78   The Stanford Daily, "Cranston urges normal relations with China", Volume 172, Issue 61, January 18, 1978, Link: https://archives.stanforddaily.com/1978/01/18?page=5&section=MODSMD_ARTICLE19

79   Ibid.

80   Ibid.

81   Communists in the Democratic Party, page 37 January 1, 1990 by Inc. Concerned Voters, ISBN-13 : 978-0962742705

82   Global Security Institute. "Mission and Overview". Link: https://gsinstitute.org/about-gsi/

83   London, Scott. "Toward a Nuclear Weapons-Free World: An Interview with Alan Cranston, December 1997. Link: https://scott.london/interviews/cranston.html

84   UC Hastings Congratulates Kamala Harris '89: California's next US Senator". UC Hastings Law. San Francisco. November 9, 2016.

85   "Kamala Harris '89 Wins Race for California Attorney General".
UC Hastings Newsroom. November 24, 2010. Archived from the original on
November 30, 2010. Retrieved February 2, 2011.

86   "Attorney Licensee Profile, Kamala Devi Harris #146672". The State
Bar of California. Retrieved August 1, 2020.

CHAPTER 2

1   Byrne, Peter SF Weekly Kamala's Karma 09.214.03 Link: https://
www.sfweekly.com/news/kamalas-karma/

2   Richardson, James, CalMatters, "Follow the trail of Kamala Harris' rise
to VP nomination back to Phil Burton's influence on California politics", August
29, 2020, Link: https://calmatters.org/commentary/my-turn/2020/08/follow-
the-trail-of-kamala-harris-rise-to-vp-nomination-back-to-phil-burtons-influence-
on-california-politics/

3   Jacobs, John A Rage for Justice: The Passion and Politics of Phillip
Burton page 22/23

4   Shafer, Scott KQED When and Why Did the Bay Area Become So
Liberal?
August 20, 2020, Link: https://web.archive.org/web/20201023121023/https://
www.kqed.org/news/11833960/when-and-why-did-the-bay-area-become-so-liberal

5   Ibid.

6   Ibid.

7   Ibid.

8   Comrades—1963 Vietnam and Peace Movement Summary—the Lead
Link: https://web.archive.org/web/20200512163439/https://www.vvfh.org/
uploads/Comrades--1963.pdf

9   Comrades—1963 Vietnam and Peace Movement Summary—the Lead
Link: https://web.archive.org/web/20200512163439/https://www.vvfh.org/
uploads/Comrades--1963.pdf

10   Wheeler, Tim, Communist Party, USA. newspaper Daily World,
October 1, 1975, p. 3.

11   Human Events", April 2, 1983

12   Bloomberg Government, "BARBARA BOXER (D-CA)", Link: https://
www.asn-online.org/policy/webdocs/CA-Barbara%20Boxer.pdf

13   Robinson, Matthew and Anderson, Brian C., City Journal,
"Willie Brown Shows How Not to Run a City", Autumn 1998, Link:
https://web.archive.org/save/https://www.city-journal.org/article/
willie-brown-shows-how-not-to-run-a-city

14   Richardson, James, "Willie Brown: A Biography", University of
California Press, page 97, November 10, 1996, ISBN-13': '978-0520213159

15   CIA report on Ramparts, "Briefing Notes on Ramparts", Link: https://
www.cia.gov/readingroom/docs/CIA-RDP70B00338R000200230132-5.pdf

16   Castro's Network in the United States (Fair Play for Cuba Committee):
Hearings Before the Subcommittee to Investigate the Administration of the
Internal Security Act and Other Internal Security Laws of the Committee on the
Judiciary, United States Senate, Eighty-eighth Congress, First Session.... United
States: Superintendent of Documents, U. S. Government Print., Office, 1963.

17   Communist Legal Subversion: The Role of the Communist Lawyer

- Report, February 16, 1959, HCUA, House Report No. 41, 86th Congress, 1st Session

18   NYU Libraries, Guide to the Robert E. Treuhaft Papers TAM.664, "Robert E. Treuhaft Papers", Link: https://findingaids.library.nyu.edu/tamwag/tam_664/

19   People's World, "Pioneering lawyer Doris Brin Walker dies at 90", August 27, 2009, Link: https://peoplesworld.org/article/pioneering-lawyer-doris-brin-walker-dies-at-9/

20   NYU Libraries, Guide to the Robert E. Treuhaft Papers TAM.664, "Robert E. Treuhaft Papers", Link: https://findingaids.library.nyu.edu/tamwag/tam_664/

21   Martin, Douglas, New York Times. "Doris Walker, Leader of Angela Davis's Defense, Is Dead at 90", August 28, 2009. Link: https://www.nytimes.com/2009/08/29/us/29walker.html

22   Atkins, C.J., People's World. Angela Davis: Electing Harris will open space for more radical struggles, September 17, 2024. Link: https://www.peoplesworld.org/article/angela-davis-electing-harris-will-open-space-for-more-radical-struggles/

23   Peoples weekly World, May 4, 1991, page 2

24   Michigan State University, Chris Hani, US Tour Invitation via "African Activist Archive". Archive Link: https://web.archive.org/web/20240815220903/https://africanactivist.msu.edu/recordFiles/210-849-26065/hanitourcard.pdf

25   [xxiv] Peoples Weekly World, September 11, 1999

26   Peoples Weekly World September 23, 2000, page 2

27   C-Span, "Evelina Alarcon", Link: https://www.c-span.org/person/evelina-alarcon/86991/

28   Goodlett, Carlton B. (1914–1997) - Chronology, Serves as Publisher, Political Leader, and Mentor, Affiliates with Socialist Activities Link: http://encyclopedia.jrank.org/articles/pages/4263/Goodlett-Carlton-B-1914-1997.html#ixzz2NoLkUM6fhttps://web.archive.org/web/20130317152441/http://encyclopedia.jrank.org/articles/pages/4263/Goodlett-Carlton-B-1914-1997.html

29   Congressional Record, House of Representative, February 11, 1997, H425, Link: https://www.congress.gov/crec/1997/02/11/CREC-1997-02-11.pdf

30   Ibid.

31   Richardson, James, "Willie Brown A Biography - Chapter Eight—Forest Knolls" page 74, UNIVERSITY OF CALIFORNIA PRESS 1996. Link: https://publishing.cdlib.org/ucpressebooks/view?docId=ft0m3nb07q&chunk.id=d0e1902&toc.id=d0e1146&brand=ucpress

32   Ibid.

33   Ibid.

34   Chakraborty, Sudeepto Changemakers DR. CARLTON B. GOODLETT 3 July 2020, Link: https://usfblogs.usfca.edu/sfchangemakers/2020/07/03/dr-carlton-b-goodlett/

35   Fikes, Robert, BLACK PAST, "Carlton B. Goodlett (1914-1997)", January 28, 2007, Link: https://www.blackpast.org/african-american-history/goodlett-carlton-b-1914-1997/

36   Fleming, Thomas C., Columbus Free Press, "Carlton B. Goodlett,

champion of the people", June 4, 1999Link: https://www.freepress.org/fleming/flemng77.html

37   The Sun-Reporter, History. Link: https://thesunreporter.com/history/

38   La Riva, Gloria, Workers World News, "Dr. Carlton Goodlett, African American pioneer", February 20, 1997, Link: https://web.archive.org/web/20090731232006/https://www.workers.org/ww/1997/goodlett.html

39   American Psychological Association, "Carlton Goodlett, PhD", Link: https://www.apa.org/pi/oema/resources/ethnicity-health/psychologists/carlton-goodlett

40   Black Press Institute Letterhead, October 5, 1987, Alice palmer Collection, Vivian G. Harsh Research Collection, Chicago Public Library

41   People's Daily World December 24, 1986, page 10

42   Ibid.

43   People's Daily World December 24, 1986, page 11

44   Ibid.

45   Ibid.

46   People's Daily World December 24, 1986, page 10

47   Yearbook on International Communist Affairs, 1991 page 437

48   Education Resources Information Center, "The Role of the International Organization of Journalists in the Debate about the 'New International Information Order'", 1958-1978 Link: https://web.archive.org/web/20120323174435/http://www.eric.ed.gov/ERICWebPortal/search/detailmini.jsp?_nfpb=true&_&ERICExtSearch_SearchValue_0=ED189654&ERICExtSearch_SearchType_0=no&accno=ED189654

49   Smith, Ben, Politico, "Obama once visited '60s radicals", February 22, 2008, Link: https://www.politico.com/story/2008/02/obama-once-visited-60s-radicals-008630

50   Democratic Left, "Remembering Dr. Quentin Young", March 12, 2016, Link: https://www.dsausa.org/democratic-left/remembering_dr_quentin_young_dl/

51   People's World, "California's new top cop is 'on the people's side'", December 6, 2010, Link: https://www.peoplesworld.org/article/california-s-new-top-cop-is-on-the-people-s-side/

52   Dorfman, Zach, Politico. "How Silicon Valley Became a Den of Spies", July 27, 2018. Link: https://www.politico.com/magazine/story/2018/07/27/silicon-valley-spies-china-russia-219071/

53   Smith, Chris Modern Luxury "Rose Pak is Winning " Link: https://digital.modernluxury.com/publication/?i=134966&article_id=1236169&view=articleBrowser&ver=html5

54   Saracevic, Al. San Francisco Examiner "Willie and Rose: How an alliance for the ages shaped SF" June 16, 2022 "Feinstein Statement on Passing of Rose Pak" September 19, 2016. Link: https://www.sfexaminer.com/archives/willie-and-rose-how-an-alliance-for-the-ages-shaped-sf/article_83f61925-2127-5ad7-948d-ce0349a9266f.html

55   Gathright, Alan and Armstrong, David SFGate: "Chinese leader's friendly Bay Area visit / S.F. and Jiang Zemin, the outgoing president, nurture long-standing ties", October 29, 2002, Link: https://www.sfgate.com/business/article/Chinese-leader-s-friendly-Bay-Area-visit-S-F-2758596.php

56   Senator Feinstein, Dianne "Feinstein Statement on Passing of Rose Pak" September 19, 2016, Link: https://webcache.googleusercontent.com/ search?q=cache:6nGR_yNgyq0J:https://www.feinstein.senate.gov/public/index. cfm/press-releases%3FID%3DA9D30930-E70F-4A76-A0FD-A69999C0185F&c d=1&hl=en&ct=clnk&gl=us

57   State of California Department of Justice, "Attorney General Kamala D. Harris Issues Statement on Passing of Rose Pak", September 19, 2016, Link: https://oag.ca.gov/news/press-releases/ attorney-general-kamala-d-harris-issues-statement-passing-rose-pak

CHAPTER 3

1   Unity Archive Project, "What was the League of Revolutionary Struggle?", Link: https://unityarchiveproject.org/what-is-lrs/

2   Ibid.

3   Friedly, Michael, Stanford Daily, "League has played little known role in campus politics", May 23, 1990, page 1, Link: https://archives.stanforddaily. com/1990/05/23?page=1&section=MODSMD_ARTICLE2

4   Ibid.

5   Ibid.

6   Ibid.

7   Phillips, Steve, Democracy in Color, "A Day I Thought Would Never Come", April 13, 2016, Link: https://ourwork.democracyincolor. com/a-day-i-thought-would-never-come-f36251b3d382

8   Friedly, Michael, Stanford Daily, "League has played little known role in campus politics", May 23, 1990, page 1, Link: https://archives.stanforddaily. com/1990/05/23?page=1&section=MODSMD_ARTICLE2

9   Ibid.

10   Ibid.

11   Michael Pugliese email. Link: KeyWiki screenshot: https://keywiki. org/Mabel_Teng#/media/File:Tengie.JPG

12   East Wind, "Asian Americans and Jesse Jackson – From Vincent Chin to the Rainbow Coalition – A Conversation with the Rev. Jesse Jackson", https:// eastwindezine.com/asian-americans-and-jesse-jackson-from-vincent-chin-to-the- rainbow-coalition-a-conversation-with-the-rev-jesse-jackson/

13   Phillips, Steve, PowerPAC+, "The Progressive Case for Cory Booker", December 20, 2012, Link: https://web.archive.org/web/20180709003742/http:// www.powerpacplus.org/the_progressive_case_for_cory_booker

14   Wei, William (2010-06-18). The Asian American Movement. Temple University Press. ISBN 9781439903742.

15   East Wind zine, "In Memoriam Wilma Chan", Link: https://eastwind- ezine.com/in-memoriam-wilma-chan/

16   Chan, Wilma (Fall–Winter 1982). "Chinese Immigrants". East Wind Magazine. Archived from the original on 2012-01-20. Retrieved 2013-07-02 – via Azine September 26, 2009.

17   Northeastern University School of Law, "Ingrid Nava '03", Link: https://law.northeastern.edu/pathway/ingrid-nava-03/

18   KCRA3, "'Full of integrity': California attorney remembers time as

clerk for Justice Breyer", January 27, 2022, Link: https://www.kcra.com/article/california-attorney-remembers-time-clerk-justice-breyer/38905723

19   Finz, Stacy, SFGATE, "Brown's Choice for S.F. School Board Withdraws", August 31, 2000, Link: https://www.sfgate.com/education/article/Brown-s-Choice-for-S-F-School-Board-Withdraws-2741351.php

20   Adenji, Ade, Inside Philanthropy, "Steve Phillips Talks Progressive Philanthropy, the Sandler Legacy, and More", January 09, 2024, Link: https://www.insidephilanthropy.com/home/2024/1/9/steve-phillips-talks-about-his-progressive-philanthropy-and-the-sandler-foundation

21   Steven Phillips, "About Steve", Link: https://www.stevephillips.com/about

22   Netroots Nation, "Netroots Nation: Speaker/Trainer Profile: Steve Phillips", Link: https://www.netrootsnation.org/profile/steve-philips/

23   Kerpen, Phil, Fox News. "Van Jones Returns", February 22, 2010. Link: https://www.foxnews.com/opinion/van-jones-returns

24   Time Magazine, "25 People to Blame for the Financial Crisis: The good intentions, bad managers and greed behind the meltdown Blameworthy: Marion and Herb Sandler", 2009. Link: https://content.time.com/time/specials/packages/article/0,28804,1877351_1877350_1877343,00.html

25   Forbes, "Bernard Osher", Link: https://www.forbes.com/static/bill2005/LIRXFVQ.html?passListId=10&passYear=2005&passListType=Person&uniqueId=XFVQ&datatype=Person

26   Said, Carolyn, SF Gate, "Why Sandlers sold their S&L / Wachovia's deal for Golden West called a good fit", May 9, 2006, Link: https://www.sfgate.com/business/article/why-sandlers-sold-their-s-l-wachovia-s-deal-for-2497431.php

27   "The 60 largest American charitable contributions of the year". Slate.com. February 15, 2007

28   Nocera, Joe, The New York Times Magazine, "Self-Made Philanthropists", March 9, 2008, Link: https://www.nytimes.com/2008/03/09/magazine/09Sandlers-t.html?pagewanted=all

29   Matt Bai: The argument, "Billionaires, Bloggers, and the Battle to Remake Democratic Politics", Link: https://web.archive.org/web/20080213003521/https://www.mattbai.com/argument-book

30   Ibid.

31   Adenji, Ade, Inside Philanthropy, "Steve Phillips Talks Progressive Philanthropy, the Sandler Legacy, and More", January 09, 2024, Link: https://www.insidephilanthropy.com/home/2024/1/9/steve-phillips-talks-about-his-progressive-philanthropy-and-the-sandler-foundation

32   Sandler Phillips Center, "ABOUT", Link: https://www.sandlerphillipscenter.com/about

33   Adenji, Ade, Inside Philanthropy, "Steve Phillips Talks Progressive Philanthropy, the Sandler Legacy, and More", January 09, 2024, Link: https://www.insidephilanthropy.com/home/2024/1/9/steve-phillips-talks-about-his-progressive-philanthropy-and-the-sandler-foundation

34   PowerPAC+, "Board of Directors, "Link: https://web.archive.org/web/20170408213431/http://www.powerpacplus.org/board_of_directors

35   Scher, Brent and Joe Schoffstall, Washington Free Beacon. "Resistance Royalty: Pelosi, Soros Headline Left's Biggest Dark Money

Conference," November 17, 2017. Link: https://freebeacon.com/politics/
resistance-royalty-pelosi-soros-headline-lefts-biggest-dark-money-conference/

36   Exendra Staff, "Kamala Harris makes fundraising stop in
Piedmont," November 17, 2023. Link: https://piedmontexedra.com/2023/11/
vp-kamala-harris-makes-fundraising-stop-in-piedmont

37   Emerge California, Facebook Post dated January 20, 2021.
Link: https://www.facebook.com/photo?fbid=3761695570545196&s
et=a.173106602737462

38   Sandler, Susan, Sandler Phillips Center. "About". Archive Link:
https://web.archive.org/web/20240821200956/https://www.sandlerphillip-
scenter.com/about

39   Democracy in Color with Steve Phillips, Apple Podcasts. "The Kamala
Harris We Know", August 20, 2020. Link: https://podcasts.apple.com/us/
podcast/the-kamala-harris-we-know/id1119065616?i=1000488676283

40   5Chicago, "How Mayor Washington Influenced Barack Obama",
November 26, 2012, Link: https://www.nbcchicago.com/news/local/
how-mayor-washington-led-to-president-obama/1946198/

41   Kwon, Tre and Vergara, Jemena, Left Voice, "The DSA in the
Democratic Party Labyrinth", June 19, 2017, Link: https://www.leftvoice.org/
The-DSA-in-the-Democratic-Party-Labyrinth/

42   Communists in the Democratic Party, page 43, January 1, 1990
by Concerned Voters Inc (Author), ISBN-13: 978-0962742705

43   Schrader, Bobby, Stanford Daily, "Jackson cancels Farm appearance",
January 15, 1988, page 1, Link: https://archives.stanforddaily.com/1988/01/15?pa
ge=1&section=MODSMD_ARTICLE6

44   Kwon, Tre and Vergara, Jemena, Left Voice, "The DSA in the
Democratic Party Labyrinth", June 19, 2017, Link: https://www.leftvoice.org/
The-DSA-in-the-Democratic-Party-Labyrinth/

45   Edsall, Thomas B. (March 13, 1988). "JACKSON WINS WITH
MAJORITY IN SOUTH CAROLINA CAUCUSES". Washington Post

46   Phillips, Steve, "Democrats: You're Falling Into the #TrumpTrap
Medium",
May 6, 2016, Link: https://ourwork.democracyincolor.com/
democrats-stop-falling-into-the-trumptrap-a37b522a2b28

47   Phillips, Steve. How We Win the Civil War: A Blueprint for Defeating
the Extremist Right and Building a Multiracial Democracy. Bold Type Books,
2022.

48   Phillips, Steve. Brown Is the New White: How the Demographic
Revolution Has Created a New American Majority. The New Press, 2016.
Archive Link: https://web.archive.org/web/20240820142416/https://not-equal.
org/content/pdf/misc/brownisthenewwhite.pdf

49   Forward, Volume 9, number 1, Spring 1989, pages 4 and 5, Link:
https://unityarchiveproject.org/wp-content/uploads/Forward_Vol.9_No.1_
Spring_Summer_1989_edit.pdf

50   Emerge, "The New American Majority". Link: https://emergeamerica.
org/nam/

51   Gholar, A'Shanti, Ms. "The Kamala Harris I Know, and What
It Could Mean for America", July 23, 2024. Archive Link: https://web.

archive.org/web/20240820182629/https://msmagazine.com/2024/07/23/
kamala-harris-first-woman-president-usa/

52   Onward Together, "Emerge". Hillary Clinton PAC Link: https://www.
onwardtogether.org/organization/emerge-america/

53   Sandler Phillips Center, "ABOUT", Link: https://www.sandlerphillip-
scenter.com/about

54   Youtube, PowerPAC+, "Celebrating 10 Years of PowerPAC", December
1, 2014, Link: https://www.youtube.com/watch?v=cmfDDSn6ibs&t=12s

55   PowerPAC+, "Conference Speakers", Link: https://web.archive.org/
web/20170701075421/http://www.powerpacplus.org/conference_speakers

56   Jang, Jon, East Wind, "Jon Jang & The Sounds of Struggle Part III –
Revolutionary Musings & Music", March 15, 2019, Link: https://eastwindezine.
com/jon-jang-sounds-of-struggle-part-iii-revolutionary-musings-music/

57   Hsiang, Bob, Mother Jones, "Jon Jang speaks out about his recent
album, Amiri Baraka, and Malcolm X", https://www.motherjones.com/
media/2020/06/jon-jang-on-his-recent-black-asian-solidarity-album-amiri-
baraka-malcolm-x/, Link: https://www.motherjones.com/media/2020/06/
jon-jang-on-his-recent-black-asian-solidarity-album-amiri-baraka-malcolm-x/

58   Bioneers, "Steve Phillips Says Brown Is the New White", August 28,
2017, Link: https://bioneers.org/steve-phillips-says-brown-new-white-ze0z1709/

59   Phillips, Steve, Netroots Nation: Speaker/Trainer Profile. Archive
Link: https://web.archive.org/web/20240821201101/https://www.netrootsnation.
org/profile/steve-philips/

60   PowerPAC+, "Board of Directors, "Link: https://web.archive.org/
web/20170408213431/http://www.powerpacplus.org/board_of_directors

61   Ibid.

62   Ibid.

63   AJW Inc., "Steve Phillips" Link: https://web.archive.org/
web/20180814082510/https://ajwi.com/bios/DetailedBio.asp?BioID=2

64   Wong, Andy, Leyton, Stacey, Unity, "Student Unity Network",
November 26, 1990

65   PowerPAC, "The Team", Link: https://www.powerpac.org/the_team/

66   PowerPAC, "Voter Enhancement", Link: https://www.powerpac.org/
our-work/campaign-strategy/

67   PowerPAC+, "Board of Directors, "Link: https://web.archive.org/
web/20170408213431/http://www.powerpacplus.org/board_of_directors

68   Schweers, Jeffrey, Tallahassee Democrat, "Andrew
Gillum's fundraising PAC took shape in city email", April 25,
2017, Link: https://www.tallahassee.com/story/news/2017/04/25/
andrew-gillums-fundraising-pac-took-shape-city-email/100857650/

69   Caputo, Marc, Politico, Steyer boosts Gillum's strug-
gling campaign with $1M", June 28, 2018, Link: https://
www.politico.com/states/florida/story/2018/06/28/
steyer-boosts-gillums-struggling-campaign-with-1-million-494849

70   Wilson, Kirby, Tampa Bay Times, "George Soros has
picked his candidate in the Florida governor's race", May 7, 2018,
Link: https://www.tampabay.com/florida-politics/buzz/2018/05/07/
george-soros-has-picked-his-candidate-in-the-florida-governors-race/

71   Inclusv, "Our Team", Link: https://web.archive.org/web/20200420064527/https://inclusv.com/our-team/

72   PowerPAC+, "Board of Directors, "Link: https://web.archive.org/web/20170408213431/http://www.powerpacplus.org/board_of_directors

73   Allison, Aimee, "Alida Garcia On Immigration Reform Being About People Not Votes", July 17, 2014, Link: https://www.laprogressive.com/immigration-reform/alida-garcia

74   The Nation, Phillips, Steve, "Democrats Are in Danger of Repeating the Mistakes of 2016", April 26, 2018, Link: https://www.thenation.com/article/archive/democrats-are-in-danger-of-repeating-the-mistakes-of-2016/

75   Democracy in Color, "Sign the Petition: Woman Of Color For VP", Link: https://democracyincolor.com/wocpetition

76   Ibid.

77   Ibid.

78   PowerPAC+, "The Demographic Revolution: the path to a permanent progressive majority in America", Link: https://web.archive.org/web/20160806163729/https://d3n8a8pro7vhmx.cloudfront.net/pacplus/pages/244/attachments/original/1396464136/2013_plans_booklet.pdf?1396464136

79   Phillips, Steve, The Nation, "The Vice-Presidential Nominee Should Be a Woman of Color", March 16, 2020, Link: https://www.thenation.com/article/politics/biden-sanders-vp-of-color/

80   Ibid.

81   Ibid.

82   Ibid.

83   The Yankee Radical, "DSA members meeting", October 2009, page 3, Link: http://web.archive.org/web/20120118072222/http://www.dsaboston.org/yradical/yr2009-09.pdf

84   PowerPAC+, "Elected and Appointed Leadership", Link: http://web.archive.org/web/20150429185733/http://www.powerpacplus.org/elected_and_appointed_leadership

85   Allison, Aimee, Newsweek, "To Beat Trump, a Woman of Color Vice President Is More Than a Consolation Prize. It's a Necessity | Opinion", March 11, 2020, Link: https://www.newsweek.com/beat-trump-woman-color-vice-president-more-consolation-prize-its-necessity-opinion-1491694

86   Chavez, Aliyah, ICT, "Internet declares 'Deb for Interior' week" December 16, 2020, Link: https://ictnews.org/news/internet-declares-deb-for-interior-week

87   Gardner, Chris, The Hollywood Reporter, "Hollywood Stars Call on Biden Administration to Nominate Rep. Deb Haaland as Interior Secretary", December 10, 2020, Link: https://www.hollywoodreporter.com/news/general-news/hollywood-stars-call-on-biden-administration-to-nominate-rep-deb-haaland-as-interior-secretary-4103185/

88   Democratic Left, "Convention Elects DSA Leadership", Winter 2006, Page 9

89   Horon, Daily Mail, "Sarah Silverman slams Democratic Socialists of America over Palestine support and leaves the organization after being a proud lifetime member: 'F**k you and goodbye forever!'", October 10, 2023, Link:

https://www.dailymail.co.uk/tvshowbiz/article-12617251/Sarah-Silverman-slams-Democratic-Socialists-America-Palestine.html

90   Rott, Nathan, NPR, "Deb Haaland Confirmed As 1st Native American Interior Secretary", March 15, 2021, Link: https://www.npr.org/2021/03/15/977558590/deb-haaland-confirmed-as-first-native-american-interior-secretary

91   Courthouse News Service, "Interior Head Haaland Revokes Trump-Era Orders on Energy", April 16, 2021, Link: https://www.courthouse-news.com/interior-head-haaland-revokes-trump-era-orders-on-energy/

92   Doyle, Michael, E&E News, "Haaland endorses Harris", July 25, 2024, Link: https://www.eenews.net/articles/haaland-endorses-harris/

93   Democracy in Color podcast, "VP Harris Picks Her VP", August 8, 2024, Link: https://democracyincolor.com/podepisodes/2024/8/8/vp-harris-picks-her-vp

94   Sandler Phillips Center, "ABOUT", Link: https://www.sandlerphillip-scenter.com/about

95   PowerPAC+, "The Demographic Revolution: the path to a permanent progressive majority in America", Link: https://web.archive.org/web/20160806163729/https://d3n8a8pro7vhmx.cloudfront.net/pac-plus/pages/244/attachments/original/1396464136/2013_plans_booklet.pdf?1396464136

96   Rob Bonta press release, "Attorney General Kamala D. Harris Announces Appointment of Eric Casher to the Fair Political Practices Commission", March 11, 2013, Link: https://oag.ca.gov/news/press-releases/attorney-general-kamala-d-harris-announces-appointment-eric-casher-fair

97   Youtube, PowerPAC+, "Celebrating 10 Years of PowerPAC", December 1, 2014, Link: https://www.youtube.com/watch?v=cmfDDSn6ibs&t=12s

98   Ibid.

99   Public Rights Project, "Meet the Team", Link: https://www.pub-licrightsproject.org/who-we-are

100   Inclusv, "Our Team", Link: https://web.archive.org/web/20200420064527/https://inclusv.com/our-team/

101   Friedlieb, Linda, Stanford Daily, "Campus responds to verdict; rally planned for noon today", May 1, 1992, Link: https://archives.stanforddaily.com/1992/05/01?page=1&section=MODSMD_ARTICLE2

102   CAP 20, "RELEASE: Maya Harris Joins the Center for American Progress as Senior Fellow", October 29, 2013, Link: https://www.americanprogress.org/press/release-maya-harris-joins-the-center-for-american-progress-as-senior-fellow/

103   Gerstein, Josh, Politico. "Eric Holder: 'I'm still the president's wingman'", April 4, 2013. https://www.politico.com/blogs/politico44/2013/04/eric-holder-im-still-the-presidents-wingman-160861

104   PowerPAC+, "History", Link: https://web.archive.org/web/20170925152657/http://www.powerpacplus.org/history

105   Cadelago, Christopher, Politico. "Eric Holder is running Harris' veep vetting process", July 22, 2024. Link: https://www.politico.com/live-updates/2024/07/22/kamala-harris-campaign-biden-drop-out/a-familiar-name-vetting-vps-00170416

106 Ballotpedia, "National Democratic Redistricting Committee", Link: https://ballotpedia.org/National_Democratic_Redistricting_Committee

107 Orduña, Ruben, San Francisco Foundation. "Philanthropy Can Build Power and Bolster Democracy", October 14, 2020. Archive Link: https://web.archive.org/web/20240822145301/https://sff.org/philanthropy-can-build-power-and-bolster-democracy/

108 Nather, David, Politico, "Clinton names top 3 wonks for campaign", April 14, 2015, Link: https://www.politico.com/story/2015/04/clinton-names-top-three-wonks-for-campaign-116975

109 Allison, Aimee, Medium "Podcast: Senator Cory Booker: Making Our Future This Election", November 1, 2016, Link: https://ourwork.democracyincolor.com/senator-cory-booker-making-our-future-this-election-e795aad8f5f2

110 Disjecta Membra, "Hillary Rodham Clinton – What Happened", April 30, 2018, Link: https://disjectamembra2014.blogspot.com/2018/04/hillary-rodham-clinton-what-happened.html

111 Nather, David, Politico, "Clinton names top 3 wonks for campaign", April 14, 2015, Link: https://www.politico.com/story/2015/04/clinton-names-top-three-wonks-for-campaign-116975

112 MDRC,"MDRC Mourns the Passing of Susan Sandler, Former MDRC Board Member" January 2023, Link: https://www.mdrc.org/news/announcement/mdrc-mourns-passing-susan-sandler-former-mdrc-board-member#:~:text=Susan%20Sandler%20was%20a%20philanthropist,grants%20focused%20on%20racial%20justice.

113 Vogel, Kenneth P. and Schleifer, Theodore, New York Times, "Democratic Billionaires and Donors Rush to Back Harris After Biden's Exit", July 21, 2024, Link: https://www.nytimes.com/2024/07/21/us/politics/democrat-donors-harris-biden.html

114 Phillips, Steve, "Running Kamala Harris may actually be a political masterstroke for the Democrats", Guardian, July 23, 2024, Link: https://www.theguardian.com/commentisfree/article/2024/jul/23/kamala-harris-elecion-masterstroke-democrats

115 Democracy in Color podcast, "VP Harris Picks Her VP", Link: https://oliviaxe.podbean.com/e/vp-harris-picks-her-vp/

CHAPTER 4

1 Lateefah Simon: BART Rider for BART Board, "How Bay Area activists keep the flames of their passion for change burning bright". Archive Link: https://web.archive.org/web/20240911203214/https://www.lateefahforbart.com/blog/tsxf7svbgaxt5rjxqjghozt52fquqm

2 Landing page for the Meadow Fund. Link: https://meadowfund.org/

3 San Francisco Foundation, "Board of Trustees". Link: https://sff.org/about-us/board-of-trustees/

4 San Francisco Foundation, "Grantmaking to Advance Racial Equity". Link: https://sff.org/what-we-do/grantmaking-to-advance-racial-equity/

5 Simon, Lateefah, Financial Disclosure Form, Filed June 14, 2024. Archive Link: https://web.archive.org/web/20240618160639/https://disclosures-clerk.house.gov/public_disc/financial-pdfs/2024/10060189.pdf

6   Simon, Lateefah, Akonadi Foundation. "To My Beloved Community". Link: https://akonadi.org/to-my-beloved-community/

7   Schleifer, Theodore, New York Times. "Female Donors Mobilize for Harris, Moving to Stamp Out Opposition", July 22, 2024. Link: https://www.nytimes.com/2024/07/22/us/politics/kamala-harris-donors-women.html?searchResultPosition=1

8   Akonadi Foundation bio. Link: https://akonadi.org/our-team/lateefah-simon-president/

9   Lateefah Simon for Congress! "ENDORSEMENTS", Link: https://www.lateefahsimon.com/endorsements

10   Adeniji, Ade, Inside Philanthropy, "Steve Phillips Talks Progressive Philanthropy, the Sandler Legacy, and More", January 09, 2024, Link: https://www.insidephilanthropy.com/home/2024/1/9/steve-phillips-talks-about-his-progressive-philanthropy-and-the-sandler-foundation

11   Local ABC Affiliate, "Judge allows criminal history detail in BART trial", May 7, 2010. Link: https://abc7news.com/archive/7428841/

12   Hales, Larry, Workers World. "Demand justice for Oscar Grant", October 28, 2009. Link: https://www.workers.org/2009/us/oscar_grant_1105/

13   Jones, Nicole, Oakland North. "Justice for Oscar Grant Coalition ponders next steps after Mehserle release", June 28, 2011. Link: https://oaklandnorth.net/2011/06/28/justice-for-oscar-grant-coalition-ponders-next-steps-after-mehserle-release/

14   McKinney, George, Freedom Road Socialist Organization, Fight Back! News. Commentary: The Murder of Oscar Grant III and the Black Liberation Struggle", January 21, 2009. Link: https://fightbacknews.org/articles/murder-oscar-grant-iii-and-black-liberation-struggle

15   Freedom Road Socialist Organization, Fight Back! News. "Still No Justice for Oscar Grant", July 9, 2010. Link: https://fightbacknews.org/articles/still-no-justice-oscar-grant

16   Allen-Taylor, J. Douglas, Berkeley Daily Planet. "DA Moving Ahead With Charges in BART Shooting Protests", February 11, 2009. Link: https://berkeleydailyplanet.com/issue/2009-02-12/article/32256?headline=DA-Moving-Ahead-With-Charges-in-BART-Shooting-Protests

17   Dirks, Sandhya, KQED. "It Started With Oscar Grant: A Police Shooting in Oakland, and the Making of a Movement", June 5, 2020. Link: https://www.kqed.org/news/11823246/it-started-with-oscar-grant-a-police-shooting-in-oakland-and-the-making-of-a-movement-2

18   Democracy in Color with Steve Phillips, Democracy in Color. "Lateefah Simon is Taking Up the Baton", April 4, 2024. Link: https://democracyincolor.com/podepisodes/2024/4/3/lateefah-simon-is-taking-up-the-baton

19   Ibid.

20   Cadelago, Christopher and Dustin Gardiner, Politico. California Playbook. "High Praise for Lee". Link: https://www.politico.com/newsletters/california-playbook/2023/11/17/the-governor-returns-00127751

21   Political Warfare.org, "Congresswoman Barbara Lee: Still stuck in the Cold War", April ,7 2009, Link: https://jmw.typepad.com/political_warfare/2009/04/congresswoman-barbara-lee-still-stuck-in-the-cold-war.html

22   Ibid.

23   Ibid.

24   Wilhelm, Ian, The Chronicle of Philanthropy, Turning Pain Into Power, October 30, 2003, Link: https://www.philanthropy.com/article/turning-pain-into-power/

25   Young Women's Freedom Center, "Meet the Team", Archive link captured February 13, 2016: https://web.archive.org/web/20160213111924/http://www.youngwomenfree.org/who_we_are

26   Keywiki.org, Ayoka Turner. Link: https://keywiki.org/Ayoka_Turner

27   Young Women's Freedom Center, "Pamela Shifman". Archive Link: https://web.archive.org/web/20240827190323/https://youngwomenfree.org/board/pamela-shifman/

28   Ferrannini, John, Bay Area Reporter. "Gunned down SF Black trans activist remembered at vigil", May 1, 2023. Link: https://web.archive.org/web/20230506185321/https://www.ebar.com/story.php?ch=news&sc=latest_news&id=324990

29   Stoughtenborough, Ryce, San Francisco Chronicle. "Civil rights champion Rev. Amos Brown: 'San Francisco has been living a lie'", June 16, 2021, Link: https://www.sfchronicle.com/lift-every-voice/article/Amos-Brown-16219697.php

30   Ross, Chuck, Washington Free Beacon. "Kamala Harris Taps Her Radical Pastor for DNC Convention Prayer", August 23, 2024. Link: https://freebeacon.com/elections/kamala-harris-taps-her-radical-pastor-for-dnc-convention-prayer/

31   Keywiki, "Jeremiah Wright". Link: https://keywiki.org/Jeremiah_Wright

32   Garofoli, Joe, San Francisco Chronicle. "Republicans are trying to make Kamala Harris' S.F. pastor 'another Jeremiah Wright.' Here's why it won't work", August 7, 2024. Archive Link: https://archive.vn/iaTfW

33   Jones, Carolyn, SFGate "Lateefah Simon: Youth advocate nominated as Visionary of the Year January" January 5, 2015. Link: https://www.sfgate.com/visionsf/article/Lateefah-Simon-Youth-advocate-nominated-as-5993578.php

34   Circa 1996 Report of Committees of Correspondence Lesbian, Gay, Bisexual, Transgender Taskforce

35   People's Weekly World, September 21, 1996, page 2

36   Ibid.

37   Wildermuth, John, SFGate, "Kamala Harris stumps for others rather than her own Senate run", November 5, 2016, Link: https://www.sfgate.com/politics/article/Kamala-Harris-stumps-for-others-rather-than-her-10594712.php

38   Working Families Party, "About Maurice Mitchell", Link: https://workingfamilies.org/about-maurice-mitchell/

39   Working Families Party, "Our Candidates", Link: https://workingfamilies.org/candidates/

40   UNDUE INFLUENCE, "Youth Empowerment Center", Link: https://web.archive.org/web/20040620023227/http://www.undueinfluence.com/yec.htm

41   Ibid.

42   Byrne, Peter SF Weekly "SOUL Trainers", October 16, 2002, Link: https://archives.sfweekly.com/sanfrancisco/soul-trainers/Content?oid=2146061

43   Ibid.

44   SOUL, "SOUL Staff & Board", Link: https://web.archive.org/web/20101017044147/http://www.schoolofunityandliberation.org/soul_sec/about/ab-staff_board.html

45   SOUL, "SOUL Staff & Board", Link: https://web.archive.org/web/20101017044147/http://www.schoolofunityandliberation.org/soul_sec/about/ab-staff_board.html

46   UNDUE INFLUENCE, "Youth Empowerment Center", Link: https://web.archive.org/web/20040620023227/http://www.undueinfluence.com/yec.htm

47   "Reclaiming Revolution", Link: https://archive.org/details/ReclaimingRevolution/page/n1/mode/2up

48   Center for Political Action Programming History, Link: https://politicaleducation.org/programs-2/past-classes-1998-2007/

49   Center for Political Action Programming History, 2005, Link: https://politicaleducation.org/programs-2/past-classes-1998-2007/

50   WAR TIMES new biweekly newspaper opposing the "war on terrorism" January 29, 2002, Link: https://ratical.org/co-globalize/wartimes.html

51   Strickland, Eliza, East Bay Express, "The New Face of Environmentalism", November 2, 2005, Link: https://eastbayexpress.com/the-new-face-of-environmentalism-1/

52   Congressional Record (Bound Edition), Volume 155, Rep. Dan Burton. "Van Jones Radical Past", Part 16, 2009. Link: https://www.govinfo.gov/content/pkg/CRECB-2009-pt16/html/CRECB-2009-pt16-Pg21103.htm

53   Youtube, "Brown is the New White: Changing Demographics and a New American Majority", April 6, 2016, Link: https://www.youtube.com/watch?v=7QRSS0lx90I&t=22s

54   Jones, Van, X. Van Jones X Post, Dated July 24, 2024. Link: https://x.com/VanJones68/status/1816102937631789378

55   Ibid.

56   Gambino, Lauren, The Guardian, "'Who are we?' Joe Biden seizes the moment as nation's attitude shifts on race", June 15, 2020, Link: https://www.theguardian.com/us-news/2020/jun/15/joe-biden-race-reforms-democrat-seizes-moment

57   Brazile, Donna, X. X Post dated October 6, 2021. Link: https://x.com/donnabrazile/status/1445743093567803406

58   Brazile, Donna, X. X Post dated August 27, 2018. Link: https://x.com/donnabrazile/status/1034258853779656704

59   Vogel, Kenneth, P., Politico, "Dems pressed on consultant diversity", June 1, 2014, Link: https://www.politico.com/story/2014/05/democratic-consultants-diversity-106252

60   Essence, "Why Jotaka Eaddy Always Bets It All On Black Women", Link: https://www.essence.com/news/money-career/jotaka-eaddy-win-with-black-women/

61   Southern Elections Fund, "About". Link: https://www.southernelectionsfund.org/about

62   Southern Elections Fund, "Board". Link: https://www.southernelectionsfund.org/board

63   Lateefah for Congress, "Endorsements", Link: https://www.lateefah-simon.com/endorsements

64   Harris, Kamala, X. X Post dated Feb 27, 2018. Link: https://x.com/KamalaHarris/status/968624792365600769

65   Garza, Alicia, Glamour, "With Kamala Harris in the VP Slot, We Just Made History—Let's Do It Again in November", August 12, 2020, Link: https://www.glamour.com/story/alicia-garza-kamala-harris-vice-president-history

66   Ibid.

67   Linskey, Annie, and Janes, Chelsea, Washington Post, "Harris's wooing of Black activists paved a path to the ticket", August 15, 2020, Link: https://web.archive.org/web/20200910015153/https://www.washingtonpost.com/politics/har-riss-wooing-of-black-activists-paved-a-path-to-the-ticket/2020/08/15/d638b276-de70-11ea-b205-ff838e15a9a6_story.html

68   Washington Post, "Harris's wooing of Black activists paved a path to the ticket", Link: https://web.archive.org/web/20200910015153/https://www.washingtonpost.com/politics/harriss-wooing-of-black-activists-paved-a-path-to-the-ticket/2020/08/15/d638b276-de70-11ea-b205-ff838e15a9a6_story.html

69   Ford Foundation, "Alicia Garza on inequality and protecting workers" Link: https://www.fordfoundation.org/news-and-stories/big-ideas/inequalityis/alicia-garza-on-inequality-and-protecting-workers/

70   Chinese Progressive Association, "Together We Move Mountains:: Celebrating Generations of Change", Link: https://web.archive.org/web/20130411234923/https://cpasf.org/content/together-we-move-mountains-celebrating-generations-change

71   National Domestic Workers Alliance press release, "Domestic Workers Bill of Rights would ensure basic labor protections and trans-form the way people work in America", November 29, 2018, Link: https://web.archive.org/web/20210307233728/https://www.domesticworkers.org/release/senator-harris-and-congresswoman-jayapal-announce-ground-breaking-national-legislation?fbclid=IwAR0ANKzC0yEAGQWj3ms9FHHq_LJ5sF01ZUXo-IqW9ZKrDPpDRWzcZ_BJ-Gw

72   Rockwood Leadership Institute, "National Leading From The Inside Out Alums". Link: https://rockwoodleadership.org/fellowships/yearlong/yearlong-alums/

73   Rockwood Leadership Institute, "Alum News Round-Up, June 2017". Link: https://rockwoodleadership.org/alum-news-round-up-june-2017/

74   Poo, Ai-jen, Instagram. Ai-jen Poo Instagram post dated July 22, 2023. Link: https://www.instagram.com/p/C9ulQIygshF/

75   The Domestic Workers Bill of Rights was initiated and promoted by graduates of a militant training school, supported by their comrade Kamala Harris. When researching Kamala, the same radical groups and individuals con-tinually appear.

76   Tom, Alex, Linked In. Linked in Profile, "Alex T. (He/Him). Link: https://www.linkedin.com/in/alexttom/

77   Audible, "One Struggle, Many Fronts with Alex Tom", February 26, 2021, Link:https://www.audible.com/podcast/One-Struggle-Many-Fronts-with-Alex-Tom/B08VG5TYQG?clientContext=134-6271894-8320211&loginAttempt=true

78   Tsukada, Kaori, Undergraduate Honors Thesis, May 26th, 2009,

"THE INTERACTION BETWEEN SERVICE AND ORGANIZING: TWO HOUSING CAMPAIGNS BY THE CHINESE PROGRESSIVE ASSOCIATION", Page 20, Link: https://www.marxists.org/history/erol/ncm-1a/iwk-cpa.pdf

79   Tsukada, Kaori, Undergraduate Honors Thesis, May 26th, 2009, "THE INTERACTION BETWEEN SERVICE AND ORGANIZING: TWO HOUSING CAMPAIGNS BY THE CHINESE PROGRESSIVE ASSOCIATION", Pages 88, 89, Link: https://www.marxists.org/history/erol/ncm-1a/iwk-cpa.pdf

80   Tsukada, Kaori, Undergraduate Honors Thesis, May 26th, 2009, "THE INTERACTION BETWEEN SERVICE AND ORGANIZING: TWO HOUSING CAMPAIGNS BY THE CHINESE PROGRESSIVE ASSOCIATION", Page 88, Link: https://www.marxists.org/history/erol/ncm-1a/iwk-cpa.pdf

81   Mabel Teng, LRS, KeyWiki screenshot, Link: https://keywiki.org/Mabel_Teng#/media/File:Tengie.JPG

82   East Wind, "Celebrating 15 Years of Progress & Service", Volume 7, Number 1, page 13, Link: https://unityarchiveproject.org/wp-content/uploads/East-Wind-Vol-7-No-1-Spring-Summer-1989-a.pdf

83   Center for Political Education, "US and China Relations", May 22, 2020, Link: https://politicaleducation.org/event/us-and-china-relations/

84   Jang, Jon, East Wind zine, "Jon Jang Sounds of Struggle, Parts 7-9: Movement Music", May 16, 2019, Link: https://eastwindezine.com/jon-jang-sounds-of-struggle-parts-7-9-movement-music/

85   The Stanford Daily, Volume 189, Issue 22, 26 February 1986. Page 12, Link: https://archives.stanforddaily.com/1986/02/26?page=12&section=DIVL489

86   Chinese Progressive Association, "Together We Move Mountains: Celebrating Generations of Change", Link: https://web.archive.org/web/20130411234923/https://cpasf.org/content/together-we-move-mountains-celebrating-generations-change

87   Ibid.

88   Chinese Progressive Association, "Harnessing the Strength of a thousand rivers", "Host Committee", Link: https://www.athousandrivers.org/hostcommittee/

89   Chinese Progressive Association, "Harnessing the Strength of a thousand rivers", "Honorees", Link: https://www.athousandrivers.org/hostcommittee/

90   Chinese Progressive Association, "Harnessing the Strength of a thousand rivers", "Thank you to all of our sponsors", Link: https://www.athousandrivers.org/our-sponsors/

91   Gonalez, Mike, Heritage Foundation, "This BLM Co-Founder and Pro-Communist China Group Are Partnering Up. Here's Why", September 15, 2020, Link: https://www.heritage.org/progressivism/commentary/blm-co-founder-and-pro-communist-china-group-are-partnering-heres-why

92   Ibid.

93   Black Futures Lab, "Our Allies". Link: https://web.archive.org/web/20190814192110/https://blackfutureslab.org/our-allies/

94   Liberation Road, "The Young and the Leftless: An

Open Letter on Organization", Link: https://roadtoliberation.org/
the-young-and-the-leftless-an-open-letter-on-organization/

95   Chinese Progressive Association San Francisco, "Michelle Foy", Link:
https://cpasf.org/?s=foy

96   Lee, N'Tanya, and Williams, Steve, "Ear to the Ground Project", Link:
https://web.archive.org/web/20160528100736/https://eartothegroundproject.
org/wp-content/uploads/2013/05/final-ear-2-ground-single-pages.pdf

97   Ibid.

98   Ibid.

99   Ibid.

100   Ibid.

101   Ibid.

102   Ibid.

103   Lee, N'Tanya, and Williams, Steve, "Ear to the Ground Project", Link:
https://web.archive.org/web/20160528100736/https://eartothegroundproject.
org/wp-content/uploads/2013/05/final-ear-2-ground-single-pages.pdf

104   Labor/Community Strategy Center, "Symbols
Of Resistance: A conversation with Claude Marks, and
Eric Mann", Link: https://fightforthesoulofthecities.com/
symbols-of-resistance-a-conversation-with-claude-marks-and-eric-mann/

105   Tsukada, Kaori, Undergraduate Honors Thesis, May 26th, 2009,
"THE INTERACTION BETWEEN SERVICE AND ORGANIZING:
TWO HOUSING CAMPAIGNS BY THE CHINESE PROGRESSIVE
ASSOCIATION", Page 88, Link: https://www.marxists.org/history/erol/
ncm-1a/iwk-cpa.pdf

106   Forward Motion, journal of the Freedom Road Socialist Organization,
Winter 96/97

107   THE CONFERENCE "MALCOLM X: Radical Tradition and a
Legacy of Struggle", Link: https://www.brothermalcolm.net/sections/malcolm/
old/v1contributor.html

108   Gallegos, Bill, Freedom Road, Number 3, Winter 2003. "They Wanted
to Serve the People Chicanos and the Fight against National Oppression in the
New Communist Movement", Link: https://www.marxists.org/history/erol/
ncm-8/ncm-chicanos.htm

109   Fernando Marti, Freedom Road Socialist Organization, KeyWiki
Screenshot, Link: https://keywiki.org/Fernando_Marti#/media/File:Marti.JPG

110   Jon Liss, Freedom Road Socialist Organization, KeyWiki Screenshot,
Link: https://keywiki.org/Jon_Liss#/media/File:Frso2.PNG

111   Scott Kurashige, Freedom Road Socialist Organization, KeyWiki
Screenshot, Link: https://keywiki.org/Scott_Kurashige#/media/File:Scottie.
PNG

112   THE CONFERENCE "MALCOLM X: Radical Tradition and a
Legacy of Struggle", Link: https://www.brothermalcolm.net/sections/malcolm/
old/v1contributor.html

113   Uetricht, Micah, Jacobin, "Learning from the New Communist
Movement", September 30, 2018, Link: https://jacobin.com/2018/09/
max-elbaum-new-communist-movement-socialism-organizing

114   Holtzman, Benjamin, In the Middle of a Whirlwind, "An Interview

with Robin D.G. Kelley", Link: https://inthemiddleofthewhirlwind.wordpress.com/an-interview-with-robin-dg-kelley/

115   Internet Archive, "E26: The League of Revolutionary Black Workers. With Jerome Scott [55 minutes]", Link: https://archive.org/details/nyi2ekr8nzqsz2jpmbdk0kfri1oiyijvwkhfv6yq

116   The People's Tribune (Online Edition), "A Convention to Reclaim America", Volume 22, Number 20, May 15, 1995, Link: https://www.marxists.org/history/erol/ncm-7/lrna-founding.htm

117   Facing Race: A National Conference, "Shaw San Liu", Link: https://facingrace.raceforward.org/es/speaker/shaw-san-liu

118   LeftRoots, "Making the Impossible Possible: A History of LeftRoots", 2023. Page 16 Archive Link: https://web.archive.org/web/20240911175718/https://dusk.leftroots.net/resources/LeftRoots_Summation.pdf

119   Invoking the People, "2018 Grant Partner – LeftRoots", Link: https://www.invokingthepause.org/2018-grant-partner-leftroots_grant-partners-list_8734.html

120   Convergence, "Timmy Lu", Link: https://convergencemag.com/authors/timmy-lu/

121   City of Oakland, "Cinthya Muñoz Ramos", Link: https://www.oaklandca.gov/staff/cinthya-munoz-ramos

122   Left Forum 2013, Speaker: Alex Tom, Link: https://web.archive.org/web/20130503180125/https://www.leftforum.org/participant/speaker-alex-tom-0

123   Solidarity, "Solidarity Summer School 2015: Program", Link: https://web.archive.org/web/20150714210730/https://solidarity-us.org/ss2015program/

124   Tuesday Group, "Who We Are", Link: https://www.understandtheworldtochangeit.com/who-we-are

125   The Black Alliance for Peace", "LeftRoots HangOut - A Report-Back from Vietnam", Link: https://web.archive.org/web/20201105172129/https://blackallianceforpeace.com/events/leftrootsvietnamreportback

126   Ibid.

127   Ibid.

128   Lee N'Tanya and Williams, Steve, Jacobin, "No Shortcuts", June 1, 2014, Link: https://jacobin.com/2014/06/no-shortcuts

129   Right To The City Alliance, "Greed Gone Wild--A Remedy is At Hand", June 1, 201, Link: https://web.archive.org/save/https://righttothecityalliance.blogspot.com/2011/06/greed-gone-wild-remedy-is-at-hand.html

130   Forward Motion article, January 1995 issue, from Lisa Duran, Bill Gallegos, Eric Mann, and Glenn Omatsu "Prop 187 - where do we go from here?"

131   Breitbart, "Black Lives Matter Founder an Open Supporter of Socialist Venezuelan Dictator Maduro", June 13, 2020, Link: https://www.breitbart.com/politics/2020/06/13/black-lives-matter-founder-an-open-supporter-of-socialist-venezuelan-dictator-maduro/

132   Garza, Alicia, Kaufman, L.A., H+1, "A Love Note to Our Folks", June 3, 2016, Link: https://web.archive.org/web/20160605033735/https://www.nplusonemag.com/online-only/online-only/a-love-note-to-our-folks/

133   Black Leaders Organizing for Leadership & Dignity (BOLD), "Staff", Link: https://web.archive.org/web/20150131021641/http://boldorganizing.org/index.php?page=staff

134   Asian American Racial Justice Toolkit, "Acknowledgements", Link: https://www.apalanet.org/uploads/8/3/2/0/83203568/asian_american_racial_justice_toolkit.pdf

135   Ibid.

136   Phelps, Timothy M. and Michael Muskal, Los Angeles Times. "Federal report largely backs Darren Wilson in Ferguson police shooting case", March 4, 2015. Link: https://www.latimes.com/nation/la-na-darren-wilson-not-charged-20150304-story.html

137   Mann, Eric, Boston Review, "Lost Radicals", January 15, 2014, https://www.bostonreview.net/articles/eric-mann-michael-dawson-radical-black-left-history/

138   HistoryMakers, "Biographical Description for The HistoryMakers® Video Oral History with Jamala Rogers", Link: https://www.thehistorymakers.org/sites/default/files/A2007_290_EAC.pdf

139   Wheaton, Sarah, and Vogel, Kenneth, P., Politico, "Major donors consider funding Black Lives Matter", November 13, 2015.

140   Youtube, "4. Montague Simmons of OBS on Building a Movement", Link: https://www.youtube.com/watch?v=tkf664FFbqY

141   LeftRoots, "Making the Impossible Possible: A History of LeftRoots", 2023. Page 16 Archive Link: https://web.archive.org/web/20240911175718/https://dusk.leftroots.net/resources/LeftRoots_Summation.pdf

142   Wong, Julia, In These Times, "As Ferguson 'Weekend of Resistance' Begins, Organizers Weigh How to Turn a Moment into a Movement", October 10, 2014, Link: https://inthesetimes.com/article/from-a-moment-to-a-movement

143   Ibid.

144   "Department Of Justice Report Regarding The Criminal Investigation Into The Shooting Death Of Michael Brown By Ferguson, Missouri Police Officer Darren Wilson", March 4, 2015, Link: https://www.justice.gov/sites/default/files/opa/press-releases/attachments/2015/03/04/doj_report_on_shooting_of_michael_brown_1.pdf

145   Hennepin County Medical Examiner's Office Autopsy Report, "George Floyd aka Floyd Perry", May 26, 2020. Archive Link: https://web.archive.org/web/20240716204544/https://www.hennepin.us/-/media/hennepinus/residents/public-safety/medical-examiner/floyd-autopsy-6-3-20.pdf

146   Keywiki, "Twin Cities Coalition for Justice 4 Jamar". Link: https://keywiki.org/Twin_Cities_Coalition_for_Justice_4_Jamar

147   Ibid.

148   Nal, Renee, RAIR Foundation USA. "UPDATE: Minneapolis Officials Planned for Rioters to Take Over Third Precinct 'at least a day in advance'," May 29, 2020. Link: https://rairfoundation.com/watch-mayor-jacob-frey-orders-police-to-flee-as-milwaukee-rioters-take-over-third-precinct/

149   Tim Walz Press Conference, May 29, 2020. (Minute mark 50:53) Link: https://www.rev.com/transcript-editor/shared/uh-rVmxJr_dPHlgssi_dJmyEg1If-wZduj9OSl9cfqF_ZN4HDaTnPujkxoTBZiLZ0wLjTxNJDF0nnR0N72K1llD HrKlQ?loadFrom=PastedDeeplink&ts=275.06

150   X Post by Tom Hauser, Chief Political Reporter dated May 29, 2024. Link: https://x.com/thauserkstp/status/1266405097703170053

151   Nal, Renee, RAIR Foundation USA. "Unlearned Lessons from the Torched Third Precinct", February 11, 2021. Link: https://rairfoundation.com/unlearned-lessons-from-the-torched-third-precinct/

152   Nal, Renee, RAIR Foundation USA. "EXPOSED: Ilhan Omar's daughter Isra Hirsi Retweets DSA's Request for Riot 'Supplies' in Minneapolis", May 29, 2020. Link: https://rairfoundation.com/exposed-ilhan-omars-daughter-isra-hirsi-retweets-dsas-request-for-riot-supplies-in-minneapolis/

153   Twin Cities DSA X Post dated May 27, 2020. Link: https://x.com/TwinCitiesDSA/status/1265774113693372417

154   Fox 9 KMSP, "Minneapolis Fire Department responded to 30 intentionally set fires during overnight protests", May 28, 2020. Link: https://www.fox9.com/news/minneapolis-fire-department-responded-to-30-intentionally-set-fires-during-overnight-protests

155   Lange, Jason and Trevor Hunnicutt, Reuters. "Biden staff donate to group that pays bail in riot-torn Minneapolis", May 30, 2020. Link: https://www.reuters.com/article/world/us/biden-staff-donate-to-group-that-pays-bail-in-riot-torn-minneapolis-idUSKBN2360SY/

156   King, Ryan, New York Post. "Trump hammers Harris for promoting BLM-era bail fund that freed felons accused of murder and sex assault", July 28, 2024. Link: https://nypost.com/2024/07/28/us-news/trump-hammers-kamala-harris-for-promoting-minnesota-freedom-fund/

157   Mac Donald, Heather, Manhattan Institute. "The Myth of Systemic Police Racism", June 3, 2020. Link: https://manhattan.institute/article/the-myth-of-systemic-police-racism

158   The Late Show with Stephen Colbert, YouTube Clip. "Sen. Kamala Harris: The Nationwide Protests Are A Movement. They're Not Going To Stop", June 18, 2020. Link: https://www.youtube.com/watch?v=NTg1ynIPGls

159   Mann, Jim, Los Angeles Times. "Peking Returns Possessions Seized in Cultural Revolution : In China, a Chance to Recapture the Past", July 24, 1985. Link: https://www.latimes.com/archives/la-xpm-1985-07-24-mn-4710-story.html

160   Real Clear Politics, "Obama Rallies Columbia", Missouri, October 30, 2008. Link: https://www.realclearpolitics.com/articles/2008/10/obama_rallies_columbia_missour.html

161   Press Release, ACLU. "ACLU Responds to Reintroduction of George Floyd Justice in Policing Act, Calls on Congress to Address Police Brutality", May 23, 2024. Link: https://www.aclu.org/press-releases/aclu-responds-to-reintroduction-of-george-floyd-justice-in-policing-act-calls-on-congress-to-address-police-brutality

CHAPTER 5

1   Loudon, Trevor, Trevor Loudon Reports, America Out Loud. "China's sinister plan for America, a battle for sovereignty in the 2024 election", August 27, 2024. Link: https://www.americaoutloud.news/chinas-sinister-plan-for-america-a-battle-for-sovereignty-in-the-2024-election/

2   World Economic Forum, Jin Canrong. Archive Link: https://web.archive.org/web/20240903191232/https://www.weforum.org/people/jin-canrong/

3   Jennifer's Blog, "CCP's Top Strategist: We Need To Put the US Under Our Jurisdiction 中共 "國師" 金燦榮自曝 "邪招" 稱將美國管起來, Link:

https://web.archive.org/web/20210324031507/https://www.jenniferzengblog.
com/home/2021/3/21/xin-cairong-on-us-china-relations

4   Ibid.

5   Ibid.

6   Ibid.

7   Kramer, Mark and Steve Phillips, Stanford Social Innovation Review.
"Where Strategic Philanthropy Went Wrong", Summer 2024. Link: https://ssir.
org/articles/entry/strategic-philanthropy-went-wrong

8   Huey-Burns, Caitlin, November 9, 2020, Real Clear Politics, "Is
Virginia Now a Blue State?", Link: https://www.realclearpolitics.com/arti-
cles/2017/11/09/is_virginia_now_a_blue_state_135492.html

9   New Virginia Majority, "Who We Are", Link: https://www.newvirgini-
amajority.org/whoweare

10   National Committee for Independent Political Action, "Steering
Committee", Link: KeyWiki screenshot, https://keywiki.org/National_
Committee_for_Independent_Political_Action#/media/File:Ncipaooo.PNG

11   Rockwood Leadership Institute, "National Leading From The Inside
Out Alums", 2010. Link: https://rockwoodleadership.org/fellowships/yearlong/
yearlong-alums/

12   City of Alexandria, Office of Historic Alexandria, Alexandria Legacies,
Oral History Program, "Interview with Jonathan 'Jon' Liss", April 14, 2015, Link:
https://media.alexandriava.gov/docs-archives/historic/info/immigration/lissjon.
pdf

13   Airlift, "Say Hello to the New Virginia Majority", November 17, 2017,
Link: https://airlift.fund/news/2017/11/17/say-hello-to-the-new-virginia-majority

14   Nguyen, Tram, New York Times, "Democrats Could Learn a
Lot From What Happened In Virginia", November 6, 2019, Link: https://
www.nytimes.com/2019/11/06/opinion/virginia-election-democrats.
html?fbclid=IwAR1hG15uy4afrNCV_-YTgih6PPf7WSdL-48bVP5l0f400P-
NAeA3UQolrO1U

15   Phillips, Steve, The Nation, "Democrats Don't Need Trump
Supporters to Win Elections", December 1, 2017, Link: https://www.thenation.
com/article/archive/democrats-dont-need-trump-supporters-to-win-elections/

16   Sandler Phillips Center, Link: https://www.sandlerphillipscenter.com/
susan

17   Democracy Alliance, "Beyond Resistance: Reclaiming
Our Progressive Future", Fall Investment Conference,
November 15-18, 2017. Link: https://freebeacon.com/politics/
resistance-royalty-pelosi-soros-headline-lefts-biggest-dark-money-conference/

18   PowerPAC+, "Board of Directors, "Link: https://web.archive.org/
web/20170408213431/http://www.powerpacplus.org/board_of_directors

19   The Center for Popular Democracy, "Rising Together in Oakland,
California", November 27, 2016, Link: https://www.populardemocracy.org/blog/
rising-together-oakland-california

20   New Virginia Majority, "New Virginia Majority
Endorses Kamala Harris for President and Tim Walz for Vice
President", September 5, 2024. Archive link: https://web.archive.
org/web/20240911200704/https://www.newvirginiamajority.org/

new_virginia_majority_endorses_kamala_harris_for_president_and_tim_walz_for_vice_president

21   Youtube, Convergence Magazine, "Victory in Virginia", Link: https://www.youtube.com/watch?v=zilu2gVi4Z4

22   Portside, "LEFTROOTS & LEFT STRATEGIES", December 1, 2015, Link: https://portside.org/2015-11-18/hangout-strategy-liberation

23   Komodo Commander, Link: https://www.amazians.com/participant/komodo/activity/paged/30/

24   Tran, Claire, Organizing Upgrade, "From the 'Year of the Underdog' to People Power", March 15, 2018, Link: https://web.archive.org/web/20221206085812/https://convergencemag.com/articles/year-underdog-people-power/

25   Ibid.

26   Youtube, Convergence Magazine, "Victory in Virginia", Link: https://www.youtube.com/watch?v=zilu2gVi4Z4

27   Nguyen, Tram, New York Times, "Democrats Could Learn a Lot From What Happened In Virginia", November 6, 2019, Link: https://www.nytimes.com/2019/11/06/opinion/virginia-election-democrats.html?fbclid=IwAR1hG15uy4afrNCV_-YTgih6PPf7WSdL-48bVP5l0f400P-NAeA3UQolrO1U

28   New Virginia Majority, "Victories", Link: https://www.newvirginiamajority.org/victories

29   China Daily, "US man in Wuhan shares his perspective", January 31, 2020, Link: https://www.chinadaily.com.cn/a/202001/31/WS5e338fada310128217273d36.html

30   Li Lei and Zhou Lihua, Liberation Road, "Covid19, Wuhan, and the US Left", Link: https://web.archive.org/web/20220818161304/https://roadto-liberation.org/covid19-wuhan-and-the-us-left/?link_id=1&can_id=e22816799
9164ab7b8394a90e1ebbb22&source=email-monthly-update-socialists-assess-how-to-win-from-a-biden-candidacy&email_referrer=email_795315&email_subject=monthly-update-covid19-wuhan-and-the-us-left

31   Steve McClure blog "Action research, mapping and civic engagement in Virginia", August 25, 2011, Link: https://web.archive.org/web/20180718111411/http://dcsteveinwuhan.over-blog.com/article-action-research-mapping-and-civic-engagement-in-virginia-82403603.html

32   Steve McClure blog, "Actionable Intelligence and Prince William County", Link: https://web.archive.org/web/20180718111424/http://dcsteveinwuhan.over-blog.com/pages/Actionable-intelligence-and-prince-william-county-5665344.html

33   Frontline, Volume 7, Number 8, October 30, 1989

34   Wing, Bob and McClure, Steve, Organizing Upgrade, "The Importance of the Fight for the South—and Why It Can and Must be Won", September 4, 2017, Link: https://convergencemag.com/articles/the-importance-of-the-fight-for-the-south-and-why-it-can-and-must-be-won-by-bob-wing-and-stephen-c-mcclure/

35   Convergence Magazine: "Bob Wing: Ending the White Republic". Frontline Dispatches, September 22, 2021. Link: https://convergencemag.com/video/bob-wing-ending-the-white-republic/

36   Cohen, Roger, New York Times. "2nd Apparent Assassination Attempt

on Trump Prompts International Alarm", Sept. 17, 2024 Link: https://www.
nytimes.com/2024/09/17/world/trump-assassination-attempt-world-reaction.
html

37   Holt, Lester, NBC News. X Post featuring NBC Nightly News
clip by Jorge Bonilla, Sept 15, 2024. Link: https://x.com/BonillaJL/
status/1835450513694900721

38   Reid, Joy & Don Lemon featured in article at Sean
Hannity Website. "BLAME GAME: Joy Reid, Don Lemon
Blame Trump for Assassination Attempts [WATCH]",
September 17, 2024. Link: https://hannity.com/media-room/
blame-game-joy-reid-don-lemon-blame-trump-for-assassination-attempts-watch/

39   Cupp, S.E., Bakari Sellers, Sarah Longwell, Jim Acosta featured
in CNN Clip. Tom Elliot X Post dated Sept 17, 2024. Link: https://x.com/
tomselliott/status/1836053800097874427

40   PND by Candid, "Home News Susan Sandler launches $200 mil-
lion fund for racial justice", September 15, 2020, Link: https://web.archive.
org/web/20201204111842/https://philanthropynewsdigest.org/news/
susan-sandler-launches-200-million-fund-for-racial-justice

41   Ibid.

42   Green for All, "About", Link: https://www.greenforall.org/team/

43   Rockwood Leadership Institute, "National Leading From The Inside
Out Alums", 2004. Link: https://rockwoodleadership.org/fellowships/yearlong/
yearlong-alums/

44   PND by Candid, "Home News Susan Sandler launches $200 mil-
lion fund for racial justice", September 15, 2020, Link: https://web.archive.
org/web/20201204111842/https://philanthropynewsdigest.org/news/
susan-sandler-launches-200-million-fund-for-racial-justice

45   Inside Philanthropy, "Power, Not Persuasion." Behind the New Susan
Sandler Fund", October 30, 2020. Link: https://www.insidephilanthropy.com/
home/2020/10/30/power-not-persuasion-how-an-heiress-is-carving-out-her-own-
path-to-social-change

46   PND by Candid, "Home News Susan Sandler launches $200 mil-
lion fund for racial justice", September 15, 2020, Link: https://web.archive.
org/web/20201204111842/https://philanthropynewsdigest.org/news/
susan-sandler-launches-200-million-fund-for-racial-justice

47   Inside Philanthropy, "Power, Not Persuasion." Behind the New Susan
Sandler Fund", October 30, 2020. Link: https://www.insidephilanthropy.com/
home/2020/10/30/power-not-persuasion-how-an-heiress-is-carving-out-her-own-
path-to-social-change

48   Portal Project, "Bob Wing", Link: https://sjiportalproject.com/
participant/bob-wing/

49   Convergence, "Claire Tran and Jacob Swenson-Lengyel", Link: https://
convergencemag.com/authors/claire-tran-and-jacob-swenson-lengyel/

50   California Calls, "Towards a National Strategy: Building
Independent State Based Power", Link: https://www.cacalls.org/
towards-a-national-strategy-building-independent-state-based-organizations/

51   Convergence, "Twenty State Organizations Unite into State-Based
Power Caucus", Link: https://convergencemag.com/articles/power-caucus/

52   Liss, Jon, Convergence, "Seize the Moment: Paving the Road for a Mass Left", June 9, 2019, Link: https://convergencemag.com/articles/seize-the-moment/

53   Inside Philanthropy, "David Callahan". Link: https://www.insidephilanthropy.com/david-callahan

54   Higgins, Eion, Blue Tent, "The state power caucus has a nationwide coalition ready...", January 11, 2021, Link: https://web.archive.org/web/20210924234331/https://www.bluetent.us/articles/campaigns-elections/the-state-power-caucus-has-a-nationwide-coalition-ready-to-k/

55   Liss, Jon "Toward a Movement 40 Million Strong", June 1, 2019, Link: https://convergencemag.com/articles/toward-a-movement-40-million-strong/

56   Ibid.

57   Ibid.

58   State Power Caucus, "Members", Link: https://web.archive.org/web/20240825223944/https://statepowercaucus.org/membership/

59   Convergence "Seed the Vote: Political Assessment", December 5, 2019, Link: https://convergencemag.com/articles/seed-the-vote-political-assessment/

60   Ibid.

61   Ibid.

62   Ibid.

63   Convergence Magazine, "Book Events: Power Concedes Nothing: How Grassroots Organizing Wins Elections". Link: https://convergencemag.com/power-concedes-nothing/book-events/

64   Burnham, M., Elbaum, P., & Poblet, M. (Eds.). (2022). Power concedes nothing: How grassroots organizing wins elections. OR Books.

65   Rockwood Leadership Institute, "National Leading from the Inside Out Alums" (2013). Link: https://rockwoodleadership.org/fellowships/yearlong/yearlong-alums/

66   Paladino, Vickie, X (formerly Twitter), X Post from Vickie Paladino dated May 9, 2024. Link: https://x.com/VickieforNYC/status/1788751832690356522 Archive Link: https://archive.fo/u4gTZ

67   Idealist, "Seed the Vote", Link: https://www.idealist.org/en/nonprofit/814d62836222447faa40bff6d2fe0b54-seed-the-vote-oakland

68   Federal Election Commission, "Everyday People", Link: https://www.fec.gov/data/committee/C00720029/?tab=about-committee

69   Chinese Progressive Association San Francisco, "Michelle Foy", Link: https://cpasf.org/?s=foy

70   Racial Equity 2030, "Alex Tom", Link: https://www.racialequity2030.org/ep/alex-tom

71   Youtube, Center for Political Education, "US and China Relations", May 22, 2020, Link: https://politicaleducation.org/event/us-and-china-relations/

72   In These Times, "Dump Trump, Defeat Racism and Misogyny, Build the Left", October 17, 2016, Link: https://inthesetimes.com/features/open_letter_left_clinton_trump.html

73   Seed the Vote, "Biden dropped - what's next?", Link: https://www.youtube.com/watch?v=jsppZyXnloM&list=PL3NihSj1mMfR2HAUlsUQ23TgppYETxwnb&t=70s

74   Chinese Progressive Association, "Resistance and Resilience: Summer

Dinner Series on the Current Political Moment and the Vision Forward", Link: https://cpasf.org/updates/resistance-and-resilience-summerdinnerseries/

75   Seed the Vote, "It took all of us", page 4, Link: https://seed-thevote.org/resources/?fbclid=IwY2xjawE50k9leHRuA2FlbQIxMAABH YrF7qP_ZdGHaQ5DFZ-tjBxRxTBhy0e2xKk4Qx6rBke4gqXZpjHakH rYGA_aem_bj_JFMqq3gBy-7FM-NxLKw#videos

76   Seed the Vote, "Meet the Team", Link: https://seedthevote.org/who-we-are/

77   The Org. "Le Tim Ly", Link: https://theorg.com/org/chinese-progressive-association-san-francisco/org-chart/le-tim-ly

78   East Bay Indymedia, "Critical Resistance 10: Strategies & Struggle to Abolish the Prison Industrial Complex", September 26, 2008, Link: https://www.indybay.org/newsitems/2008/09/22/18540833.php

79   Open Secrets, "Everyday People PAC", Link: https://www.opensecrets.org/political-action-committees-pacs/everyday-people-pac/C00720029/donors/2020?start=50&page_length=25

80   Open Secrets, "Sandler Foundation - All Recipients", Link: https://www.opensecrets.org/orgs/sandler-foundation-recipients?cycle=2022&id=D000063260

81   LeftRoots, "Out to Win", Issue 1, page 7

82   Misumi. Laura, East Wind, "Connecting Threads: Weaving the Past and Present of Asian American Activism. Book Review of Contemporary Asian American Activism- Building Movements for Liberation by Laura Misumi", March 23, 2022, Link: https://eastwindezine.com/connecting-threads-weaving-the-past-and-present-of-asian-american-activism-book-review-of-contemporary-asian-american-activism-building-movements-for-liberation-by-laura-misumi/

83   Convergence, "Jennifer Disla", https://convergencemag.com/authors/jennifer-disla/

84   SPLC Action Fund, "Andrea Cristina Mercado", Link: https://www.splcactionfund.org/about/board-member/andrea-cristina-mercado

85   Riddiough, Chris, Washington Socialist, "Left Unity call sets path for organizational coordination, capacity building", June 2018, Link: https://washingtonsocialist.mdcdsa.org/ws-articles/2018-06-left-unity

86   PowerPAC+, "Board of Directors, "Link: https://web.archive.org/web/20170408213431/http://www.powerpacplus.org/board_of_directors

87   Detroit Action Facebook page, November 4, 2020, Link: https://www.facebook.com/DetroitActionOrganizing/videos/2559256261032900

88   Ibid.

89   Facebook, Converge, "This is not a drill", November 10, 2020, Link: https://archive.vn/wip/H50mr

90   Bachtell, John, People's World, "New book, 'Power Concedes Nothing,' collects insights from on-the-ground electoral organizers", October 5, 2022, Link: https://peoplesworld.org/article/new-book-power-concedes-nothing-collects-insights-from-on-the-ground-electoral-organizers/

91   Seed the Vote, "It took all of us", page 7, Link: https://seedthevote.org/wp-content/uploads/2024/07/STV_Report_August2021_FINAL.pdf

92   Seed the Vote, "Clear strategy, strong knocks can't lose", Link: https://seedthevote.org/wp-content/uploads/2024/07/2022-Report.pdf

93   Ibid.

94   Elbaum, Max, Convergence, "The Energy Has Changed. The Underlying Politics Have Not",
July 31, 2024, Link: https://convergencemag.com/articles/the-energy-has-changed-the-underlying-politics-have-not/?fbclid=IwY2xjawFACVpleHRuA2Flb QIxMQABHbNq9IbsILAJqe_nLLY6QD6EZhLj3O-oPDVFvrE89P5dXX1rrvl-Giro3NA_aem_HSv44Gf-QSQUAK5nh8iGMA

95   Lee, N'Tanya and Williams, Steve, "Ear to the Ground Project", page 51, Link: https://web.archive.org/web/20180716043334/https://eartotheground-project.org/wp-content/uploads/2013/05/final-ear-2-ground-single-pages.pdf

96   Ibid.

97   Socialism2024, "2024 Schedule", Link: https://web.archive.org/save/https://socialismconference.org/2024-schedule/

98   North Star Socialist Organization's
National Leadership, "MOVEMENT MISSION 2024", Link: https://www.northstarsocialist.org/sites/default/files/2024-07/Movement_Mission_2024_by_NSSO.pdf

99   Ibid.

CHAPTER 6

1   Green New Deal Network, "The Green New Deal Network Endorses Kamala Harris for President", August 1, 2024. Link: https://greennewdealnet-work.org/the-green-new-deal-network-endorses-kamala-harris-for-president/

2   Ibid.

3   Inclusv "or Team", Link: https://inclusv.com/our-team/

4   Native Sun News Today, August 9, 2021, Link: https://www.nativesun-news.today/articles/killer-meets-with-vp-and-interior-secretary-in-washington/

5   Ibid.

6   Ibid.

7   Harris, Meena, Glamour "It's Black Women's Equal Pay Day. No Matter Who You Are, That Should Matter to You", August 22, 2019, Link: https://www.glamour.com/story/black-womens-equal-pay-day-alicia-garza-meena-harris

8   vi Ibid.

9   Nal, Renee, RAIR Foundation USA. "No, Hate Crimes Are Not Rising Against Asian Americans", April 18, 2020. Link: https://rairfoundation.com/no-hate-crimes-are-not-rising-against-asian-americans/

10   Labong, Leilani Marie, San Francisco Chronicle, "How Bay Area activ-ists keep the flames of their passion for change burning bright", July 3, 2020, Link: https://web.archive.org/web/20200712215010/https://www.sfchronicle.com/bayarea/article/How-Bay-Area-activists-to-keep-the-flames-of-15383840.php

11   Phenomenal, About. Archive Link: https://web.archive.org/web/20240916000930/https://www.phenomenalmedia.com/pages/about

12   CBS News, Bay Area. "'Phenomenally Asian' Campaign Responds To Rising Discrimination During Coronavirus Pandemic", April 27, 2020. Link: https://www.cbsnews.com/sanfrancisco/news/phenomenally-asian-campaign-responds-discrimination-coronavirus-pandemic/

13   Rockefeller Philanthropy Advisors, "Visibility, Voice, Vision: Asian

American and Pacific Islander Reproductive Justice Agenda." Link: https://www.apnaghar.org/uploads/9/6/4/4/9644061/reproductive_justice_agenda.pdf

14   National Asian Pacific American Women's Forum, "About". Link: https://napawf.org/about/

15   Pillai, Drishti & Lindsey, Alyssa, "The State of Safety for Asian American and Pacificn Islander Women in the US National Asian Pacific American Women's Forum," Washington, DC. , March 2022. Link: https://www.napawf.org/wp-content/uploads/2023/07/napawf-state-of-safety-report.pdf

16   People's Daily, China, X (formerly Twitter). X Post dated March 9, 2022. Link: https://x.com/PDChina/status/1501437628637491202 Archive Link: https://archive.fo/xEJ8U

17   Schneider, Sonya, https://www.northstarsocialist.org/sites/default/files/2024-07/Movement_Mission_2024_by_NSSO.pdf Stanford Daily, "May looks at Asian-American culture", May 4, 1998, Link: https://archives.stanford-daily.com/1998/05/04?page=2&section=MODSMD_ARTICLE10

18   The Stanford Daily, Volume 209, Issue 2, February 6, 1996

19   The Stanford Daily, "Campus Viewpoint: Jane Kim", February 4, 1998, Link: https://archives.stanforddaily.com/1998/02/04?page=4&section=MODSMD_ARTICLE19

20   Chinese Progressive Association – San Francisco, "Together We Move Mountains: Celebrating Generations of Change", Link: https://web.archive.org/web/20130411234923/https://cpasf.org/content/together-we-move-mountains-celebrating-generations-change

21   Chinese Progressive Association – San Francisco, "Harnessing the Strength of a thousand rivers", "Link: https://www.athousandrivers.org/hostcommittee/

22   Matier & Ross, San Francisco Chronicle, "City Hall crowd rolls out red carpet for Rose Pak's royal return", May 24, 2016, Link: https://www.sfchronicle.com/bayarea/matier-ross/article/City-Hall-crowd-rolls-out-red-carpet-for-Rose-7943343.php

23   Chinese Progressive Association – San Francisco, "Harnessing the Strength of a thousand rivers", "Link: https://www.athousandrivers.org/hostcommittee/

24   PAC+, Board of Directors, Link: https://web.archive.org/web/20120928005532/http://pacplus.org/index.php?/main/directors

25   Rose Pak Democratic Club, Facebook page, March 14, 2018, Link: https://archive.vn/wip/qvKzd

26   The New Press, "Brown Is the New White Book Launch at Impact Hub Oakland", Link: https://thenewpress.com/events/brown-new-white-book-launch-impact-hub-oakland

27   "Together We Win: How the California Donor Table moved California to the left by investing in communities of color", Link: https://californiadonortable.org/wp-content/uploads/2020/06/Impact-Report-1.pdf

28   De Rivera, Sarah Demarest, Rockwood Leadership Institute, "Announcing The 2023 National Leading From The Inside Out Yearlong Fellows", January 18, 2023, Link: https://rockwoodleadership.org/announcing-the-2023-national-leading-from-the-inside-out-yearlong-fellows/

29   Supreme Court of California, "Associate Justice Goodwin H. Liu", Link: https://supreme.courts.ca.gov/about-court/justices-court/associate-justice-goodwin-h-liu

30   Liu, Goodwin, SCOTUSblog, "Clerking for Justice Ginsburg was a gift beyond measure", September 22, 2020, Link: https://www.scotusblog.com/2020/09/clerking-for-justice-ginsburg-was-a-gift-beyond-measure/

31   Chinese for Affirmative Action 2011 Annual Report, page 14, Link: https://caasf.org/wp-content/uploads/2019/03/CAA_2011_Annual_Report_web.pdf

32   Chinese for Affirmative Action Facebook page, August 8, 2018, Link: KeyWiki Screenshot: https://keywiki.org/Russell_Lowe#/media/File:Ddddddhhfffjtutu.JPG

33   Matier & Ross, San Francisco Chronicle, "Feinstein had a Chinese spy connection she didn't know about — her driver" August 1, 2018, Link: https://www.sfchronicle.com/bayarea/matier-ross/article/Sen-Feinstein-had-a-Chinese-connection-she-13121441.php

34   Loudon, Trevor, Epoch Times. "Feinstein's Spy: Russell Lowe and San Francisco's Pro-China Left", August 20, 2018. Link: https://www.theepochtimes.com/us/feinsteins-spy-russell-lowe-and-san-franciscos-pro-china-left-2628597

35   Official US Military Website, "Final Environmental Impact Statement for the Disposal and Reuse of the Department of Defense Housing Facility Novato, California", November 1997. Archive Link: https://web.archive.org/web/20240908165457/https://apps.dtic.mil/sti/tr/pdf/ADA331836.pdf

36   Evans, Zachary, National Review, "Swalwell Spoke at 2013 Event With Feinstein Staffer Accused of Spying for China", December 11, 2020, Link: https://www.nationalreview.com/news/swalwell-spoke-at-2013-event-with-feinstein-staffer-accused-of-spying-for-china/

37   Solender, Andrew, "McCarthy formally kicks Schiff, Swalwell off Intelligence Committee", January 24, 2023, Link: https://www.axios.com/2023/01/25/mccarthy-removes-schiff-swalwell-intelligence-committee

38   ABC News, "Eric Mar", May 17, 2011, Link: https://abc7news.com/archive/8136658/

39   Ortiz, Paul, Truthout, "On the Shoulders of Giants" November 25, 2008, Link: https://web.archive.org/web/20181106202252/https://truthout.org/articles/on-the-shoulders-of-giants/

40   Eric Mar, a law student at the New College of California, interviewed Renee Saucedo, president of the Boat Hall Law Students Association, published on page 6 of League of Revolutionary Struggle's Unity March 19, 1990.

41   Mar, Eric, Threads. Eric Mar Threads Post dated July 22, 2024. Link: https://www.threads.net/@ericmar415/post/C9tn8fFRw8W Archive Link: https://archive.vn/Vg9zY

42   Convergence Magazine, "About Convergence". Link: https://convergencemag.com/about/

43   Convergence Magazine, "BLOCK AND BUILD: Left Strategy in the MAGA Era". Link: https://convergencemag.com/syllabus/block-build-left-strategy-in-the-maga-era/

44   Committee of 100, "Committee of 100 Supports Confirmation of Goodwin H. Liu to the US Circuit Court of Appeals for the Ninth Circuit", May

26, 2010, Link: https://www.committee100.org/media-center/press-release-com-mittee-of-100-supports-confirmation-of-goodwin-h-liu-to-the-us-circuit-court-of-appeals-for-the-ninth-circuit/

45   Simon, Mark (May 1, 2019). "How the 'Committee of 100' is doing Beijing's bidding in the US". Hong Kong Free Press, Link: https://hongkongfp.com/2019/05/01/committee-100-beijings-bidding-us/

46   Newsweek, "Exclusive: 600 US Groups Linked to Chinese Communist Party Influence Effort with Ambition Beyond Election", October 26, 2020, Link: https://www.newsweek.com/2020/11/13/exclusive-600-us-groups-linked-chinese-communist-party-influence-effort-ambition-beyond-1541624.html

47   Committee of 100, "Gordon Chang", Link: https://www.committee100.org/?s=gordon+chang

48   Wei, William, "The Asian American Movement", page 234, Temple University Press (October 6, 1993), ISBN-13: 978-1566391832

49   Phillip, Abby, Politico, "Goodwin Liu withdraws nomina-tion", June 25, 2011, Link: https://www.politico.com/story/2011/05/goodwin-liu-withdraws-nomination-055724

50   Gluss, Susan, Berkeley Law, "Goodwin Liu Confirmed to California Supreme Court, sworn in", September 1, 2011, Link: https://www.law.berkeley.edu/press-release/goodwin-liu-confirmed-to-california-supreme-court-sworn-in/

51   Ibid.

52   Fiduccia, Dan, The Stanford Daily, "Groups Plan Alternate Graduation Ceremony", May 5, 1975, Link: https://archives.stanforddaily.com/1975/05/05?page=1&section=MODSMD_ARTICLE4

53   Walsh, Susan, NBC News, "Obama Nominates Maria Echaveste for Ambassador to Mexico", September 18, 2014, Link: https://www.nbcnews.com/news/latino/obama-nominates-maria-echaveste-ambassador-mexico-n206576

54   PAC+, Board of Directors, Link: https://web.archive.org/web/20120928005532/http://pacplus.org/index.php?/main/directors

55   Gluss, Susan, Berkeley Law, "Goodwin Liu Confirmed to California Supreme Court, sworn in", September 1, 2011, Link: https://www.law.berkeley.edu/press-release/goodwin-liu-confirmed-to-california-supreme-court-sworn-in/

56   Ettinger, David, At the Lectern, "Justice Liu not chosen to be California Attorney General, congratulates the nominee [Updated]", March 24, 2021, Link: https://www.atthelectern.com/justice-liu-not-chosen-to-be-california-attorney-general-congratulates-the-nominee/

57   Miller, Cheryl, Law.com, "Yale Law Classmates Goodwin Liu and Rob Bonta Vie, Through Friends, for Attorney General", February 22, 2021, Link: https://www.law.com/therecorder/2021/02/02/yale-law-classmates-goodwin-liu-and-rob-bonta-vie-through-friends-for-attorney-general/?slreturn=20240731143854

58   Gluss, Susan, Berkeley Law, "Goodwin Liu Confirmed to California Supreme Court, sworn in", September 1, 2011, Link: https://www.law.berkeley.edu/press-release/goodwin-liu-confirmed-to-california-supreme-court-sworn-in/

59   Rob Bonta press release, "Supervisor Wilma Chan backs Bonta for Assembly", Link: KeyWiki screenshot, https://keywiki.org/Rob_Bonta#/media/File:Bontalicious.JPG

60   Ibid.

61   NBC News, Date: November 10, 1980 ," CONTROVERSY OVER THE COMMUNIST WORKERS PARTY", Link: KeyWiki screenshot https://keywiki.org/Kent_Wong#/media/File:Kento.PNG

62   PAC+, Board of Directors, Link: https://web.archive.org/web/20120928005532/http://pacplus.org/index.php?/main/directors

63   Inclusv, "Founders and Staff", Link: https://web.archive.org/web/20170115003835/https://inclusv.com/our-team/

64   APALA, "Sign up to become a Lifetime Warrior today!", Link: https://www.apalanet.org/august2016.html

65   Bulosan Center for Filipino Studies, "Cynthia Bonta", Link: https://bulosancenter.ucdavis.edu/meet-team

66   Chan, Louis, Asam News, "Rob Bonta wins support for California Attorney General", January 7, 2021, Link: https://asamnews.com/2021/01/07/rob-bonta-would-be-the-first-filipino-american-to-hold-a-statewide-office-in-california/

67   Munguia, Hayley, Press-Telegraph, "Long Beach's Robert Garcia is the only mayor to join state leaders as a Kamala Harris campaign co-chair", May 31, 2019, Link: https://www.presstelegram.com/2019/05/31/long-beachs-robert-garcia-is-the-only-mayor-to-join-state-leaders-as-a-kamala-harris-campaign-co-chair/

68   Chan, Louis, Asam News, "Rob Bonta wins support for California Attorney General", January 7, 2021, Link: https://asamnews.com/2021/01/07/rob-bonta-would-be-the-first-filipino-american-to-hold-a-statewide-office-in-california/

69   Ibid.

70   De Guzman, Mila, Positively Filipino, "From Grassroots Activist to LA City Commissioner", Link: https://www.positivelyfilipino.com/magazine/from-grassroots-activist-to-la-city-commissioner

71   Ibid.

72   De Guzman, Mila, Inquirer.net, "Lillian Galedo, Top Community Organizer-leader,

Retires After Decades of Service", June 27, 2017, Link: https://carlosbulosanbookclub.org/wp-content/uploads/2021/03/Lillian-Galedo-by-MDG-2.pdf

73   Ang Katipunan, July 1984, page 9

74   Filipino Advocates for Justice, "Staff and Board" Link: https://web.archive.org/web/20100926122648/http://www.filipinos4justice.org/about/board-staff/

75   Allen Gary, "The Grapes: Communist Wrath In Delano", page 7, Link: https://libraries.ucsd.edu/farmworkermovement/essays/essays/MillerArchive/018%20The%20Grapes%20Communist%20Wrath.pdf

76   Chappell, Bill, NPR, "California's Assembly Votes To Allow Communists To Hold State Jobs", May 9, 2017, Link: https://www.npr.org/sections/thetwo-way/2017/05/09/527586682/california-assembly-votes-to-allow-communists-to-hold-state-jobs

77   Bollagass, Sophia, AP, "California lawmaker pulls bill on Cold War-era communist ban", May 17, 2017, Link: https://www.apnews.com/4e9dd0f1d3334f2189dc61046bca3fa6/California-lawmaker-pulls-bill-on-Cold-War-era-communist-ban

78   Asian Journal News, Link: https://asianjournal.com/tag/rob-bonta/page/2/

79   Nal, Renee, RAIR Foundation USA. "WARNING: Communists Weaponize Fake Asian Hate Crime Narrative - Plot March 27th US Protest". Link: https://rairfoundation.com/warning-communists-weaponize-fake-asian-hate-crime-narrative-plot-march-27th-u-s-protest/

80   Ibid.

81   Jeung, Russell Ph.D., Aggie Yellow Horse, Ph.D., Tara Popovic, and Richard Lim, Stop AAPI Hate. "Stop AAPI Hate National Report 3/19/2020 – 2/28/2021. Archive Link: https://web.archive.org/web/20210531232911/https://secureservercdn.net/104.238.69.231/a1w.90d.myftpupload.com/wp-content/uploads/2021/03/210312-Stop-AAPI-Hate-National-Report-.pdf

82   Jeung, Russell, Manjusha Kulkarni and Cynthia Choi, Los Angeles Times. "Op-Ed: Trump's racist comments are fueling hate crimes against Asian Americans. Time for state leaders to step in." April 1, 2020. Link: https://www.latimes.com/opinion/story/2020-04-01/coronavirus-anti-asian-discrimination-threats

83   Commission on Asian & Pacific Islander American Affairs, "Stop the Hate Resources". Link: https://capiaa.ca.gov/stop-the-hate/

84   Wong, Ashley. "California passes bill allocating $1.4 million to track anti-Asian bias and hate crimes". Fresno Bee, February 23, 2021. Link: https://www.fresnobee.com/news/california/article249437955.html

85   Wire, Sarah D., Los Angeles Times. "Californian to help lead super pac focused on registering Asian American voters", January 14, 2016. Link: https://www.latimes.com/politics/la-pol-ca-aapi-super-pac-story.html

86   AAPI Victory Fund, Home page. Link: https://www.aapivictoryfund.com/

87   Democracy Alliance, Shekar Narasimhan, Link: https://www.democracyalliance.org/people/shekar-narasimhan/

88   Huang, Zhengyu, Committee of 100, "Committee of 100 Statement on the US Election Results", November 9, 2020, Link: https://web.archive.org/web/20231128220859/https://www.committee100.org/media-center/2020elections/

89   Committee of 100, "AAPI Victory Fund, Committee of 100, Council of Korean Americans, and Japanese American Citizens League Celebrate Lunar New Year with Vice President Kamala Harris", February 17, 2023, Link: https://web.archive.org/web/20240717150007/https://www.committee100.org/media-center/aapi-victory-fund-committee-of-100-council-of-korean-americans-and-japanese-american-citizens-league-celebrate-lunar-new-year-with-vice-president-kamala-harris/

CHAPTER 7

1   Tim Walz for Congress, "Meet Tim" Link: https://web.archive.org/web/20080506105628/http://www.timwalz.org/free_details.asp?id=46

2   Ibid.

3   Johnson, Eliana, Washington Free Beacon. "For Tim Walz, a Pattern of Prevarications Stretches Back Almost Two

Decades", August 24, 2024. Link: https://freebeacon.com/democrats/for-tim-walz-a-pattern-of-prevarications-stretches-back-almost-two-decades/

4   General CIA Records China, Freedom of Information Act Electronic Reading Room. "The Anti-Bourgeois Liberalization Campaign In The Provinces", Publication Date: July 22, 1987. Archive Link: https://web.archive.org/web/20240829144633/https://www.cia.gov/readingroom/document/cia-rdp90t00114r000200780001-1

5   Time Magazine, "How Many Really Died? Tiananmen Square Fatalities", June 4, 1990. Link: https://time.com/archive/6715033/how-many-really-died-tiananmen-square-fatalities/

6   Marshall, Con, Chadron Record, "Chadron grad gets royal treatment in China", September 04, 1990

7   Hains, Tim, RealClearPolitics. "Schweizer: Chinese Communist Party Has "Groomed" Tim Walz; "Big Help With A Little Bad-Mouth"", August 25, 2024. Link: https://www.realclearpolitics.com/video/2024/08/25/schweizer_chinese_communist_party_has_been_grooming_tim_walz_he_brought_lots_of_copies_of_maos_little_red_book_back_from_china.html

8   Rob Schmitt Tonight, Newsmax, "Kamala's VP Pick: Compromised by China?", August 2024. Link: https://x.com/Govt_Acct_Inst/status/1823020983466279058 (video clip)

9   Coolican, J. Patrick, Star-Tribune, "Tim Walz's campaign for Minnesota governor aims to bridge the great divide", October 13, 2018, Link: https://www.startribune.com/tim-walz-s-campaign-for-minnesota-governor-aims-to-bridge-the-great-divide/495297961

10   Wernke, Mary, Star-Herald, Scottsbluff, Nebraska. "Honeymoon in China", January 09, 1994.

11   Ibid.

12   Greenfield, Daniel, IsraPundit, "Tim Walz's troubling China ties exposed", August 7, 2024, Link: https://www.israpundit.org/kamala-picks-walz-as-a-manchurian-candidate/

13   Ibid.

14   Ibid.

15   Ibid.

16   Tim Walz for Congress, "Meet Tim" Link: https://web.archive.org/web/20080506105628/http://www.timwalz.org/free_details.asp?id=46

17   Ettinger, Morton, Daily Dot, "MAGA convinces itself Tim Walz is a Chinese sleeper agent", Aug 6, 2024, Link: https://www.dailydot.com/debug/tim-walz-china-communist-party-gop/

18   Tim Walz for Congress, "Meet Tim" Link: https://web.archive.org/web/20080506105628/http://www.timwalz.org/free_details.asp?id=46

19   University of Minnesota, "US-Dakota War of 1862". "The Dakota Trials and Their Aftermath". Link: https://cla.umn.edu/chgs/holocaust-genocide-education/resource-guides/us-dakota-war-1862#:~:text=In%20the%20end%2C%20Lincoln%20commuted,single%20execution%20in%20American%20history.

20   "The 20th Anniversary Of The Tiananmen Square Protests: Examining The Significance Of The 1989 Demonstrations In China And Implications For

US Policy", June 4, 2009. Link: https://www.govinfo.gov/content/pkg/CHRG-111jhrg51191/html/CHRG-111jhrg51191.htm

21   Greenfield, Daniel, IsraPundit, "Tim Walz's troubling China ties exposed", August 7, 2024, Link: https://www.israpundit.org/kamala-picks-walz-as-a-manchurian-candidate/

22   Hamill, Drew, and George, Evangeline, Congresswoman Nancy Pelosi press release, "Pelosi, Congressional Delegation Conclude Visit to China and Tibet". November 13, 2015, Link: https://pelosi.house.gov/news/press-releases/pelosi-congressional-delegation-conclude-visit-to-china-and-tibet

23   Sherry, Allison, Star Tribune, "Reps. Walz, McCollum tout China's progress in climate change, tolerance", November, Tibet", November 17, 2015, Link: https://www.startribune.com/reps-walz-mccollum-tout-china-s-progress-in-climate-change-tolerance-in-trip-to-tibet/351187261

24   Ettinger, Morton, Daily Dot, "MAGA convinces itself Tim Walz is a Chinese sleeper agent", Aug 6, 2024, Link: https://www.dailydot.com/debug/tim-walz-china-communist-party-gop/

25   US-China Peoples Friendship Association - Minnesota Chapter: "Forty Years and Beyond:

Friendship, Successes, and Challenges", October 18 –20, 2019. Link: https://uscpfa-mn.org/wp-content/uploads/2019/07/Attachment-1-USCR-Sum-convention-updated.pdf

26   Greenfield, Daniel, IsraPundit, "Tim Walz's troubling China ties exposed", August 7, 2024, Link: https://www.israpundit.org/kamala-picks-walz-as-a-manchurian-candidate/

27   Li, Xiaobing (2012). China at War: An Encyclopedia. ABC-CLIO. p. 226. ISBN 978-1-59884-415-3.

28   Li Xiannian (1909–1992), in Christopher R. Lew, Edwin Pak-wah Leung: Historical Dictionary of the Chinese Civil War, p.p. 120-121, Scarecrow Press, 2013

29   Holley, David. "Li Xiannian, Ex-President of China, Dies at 83: Old Guard: He was one of a ruling clique of '8 elders' who ordered the army to repress the pro-democracy movement in 1989". Los Angeles Times, 23 June 1992.

30   Chinese People 's Association for Friendship with Foreign Countries, Link: https://web.archive.org/web/20181208040750/http://cpaffc.org.cn/content/details34-627.html

31   Lenczycki, Philip, Daily Caller. "EXCLUSIVE: Tim Walz Has A History Of Rubbing Elbows With Nonprofit Linked To Chinese Intel And Influence Agency", August 27, 2024. Link: https://dailycaller.com/2024/08/27/exclusive-tim-walz-history-nonprofit-linked-chinese-intel-agency/

32   Walsh, Erin and Harding, Andrew, Heritage Foundation, "Crack Down on Illegal Chinese Police Stations in the US", June 7, 2023, Link: https://www.heritage.org/homeland-security/commentary/crack-down-illegal-chinese-police-stations-the-us

33   Lenczycki, Philip, Daily Caller. "EXCLUSIVE: Tim Walz Has A History Of Rubbing Elbows With Nonprofit Linked To Chinese Intel And Influence Agency", August 27, 2024. Link: https://dailycaller.com/2024/08/27/exclusive-tim-walz-history-nonprofit-linked-chinese-intel-agency/

34   US House of Representatives, Select Committee on the Chinese

Communist Party. "Investigative Report on the Chinese Communist Party's Influence in the United States", 2022. Link: https://selectcommitteeontheccp. house.gov/

35   Select Committee on the CCP, "Memorandum: United Front 101. Archive Link: https://web.archive.org/web/20240827232226/https://selectcommitteeontheccp.house.gov/sites/evo-subsites/selectcommitteeontheccp.house.gov/ files/evo-media-document/uf-101-memo-final-pdf-version.pdf

36   Select Committee on the CCP, Press Release. "Select Committee Unveils CCP Influence Memo, "United Front 101", November 27, 2023. Link: https://selectcommitteeontheccp.house.gov/media/press-releases/ select-committee-unveils-ccp-influence-memo-united-front-101

37   Qing, Deng, Minnesota Chinese World. "Do you know the relationship between Kamala Harris's partner, Governor Waltz, and our Minnesota Chinese community?", August 06, 2024. Archive Link: https://archive.is/vq18z

38   Lenczycki, Philip, X, X Post dated August 27, 2024. Link: https://x. com/LenczyckiPhilip/status/1828592912822616483 Archive Link: https:// archive.vn/WubuF

39   Lenczycki, Philip, Daily Caller. "EXCLUSIVE: GOP Senators Demand Biden DOJ Provide Answers On CCP Intel-Linked 'Service Centers'", July 10, 2023. Link: https://dailycaller.com/2023/07/10/ ccp-service-centers-ufwd-lawmakers/

40   House Committee on Oversight and Accountability, Letter from Chairman Representative James Comer, August 16, 2024. Link: https://oversight. house.gov/wp-content/uploads/2024/08/Letter-to-Director-Wray-08162024.pdf

41   Lenczycki, Philip, X, X Post dated August 27, 2024 (2). Link: https://x.com/LenczyckiPhilip/status/1828592939838124309 Archive Link: https://archive.vn/rxT4H

42   Chang, Gordon G., X (formerly Twitter), Gordon Chang X Post Dated August 29, 2024. Link: https://x.com/GordonGChang/ status/1829270214787072412

43   Gihring, Tim, MinnPost. "20 years after Paul Wellstone's death, his legacy may be stronger than ever", October 21, 2022. Link: https://www.minnpost.com/politics-policy/2022/10/20-years-after-paul-wellstones-death-his-legacy-may-be-stronger-than-ever/

44   Jackson, Reverend Jesse L., "Lessons from 1984", July 8, 2014, Link: https://www.stlamerican.com/news/columnists/guest-columnists/ lessons-from-1984/

45   Socialist Working Papers on Energy, NAM revised edition 1979, contents page

46   Roman, Bob, New Ground 85, "Red Baiting", November - December 2002, Link: https://chicagodsa.org/ngarchive/ng85.html

47   Democratic Left, "On the Left", November/December 1990 issue, page 5

48   Riddiough, Chris, Democratic Left, "Election Dispatches, Continued," November/December 1996 issue, page 18

49   Democratic Left, "Locals Report", Summer 2001, page 15

50   Lapin, Andrew, The Jerusalem Post, "How a tragic twist in Minnesota's

'Jewish Senate seat' helped Tim Walz break into politics", August 7, 2024, Link: https://www.jpost.com/american-politics/article-813646

51   Re:power website, "Where we've been", Link: https://repower.org/about/

52   Re:power, X. Re:Power X Post dated August 21, 2024. Link: https://x.com/repowerorg/status/1826333551261815239 Archive Link: https://archive.vn/T327N

53   Kroll, Andy, Mother Jones, "Wellstone's revenge: how Minnesota Democrats took their state back", October 2013, Link: https://www.motherjones.com/politics/2013/10/minnesota-progressives-turn-state-blue/

54   Ibid.

55   Ibid.

56   Ibid.

57   Walz, Tim, X. Tim Walz X Post dated October 7, 2017. Link: https://x.com/Tim_Walz/status/916689058679672832 Archive Link: https://archive.vn/zAuPI

58   Ibid.

59   Ellison, Keith, Facebook. Keith Ellison Facebook Post, October 25, 2020. Link: https://www.facebook.com/ellisoncampaign/photos/a.10150751188500412/10158393390960412/?type=3 Archive Link: https://archive.vn/4OOX9

60   Demko, Paul, Politico, "Inside the Three-Day Bootcamp that Launched Tim Walz's Political Career", August 19, 2024, Link: https://www.politico.com/news/magazine/2024/08/10/tim-walz-camp-wellstone-bootcamp-minnesota-00173480?fbclid=IwY2xjawFC6AtleHRuA2FlbQIxMQABHWyy6vFqpXojoqE6w4H5brDWF_rnfhOFqMgymragws_hupJtPSMBx-2e8Q_aem_qLScA-Si4AbqhxjjW7HFDgQ

61   Bunch, Sonny, Roll Call, "Candidate Camp: Wellstone's Living Minnesota Legacy", January 7, 2005, Link: https://rollcall.com/2005/01/07/candidate-camp-wellstones-living-minnesota-legacy/

62   Cohn, Roy, M., "Outlaws of Amerika' The Weather Underground" page, Western Goals; First Edition (January 1, 1982), pages 33 to 35, ASIN : B000KWKNXM

63   Ibid.

64   Marquit, Erwin "Memoirs of a Lifelong Communist," page 576

65   Loudon, Trevor. "Burn This Book: What Keith Ellison Doesn't Want You to Know: A Radical Marxist-Islamist, His Associations and Agenda". CreateSpace Independent Publishing Platform, 2018. Link: https://centerforsecuritypolicy.org/wp-content/uploads/2018/09/Ellilson_Burn_This_Book.pdf

66   Sara Olson Defense Committee; Keith Ellison's Speech UNGAGGED Forum held on February 12, 2000 (archived) LINK: https://web.archive.org/web/20000823032901/http://www.saraolsondefense.com:8 0/Articles/Ungagged/Speech%20by%20Keith%20Ellison.html

67   Committee on Un-American Activities, "Report on the National Lawyers Guild, legal bulwark of the Communist Party", 1950. Link: https://archive.org/details/reportonnational1950unit/page/n3/mode/2up

68   Special Committee on Un-American Activities, House Report 1311, on the CIO Political Action. Committee, March 29, 1944, p. 149. See Page 93 at this Link: https://www.archives.gov/files/research/jfk/releases/docid-32989757.pdf

69   Democratic Left, "Convention Election Results", November/December 1987, page 7

70   American Sociological Association, "Frances Fox Piven", Link: https://www.asanet.org/frances-fox-piven/

71   Democratic Left, January/February 1991 issue, page 16

72   FairVote California, "Staff and Leadership", Link: https://web.archive.org/web/20161026182403/http://www.fairvote.org/staff_and_leadershiphttps://web.archive.org/web/20161026182403/http://www.fairvote.org/staff_and_leadership

73   FairVote California, "Jennifer Pae", Link: https://web.archive.org/web/20161029193114/https://fairvote.org/jennifer_pae

74   PAC+, Board of Directors, Link: https://web.archive.org/web/20120928005532/http://pacplus.org/index.php?/main/directors

75   Demarest De Rivera, Sarah, Miriam, Rockwood Leadership Institute, "Announcing the 2020-2021 National Leading From The Inside Out Yearlong Fellows", Link: https://rockwoodleadership.org/announcing-the-2020-21-national-leading-from-the-inside-out-yearlong-fellows/

76   Inclusv, "Our Team", Link: https://web.archive.org/web/20200420064527/https://inclusv.com/our-team/

77   Grant, Miriam, Rockwood Leadership Institute, "Announcing the 2018-2019 National Leading From The Inside Out Yearlong Fellows", Link: https://rockwoodleadership.org/2018-2019-lio-fellows/

78   Movement Voter Project, "Advisory Board", Link: https://web.archive.org/web/20190806181120/https://movement.vote/advisors/

79   Rockwood Leadership Institute, "National Leading from the Inside Out Alums – 2003-2015", Link: https://rockwoodleadership.org/fellowships/yearlong/yearlong-alums/

80   Grant, Miriam, Rockwood Leadership Institute, "Announcing the 2017-2018 National Leading From The Inside Out Yearlong Fellows", Link: https://rockwoodleadership.org/2018-2019-lio-fellows/

81   She The People. "Advisory Board", Link: https://www.shethepeople.org/advisory

82   Movement Voter Project, "Support the Resistance", Link: https://web.archive.org/web/20180611051111/https://movement.vote/

83   Inclusv, "Our Team", Link: https://web.archive.org/web/20200420064527/https://inclusv.com/our-team/

84   Supermajority, Link: https://supermajority.com/team/jess-morales-rocketto/

85   Demarest De Rivera, Sarah, Miriam, Rockwood Leadership Institute, "Announcing the 2021-2022 National Leading From The Inside Out Yearlong Fellows", Link: https://rockwoodleadership.org/announcing-the-2021-22-national-leading-from-the-inside-out-yearlong-fellows/

86   We the People Michigan, Link: https://wethepeoplemi.org/our-team/

87   Rockwood Leadership Institute, "National Leading from the Inside Out Alums – 2003-2015", Link: https://rockwoodleadership.org/fellowships/yearlong/yearlong-alums/

88   Hua, Vanessa, SFGate, "Amnesty touches home for Bay Area Asians / About 1.5 million Chinese, Filipinos, others live here illegally -- many overstayed

visas", May 18, 2006, Link: https://www.sfgate.com/bayarea/article/Amnesty-touches-home-for-Bay-Area-Asians-About-2535060.php

89   Keywiki, Author's personal collection. Link: https://keywiki.org/Mark_Ritchie_(Communist_Party_USA_Connection)

90   Wheeler, Tim, Communist party USA Farm Commission, "Mark Ritchie (Communist Party USA Connection)", Link, KeyWiki screenshot: https://keywiki.org/Mark_Ritchie_(Communist_Party_USA_Connection)

91   Dreier, Peter, In These Times, "Paul Wellstone's Legacy", October 12, 2012, Link: https://inthesetimes.com/article/paul-wellstones-legacy

92   Ibid.

93   Mark Ritchie Secretary of State campaign website, "About Mark", Link: https://web.archive.org/web/20090208063625/http://www.markritchie06.net/aboutmark.htm

94   Communist Party USA, "This Battle Can Be Won!", July 8, 2006, Link: https://www.cpusa.org/article/this-battle-can-be-won/

95   Barnes, Ed, Fox News, "States' Secretaries of State Are Tipping Balance of Power", February 1, 2010, Link: https://www.foxnews.com/politics/states-secretaries-of-state-are-tipping-balance-of-power

96   Kucera, Barb, "Minnesota euphoria over Obama win tempered by Senate recount", November 22, 2008, Link: https://web.archive.org/web/20101212003226/http://transitional.pww.org/minnesota-euphoria-over-obama-win-tempered-by-senate-recount/

97   Barnes, Ed, Fox News, "States' Secretaries of State Are Tipping Balance of Power", February 1, 2010, Link: https://www.foxnews.com/politics/states-secretaries-of-state-are-tipping-balance-of-power

98   LinkedIn, "Mark Ritchie", https://www.linkedin.com/in/mark-ritchie-minnesota/

99   Ibid.

100   Wilmes, Sam, Albert Lea Tribune, "Former secretary of state, wife of Walz encourage people to vote in primary", Link: https://www.albertleatribune.com/2018/08/former-secretary-of-state-wife-of-walz-encourage-people-to-vote-in-primary/

101   Chanen, David, The Minnesota Star Tribune, "Mark Ritchie, former Minnesota Secretary of State, to lead nonprofit international education organization", November 19, 2018, Link: https://www.startribune.com/mark-ritchie-former-minnesota-secretary-of-state-to-lead-nonprofit-international-education-organization/500884772

102   University of St. Thomas, "Racial Justice Initiative to Host Voting Rights Symposium; Governor and Attorney General to Speak", January 24, 2024. Archive Link: https://web.archive.org/web/20240907222007/https://news.stthomas.edu/racial-justice-initiative-to-host-voting-rights-symposium-governor-and-attorney-general-to-speak/

103   All Events, "St. Paul – Symposium on Voting Rights: Our Past, Our Present, Our Future", August 7, 2024, Link: https://www.mnhum.org/event/symposium-on-voting-rights/

104   Ibid.

105   US Army, "America's link to the Army!", Link: https://www.army.mil/casa

106   Marquit, Erwin "Memoirs of a Lifelong Communist," CHAPTER 34. "CPUSA Enters 21st Century, and Jettisons the Gus Hall Stalinist Model of Party Organization, 2000–2008".

107   Marquit, Erwin, "Memoirs of a Lifelong Communist, page 576

108   Hahn, Geoff, Forward Motion, "Battling the Rise in Police Brutality", June 1989, page 22.

109   Milwaukee Journal Sentinel. Youtube, "Keith Ellison DNC speech on Tim Walz appointing him to prosecute case of George Floyd's murder", Link: https://www.youtube.com/watch?v=4aQ4HtKNWpE

110   Maki, Alan, Personal Blog, Thoughts from Podunk. "Crisis of Disinvestment: Organizing to Rebuild Our Communities", May 10, 2008. Link: https://thepodunkblog.blogspot.com/2008_05_10_archive.html

111   Bertsch, KVRR, "Local labor leader and political scientist react to Walz VP selection", August 6, 2024, Link: https://www.kvrr.com/2024/08/06/local-labor-leader-and-political-scientist-react-to-walz-vp-selection/

112   Trevor Loudon Youtube, "Joe Henry: I Have Been a Communist Since 1982", Link: https://www.youtube.com/watch?v=E_xZ4HtX5aM&t=53s

113   Polk County Democrats, "Neighborhood Groups", Link: https://www.polkdems.com/join-a-local-group

114   Times-Republican, "Smith elected as chair of the Iowa Democratic Party", February 15, 2020, Link: https://www.timesrepublican.com/news/todays-news/2020/02/smith-elected-as-chair-of-the-iowa-democratic-party/

115   Bleeding Heartland, "Des Moines hiring practices don't reflect community's diversity", June 21, 2020, Link: https://www.bleedingheartland.com/tag/joe-henry/

116   Communist Party USA, Youtube, "The Fight for Voting Rights Today", Link: https://www.youtube.com/watch?v=mIuITt_weP4&t=3870s

117   Gruenberg, Mark, People's World, "CPUSA Labor Commission makes proposals for 2024 election work", August 15, 2023, Link: https://www.peoplesworld.org/article/cpusa-labor-commission-makes-proposals-for-2024-election-work/

118   The Austin Chronicle, The Hightower Report, "The Nobel Prize for Greed; and Camp Wellstone Winners", December 22, 2006, Link: https://www.austinchronicle.com/news/2006-12-22/431147/

119   LinkedIn, "Joe Henry", Link: https://www.linkedin.com/in/joehenry/

120   Des Moines Register, "Mitch Henry: Co-founder and communications director of the Asian & Latino Coalition", Link: https://features.desmoinesregister.com/news/politics/50-most-wanted/mitch-henry-election-2020-iowa-caucus-democrats-key-people-to-know.html

121   Wang, Shirley, NBC News, "Iowa's Asian and Latino Coalition endorses Kamala Harris for the 2020 caucus", August 12, 2019, Link: https://www.nbcnews.com/news/asian-america/iowa-s-asian-latino-coalition-endorses-kamala-harris-2020-caucus-n1041681

122   The American Presidency Project, "Kamala Harris' Iowa Campaign Announces Latinx Steering Committee", August 27, 2019, Link: https://www.presidency.ucsb.edu/documents/harris-campaign-press-release-kamala-harris-iowa-campaign-announces-latinx-steering

123   Rushing, Ty, Iowa Starting Line", "The personal side of Kamala Harris

that Deidre DeJear wishes more knew", July 10, 2024, Link: https://iowastarting-line.com/2024/07/10/deidre-on-kamala-harris/oting

124   Deirdre DeJear for Iowa Secretary of State, Deirdre DeJear", Link: https://www.higherheightsforamericapac.org/candidate/deidre-dejear/

125   Rushing, Ty, Iowa Starting Line", "The personal side of Kamala Harris that Deidre DeJear wishes more knew", July 10, 2024, Link: https://iowastarting-line.com/2024/07/10/deidre-on-kamala-harris/oting

126   Siders, David, Politico, "Kamala Harris to make first Iowa endorse-ment", August 16, 2018, Link: https://www.politico.com/story/2018/08/16/kamala-harris-iowa-endorsement-deidre-dejear-782255

127   Gamboa Suzanne, NBC News, "Oldest Latino civil rights group announces its first presidential endorsement for Harris-Walz", August 9, 2024, Link: https://www.nbcnews.com/news/latino/lulac-endorses-harris-walz-historic-first-rcna165848

128   LULAC, "National Board of Directors", Link: https://web.archive.org/web/20160223223353/https://lulac.org/about/board/

129   Powell, Michael, The New York Times, "Tributes to a Father of Modern Harlem" June 6, 2010,
    Link: https://www.nytimes.com/2010/01/07/nyregion/07sutton.html

130   Daniels, Eugene; Schneider, Elena; Otterbein, Molly and Brandon, Alex, Politico, "Why Kamala Harris chose Tim Walz", August 6, 2024, Link: https://www.politico.com/news/2024/08/06/why-kamala-harris-chose-tim-walz-00172834

Made in United States
North Haven, CT
27 October 2024

59464154R00215